THE
MOVIE
LOVER'S
GUIDE
TO
NEW YORK

Also by Richard Alleman

The Movie Lover's Guide to Hollywood

THE MOVIE LOVER'S GUIDE TO NEW YORK

RICHARD ALLEMAN

PERENNIAL LIBRARY

Harper & Row, Publishers, New York
Cambridge, Philadelphia, San Francisco, Washington
London, Mexico City, São Paulo, Singapore, Sydney

To W. A. H.—with thanks

Photo credits start on page 328

THE MOVIE LOVER'S GUIDE TO NEW YORK. Copyright © 1988 by Richard Alleman. All rights reserved. Printed in the United States of America. No part of this book may be used or reproduced in any manner whatsoever without written permission except in the case of brief quotations embodied in critical articles and reviews. For information address Harper & Row, Publishers, Inc., 10 East 53rd Street, New York, N.Y. 10022. Published simultaneously in Canada by Fitzhenry & Whiteside Limited, Toronto.

FIRST EDITION

Copy editor: Brian Hotchkiss
Designer: Abigail Sturges
Maps: Heidi King
Index: Wyman Holmes for EDINDEX

Library of Congress Cataloging-in-Publication Data

Alleman, Richard.
  The movie lover's guide to New York.

  Includes index.
  1. Moving-picture industry—New York (N.Y.)   I. Title.
PN1993.5.U77A44   1988   384′.8′097471   87-16054
ISBN 0-06-096080-9 (pbk).

88 89 90 91 92 MPC 10 9 8 7 6 5 4 3 2 1

CONTENTS

INTRODUCTION

I got the idea for this book in 1984, while I was in Los Angeles researching *The Movie Lover's Guide to Hollywood.* In my efforts to track down and document the surviving monuments to L.A.'s impressive film history, I was constantly confronted by the fact that the real roots of the American movie industry lay not in Southern California, but in the New York metropolitan area. Practically without exception, almost every important film name and film company in early Hollywood either started off in or had strong ties to the East Coast. Someday, I remember thinking at the time, it would be interesting to take a closer look at those ties. But while I entertained the possibility of a *Movie Lover's Guide to New York,* I feared that most of the studios and sites relevant to New York's early film history—which goes back to the 1890s—had long since been torn down.

Nevertheless, when I returned to the East Coast the following year, my curiosity got the better of me, and I started poking around New York in search of lost movie landmarks. To my delight, I found that there was a lot more for a movie lover to discover than I had previously surmised—early studios, theaters, and film locations; landmark hotels and townhouses where silent screen idols stayed and played; superstar cemeteries; even an occasional scandal. In fact, I quickly realized that New York was crammed with as many movie landmarks as L.A. Only here, they were less obvious, since film is just one of New York's many personalities and dimensions.

Ultimately, though, it wasn't New York's rich film past that convinced me the time had come for a *Movie Lover's Guide to New York;* it was its vital film-making present. As this book goes to press, movie and television production in the city account for almost $3 billion in annual gross revenues—and the figure grows higher every year. No longer just a "location" city, New York is coming into its own again as a full-service studio town. Witness the exciting rebirth of Kaufman-Astoria Studios in Queens, where contemporary film greats like Robert Redford, Jane Fonda, Woody Allen, and Sidney Lumet work on the stages that were broken in by legends like Gloria Swanson, Rudolph Valentino, and D. W. Griffith. Indeed, in many ways, Astoria's comeback represents New York's having come full circle as one of the world's great centers of film production.

Like my Hollywood book, *The Movie Lover's Guide to New York* is meant for arm-chair travelers as well as for movie buffs who actually wish to visit the sites it documents. For those in the latter group, a numbered map precedes each chapter; but since most of these are not drawn to scale, it is suggested that movie lovers also use an additional, more detailed map in conjunction with any sight-seeing they do. This is especially necessary for the outer boroughs and for New Jersey and Westchester County, where a car is also a good idea, since the attractions described in these areas are more spread out than in Manhattan. Needless to say, because many of the places covered by this book are private property, movie lovers are requested to respect the privacy of tenants and owners at all times. Keeping all that in mind, let's start traveling. We have a lot of ground to cover—not to mention some hundred years of history—on our movie lover's odyssey through America's greatest city. Hooray for Hollywood . . . on the Hudson!

April 1988

Special thanks to my editor, Margaret Wimberger, for her hard work and strong involvement in this project; also to Larry Ashmead for giving me another shot; Martin J. Walsh for his superior research; Chris Steinbrenner for organizing *The Movie Lover's Guide to New York* cine-club; Roy Barnitt for sharing all the videos, the books, and the memories; Mary Ellen Rich for the ultimate clipping service; Bill Reilly for showing me his New Jersey; Stephen Drucker for showing me his Bronx; Jessica Harris for showing me her Queens; Lisa Shelkin for showing me her Staten Island; Tom Hanlon for his noble efforts to keep Fort Lee's film past alive; Joan Alleman and Arthur Birsh for launching *The Movie Lover's Guide to Hollywood* in great style; Pat Scott, Joyce Saffir, and Beverly Sammartino at the Mayor's Office of Film, Theatre, & Broadcasting; Richard Koszarski and Rochelle Slovin at The American Museum of the Moving Image; Michael P. Miller and the New York branch of the Theater Historical Society; Louis Botto; Ann Roth; Sam Robert; David Stark; Itzy Atkins; Jerome Hellman and Nancy Ellison; Leo Lerman; Amy Gross; Joan Micklin Silver; Jack MacBean; Linda Kirland; Diane Lampert and Fred Stewart; Guy LeBow; Barry Lewis; Jeff Gottlieb; Hyman Brown; Howard Feinstein; Janet Martin; Lois Cohn; Harry Medved; Marlene Landau; Howard Otway; Marc Wanamaker; David Bourdon; Nancy Jo Friedman; Charles Maguire; William Nadel; David Loehr; Dale Seuss; Andrew Achsen; Brian Donovan; Bill Kirkwood; Frank Wood; Joe Henehan; Marvin Usavitch; Eileen Shanahan; Mitchell-Manning-Vatter Associates; Playbill Magazine; The Bayside Historical Society; The Brooklyn Historical Society; The Flatbush Development Corporation; and The Urban Kin—always.

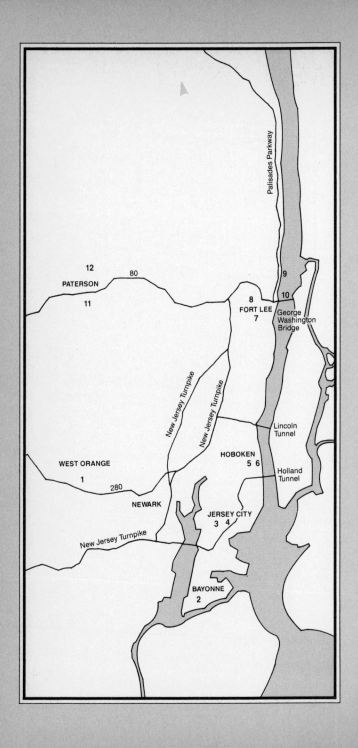

NEW JERSEY

In the Beginning

The first mogul:
Thomas Alva Edison

FOR ALL intents and purposes, the motion picture as we have come to know it was born some sixteen miles due west of the island of Manhattan at the Edison laboratories in West Orange, New Jersey. Recognizing that fact, we begin our movie lover's odyssey there. It wasn't just the Edison Company, however, that made New Jersey a powerful force in the early motion picture industry, because, from the very beginning, the state was home to scores of other film companies. These included long-forgotten studios with names like Centaur, Nestor, Champion, Eclair, Victor, Solax, and World—as well as many that are still familiar, like Fox, Metro, Selznick, Goldwyn, and Universal. All took advantage of New Jersey's then wide open spaces, its pristine fields and forests for location shooting. The world's first Westerns were not done in Colorado or California—they were done in New Jersey.

Needless to say, today's New Jersey is a very different place from the New Jersey of around the turn of the century, and tracking down traces of the state's early film history can be as challenging as working on an archaeological dig. But for the intrepid movie lover who knows where to dig and what to look for, the rewards to be unearthed along the *west* bank of the Hudson River are many. These range from ancient movie studios to famous and "infamous" silent film locations and even to the world's first screening room! Happy hunting!

1. EDISON LABORATORY
Main Street and Lakeside Avenue, West Orange

For the movie lover, this is probably the single most important site connected with the development of the motion picture in America—if not the world—for it was here that, toward the end of the last century, Edison researchers perfected and successfully marketed a practical system for photographing and exhibiting moving images. Thomas Alva Edison is often credited as the inventor of the movies, but it is difficult to attribute this achievement to any one person since various inventors in America and abroad were experimenting with "moving pictures" at around the same time. And, indeed, even if we credit the Edison Laboratory with coming up with the first commercially viable motion pictures, it seems that Edison himself had relatively little to do with the project.

The real force behind the endeavor was Edison's assistant, an Englishman named W. K. L. Dickson who, as early as 1889, came up with a machine called the Kinetograph that showed moving pictures backed up by synchronized sound provided by an Edison phonograph. (It is said that the main reason Edison gave his go-ahead to motion picture development was because he saw the new medium as a way to further enhance—and thus further capitalize on—his already immensely successful phonograph.) The big breakthrough of Dickson's device, however, was not the fact that it employed synchronized sound, but the incredible realism of the moving images it recorded. To achieve this, Dickson had taken advantage

The first movie studio: Edison's "Black Maria"

of George Eastman's newly invented celluloid film, which was thin, tough, and flexible. Cut into continuous 35mm strips and perforated with four holes per frame, the film was fed through the Kinetograph by means of sprockets, another key design element because these regularly stopped the film for that fraction of a second needed to record the image on the frame. Today, almost one hundred years later, most motion pictures still use 35mm film as well as this same basic stop-and-go sprocket mechanism.

In 1893, an improved version of this Kinetograph—redubbed the Kinetoscope, and minus the synchronized phonograph—was unveiled at the Chicago World's Fair. Essentially a coin-operated "peep show," the Kinetoscope was housed in a large wooden box into which the viewer peered to see a silent movie lasting less than a minute. Before long, Kinetoscope parlors started springing up all across the country and Edison was in the motion picture business in a big way. To provide products for these Kinetoscope parlors, and later for the storefront nickelodeons, where motion pictures were projected onto screens, Dickson built the world's first movie studio at the West Orange laboratory in 1893. It was really nothing more than a tar-paper-covered shack with a roof that could be opened up and adjusted to let in sunlight. In addition, the bizarre structure was mounted on wheels so that it could be rotated to keep up with the sun throughout the day. The studio was dubbed "the Black Maria," because it resembled the police patrol wagons of the period, which bore the same nickname.

What were the first Edison movies like? Directed by W. K. L. Dickson, they relied heavily on vaudeville and circus performers

Edison's epic: The Great Train Robbery, *1903*

for talent—and showed snippets of everything from animal acts, exotic dancers, and Gaiety Girls to 1890s superstars like Annie Oakley and Buffalo Bill Cody. By the turn of the century, however, with the arrival of director Edwin S. Porter on the Edison scene, the company's films became longer, more sophisticated, and started to tell stories. It was Porter who in 1903 directed what is considered the milestone of early story films, the eleven-minute-long *The Great Train Robbery.*

Today, one of the treats in store for the movie lover who visits the Edison Laboratory site (now a museum administered by the National Park Service) is the chance to see *The Great Train Robbery* in its entirety. Several less-well-known early Edison films are also shown; one features the original "Little Egypt" doing her famous Hoochie-Coochie; another is a slapstick comedy centering on a husband and wife's attempts to swat a giant fly. There's even a bizarre sketch using trick photography about a barber who removes the heads of his customers, shaves them, and then replaces them!

For movie lovers, other highlights of the Edison Laboratory site are the full-scale mock-up of the Black Maria studio, a working Kinetoscope from the 1890s, and Edison's handsome private library and study. A grand wood-paneled room with two balconied stories and a huge chandelier, the library has been left exactly as it was—down to the half-smoked cigars on the roll-top desk—when Edison died in 1931. Especially interesting is the little second-story projection booth that faces a large rolled-up screen suspended from the ceiling across the way. Edison's library, it turns out, was one of the world's first screening rooms.

Edison's West Orange Laboratory today

While Edison's name is linked with many motion picture firsts, it is ironic how small a role his company played in the ultimate flourishing of the film industry. Immediately besieged by rival producers using what Edison considered to be pirated equipment, the Edison Company fought hard to retain supremacy in the movie business and summarily sued all competitors for patent infringement. Eventually some of these competitors became so strong that Edison stopped fighting and joined with them in 1908 to form the Motion Picture Patents Company. Effectively, this new organization was a business "trust," and it was ruled illegal and dissolved in 1915. By that time, however, the competition from the outside was too strong, too innovative, and the company that started it all was out of the film business by 1918. But at the West Orange laboratory, the movie lover witnesses beginnings, not endings.

NOTE: *The Edison Laboratory offers guided tours of its vintage 1880s factory complex Wednesdays through Sundays between 9:30 A.M. and 3:30 P.M. The Visitors' Center has a bookshop as well as exhibits that celebrate a number of Edison's inventions—the phonograph, storage battery, dictaphone, and Kinetoscope. Closed Thanksgiving, Christmas, and New Year's Day. Nearby, Glenmont, Edison's spectacular twenty-three-room, red-brick Victorian mansion is open to the public on weekends. Glenmont tour groups (of no more than fifteen people) are put together at the Edison Lab on a first-come, first-served basis. For information: (201) 736–5050.*

2. CENTAUR FILM COMPANY SITE
900 Broadway, Bayonne

Strange as it may seem, Hollywood has its roots in Bayonne. In 1911 the Bayonne-based producer David Horsley took his company of New Jersey cowboys and Indians and relocated in the small Southern California community of Hollywood. While several other

East Coast film companies had already discovered the sunshine of Los Angeles (as well as its convenient location some 2,500 miles from the strong arm of the Edison-led Motion Picture Patents Company trust), Horsley's was the first to set up a permanent studio within the borders of Hollywood proper.

But back to Bayonne, where a storefront—equipped with bathtubs for developing film—was the Centaur Company's headquarters from 1907 to 1911. Specializing in westerns, Centaur came out with such provocative titles as *A Cowboy's Escapade* (1908), *Johnny and the Indian* (1909), *Redman's Honor* (1910), *The Cowboy Preacher* (1910), and *Those Jersey Cowpunchers* (1910), which was a spoof on its own horse operas. When Centaur first came on the scene in 1907, unsophisticated nickelodeon audiences didn't know the difference between rural New Jersey and the wilds of Wyoming, but as directors started to shoot in the real West a few years later, a demand for more authentic locations soon arose. This prompted Centaur to move into other genres, including a series based on the "Mutt and Jeff" comic strip. It also prompted the company's 1911 move to the West Coast.

Today, the spot where Centaur once had its Bayonne headquarters is occupied by a beauty parlor called Chicks Only. While this is not the original Centaur office building, those on either side of it—Vector Books and Thomas Bros. Furniture respectively—were around in 1907. In fact, much of this section of Broadway, Bayonne's main street, is made up of little clapboard buildings that, in an odd way, do not look unlike those of a small town out West.

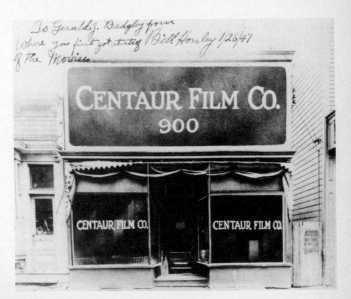

Centaur Film Company, Bayonne, 1908

Stanley Theater, Jersey City

3. STANLEY THEATER SITE
2932 John F. Kennedy Boulevard, Jersey City

Old-timers will remember the enormous rooftop sign that once proclaimed, "The Stanley . . . One of America's Great Theaters." And that it was. With 4,332 seats, the Stanley was one of the largest movie palaces ever built. Then there was its lobby, a spectacular space of faux-marble columns, grand staircases, cloud-painted ceilings, and glittering chandeliers. Finally, the house itself was a stunner—with walls of back-lit, three-dimensional Gothic façades, including a replica of Venice's Rialto Bridge spanning the stage.

The Stanley opened its ornate brass doors back in 1928 with a mixed bill that featured a prerecorded welcome message by Norma Talmadge, a performance by the house orchestra, a stage show called "Sky Blues," a newsreel, musical selections on the Wurlitzer organ, and eventually the film presentation, which was *The Dove,* starring the aforementioned Miss Talmadge and Gilbert Roland.

The Stanley survived as a theater for fifty years and, despite its enormous size, never suffered the ignominy of multiplexing. When it finally closed down in 1978, however, it was a prime candidate for the wrecking ball. Luckily, it escaped this fate when the Jehovah's Witnesses purchased the building in the early 1980s to use as a convention center, bringing some 5,500 volunteers to Jersey City to help with its restoration. While most preservationists applaud the saving of the Stanley, some regret that the theater's original Willy Pogany murals, which featured scantily-clad Greek gods and goddesses, have been replaced by Biblical scenes. Nonetheless, the good news is that the Stanley still stands, and movie lovers who wish to take a peek at it can stop by on a weekend when thousands of Jehovah's Witnesses converge on the place for meetings, religious services, and baptisms. A far cry from Norma Talmadge, Gilbert Roland, and "Sky Blues," however.

4. LOEW'S JERSEY THEATER
54 Journal Square, Jersey City

Opened in 1929, this Journal Square landmark—boasting a wonderful baroque façade with a mechanical statue of the mounted St. George which periodically slayed a dragon—was the most opulent movie palace ever built in New Jersey. Designed by the noted theatrical architectural firm of Rapp and Rapp, the dazzling gold Loew's Jersey auditorium seated 3,187 movie lovers who had first passed under an equally dramatic three-story lobby rotunda supported by jade-green columns. Although triplexed in 1974, the Jersey retained much of its original splendor right up to the day it closed its doors in the summer of 1986.

Today, the future of this extraordinary structure is the subject of much speculation—and some controversy. Whether it will be demolished, restored, or wind up with its façade and lobby as part of a high-rise office building remains to be seen. The only thing that is certain in all of this is that they'll never build another theater quite like Loew's Jersey.

*Loew's Jersey Theater,
Jersey City, ca. 1930*

On the Waterfront *in Hoboken: Eva Marie Saint and Marlon Brando at Our Lady of Grace Church*

5.   OUR LADY OF GRACE CHURCH
400 Willow Avenue, Hoboken

It was *the* picture of 1954; an incredible collaboration of New York–based talent that brought together director Elia Kazan, screenwriter Budd Schulberg, composer Leonard Bernstein, plus a cast headed by Marlon Brando, and featuring Eva Marie Saint, Karl Malden, Lee J. Cobb, Martin Balsam, and Rod Steiger. And when Hollywood handed out the Academy Awards that year, *On the Waterfront* received no less than eight of them, including best picture, director, actor (Brando), and supporting actress (Saint). Not bad for an independent, low-budget, made-in-New York film.

Made in New York perhaps, but it was shot largely on location in Hoboken, the little town directly across the Hudson River from Greenwich Village in lower Manhattan. In the 1950s, Hoboken, like New York City, was a thriving port, and it provided an ideal setting for Kazan's hard-nosed look at the very real corruption that was an ugly fact of waterfront life in New York and New Jersey. (The film was based on a series of shocking newspaper articles by muckraking journalist Malcolm Johnson.) Today, the Hoboken docks and warehouses that served as backgrounds for *On the Waterfront* are being transformed into a slick multi-million-dollar development of shops, offices, condos, and marinas. One important location from the film does survive, however: the Roman Catholic church where the crusading priest played by Karl Malden helped Brando's failed prizefighter-turned-longshoreman realize the forces of evil lurking in his union. For the church, Kazan chose Hoboken's historic 1874 Our Lady of Grace, a striking brick structure with a statue-studded Gothic façade and an ornate interior. Perhaps this interior was a bit too grand for Kazan, because a different, much more austere church (Hoboken's St. Peter and St. Paul at 400 Hudson Street) was used for the interior scenes.

Fans of *On the Waterfront* may also remember that a number

of scenes take place in front of the church, including a touching love scene between Brando and Eva Marie Saint, where the two of them are sitting on a children's swing set. A bit of cinematic trickery was involved in these sequences as well. The shots that show Our Lady of Grace Church in the background were done in the park that's directly across the street; but when we see Brando and Saint looking out at the murky waterfront in the same scene, a different park (Stevens Park, which fronts St. Peter and St. Paul Church) was used. Films often use a combination of sites to create one location. By "cheating the location," i.e., using two churches and two parks, Kazan was able to move the more photogenic Our Lady of Grace some four blocks away from where it really stood and magically reposition it . . . on the waterfront.

6. FRANK SINATRA HOUSE
841 Garden Street, Hoboken

The house where Albert Francis Sinatra was born stood at 415 Monroe Street in Hoboken. It was demolished in 1968, and a parking lot now marks the spot. But Sinatra fans can still check out the skinny three-story brownstone on Garden Street, where Hoboken's most famous native son spent his late teen years. Sinatra's father, Marty, was an Italian immigrant who had a string of jobs—boxer, bootlegger, saloon keeper, and fireman. Sinatra's mother, Dolly, as the world has learned from Kitty Kelley's "unauthorized" Sinatra biography, *His Way* (Bantam Books, 1986), was said to have performed illegal abortions in the basement of this same Hoboken house.

Frank Sinatra's
Hoboken home

Young Sinatra, who attended Hoboken High School but never graduated, got his first break as a singer when he and three friends, appearing as The Hoboken Four, won a "Major Bowes Amateur Hour" radio show contest in 1935. This led to a tour, nightclub gigs, stints as vocalist with both Harry James's and Tommy Dorsey's bands, and by the early 1940s Sinatra had become the country's number-one teen idol.

With his great success as a singer, Sinatra was tapped by Hollywood to appear in a number of fluffy 1940s musicals, but by the early 1950s, both his singing and film careers were on the downswing. Attacked by the House Committee on Un-American Activities for supposed Communist affiliations, and by the press for alleged Mafia contacts, Sinatra was, as he said in a recent talk at the Yale Law School, "busted."

The surprise was that his acting ability, not his singing voice, brought about his comeback—notably through his Oscar-winning performance as Private Angelo Maggio in the 1953 film *From Here to Eternity*. With the roles that followed—in *The Man with the Golden Arm, Pal Joey,* and *High Society*—the kid from Hoboken wound up one of the most powerful figures in the entertainment industry.

Throughout the years, Sinatra's associations with his hometown have been mysteriously strained. Indeed, with the exception of a highly publicized return visit in 1947 for Frank Sinatra Day and an appearance at a benefit for the International Firefighters orchestrated by his fireman father in 1952, Sinatra seems to have stayed away from his hometown deliberately. There are even stories that, at one point in his career, Sinatra gave his birthplace as Hasbrouck Heights, a nearby and at the time more fashionable New Jersey community. With the revelations of the Kitty Kelley book, however, Frank's reluctance to own up to his Hoboken origins becomes more understandable. In 1984, Sinatra did make a quick Hoboken appearance. Possibly owing to an offer he couldn't refuse, Sinatra accompanied Ronald Reagan to St. Ann's Church on the Feast of St. Ann (a holy day dedicated to pregnant women), where the president was to deliver a nationwide message against legalized abortions. Needless to say, the irony of Sinatra's presence at the event was not lost on some Hoboken old-timers who remembered what supposedly once went on in the basement of 841 Garden Street.

7. FORT LEE

Known to most New Yorkers as the town on the Jersey side of the George Washington Bridge (and to today's movie audiences as the suburb Rosanna Arquette called home in *Desperately Seeking Susan*), Fort Lee is a booming community of cushy condos, corporate headquarters, new hotels, and some of the highest commercial real estate prices in the Northeast. It wasn't always like this. At the beginning of the century, Fort Lee was a rural village surrounded by green hills, forests, and farms, with the added geographic distinction of being bounded by the dramatic Palisades cliffs and the Hudson River. Despite the fact that Fort Lee was easy to get to from Upper Manhattan via ferry boat (the George Washington Bridge wasn't built until 1931), the town was worlds away from the big city on the other side of the Hudson, and this fact was not lost on early film directors, who quickly came to see Fort Lee as the ultimate rural "location."

One of the first directors to discover Fort Lee was Edwin S. Porter, who in 1907 (working out of Edison's Manhattan studio at 41 East 21st Street) used the towering cliffs of Fort Lee's Palisades for the exteriors of *Rescued from the Eagle's Nest,* a melodramatic yarn about a baby kidnapped by an eagle. In the film, the role of the mountaineer who saves the baby was played by a young actor named D. W. Griffith. A year later, Griffith would move to the other side of the camera to become a director at Biograph, and in this new role, he would often return to shoot in Fort Lee. Among Griffith's most important Fort Lee films are *The Curtain Pole* (1908), a slapstick comedy starring Mack Sennett before he, too, became an important director/producer; *The Lonely Villa* (1909), featuring Mary Pickford in her first performance on screen; *The Battle* (1911), in which Griffith developed many of the photographic techniques that he would later employ in his landmark *The Birth of a Nation;* and *The New York Hat* (1912), with its all-star cast including Pickford and Sennett, as well as Lionel Barrymore, Mae Marsh, and Lillian and Dorothy Gish in a story written by a fifteen-year-old schoolgirl from San Diego named Anita Loos.

Besides the scenic variety that Fort Lee offered as a location,

Fort Lee epic: Les Misérables, *1918*

the town provided an even more important commodity to the rapidly growing film industry—low-cost real estate—and soon a number of companies had built studios within its borders. The first company to set up shop in Fort Lee was the Champion Film Company, opening on Fifth Street in 1909. Since Champion, which specialized in Eastern-made westerns, was not a member of the Edison-led Motion Picture Patents Company, its Fort Lee facility was in constant danger of being closed down by this all-powerful trust of supposedly "legitimate" film producers. For this reason, Champion built its studio partially below ground level in order to disguise the fact that the building had a high ceiling and was actually a moviemaking installation.

Ironically, this little 1909 building is one of just two of Fort Lee's many early movie studio structures that survive. Used today as a printing plant, it sits where Fifth Street comes to a dead end just beyond Washington Avenue. Across the street—actually more of an alleyway—from the Champion site, the house at 2486 Fifth Street was frequently used as a location in early westerns.

The great flourishing of Fort Lee's film industry was from 1914 to 1919. By then, the Motion Picture Patents Company was no longer a force to be reckoned with (it was declared illegal in 1915), the feature-length film had become the staple of the movie business, and practically every major, and a number of minor, film companies had some kind of Fort Lee operation. Some of the more memorable Fort Lee movie names—Goldwyn, Selznick, Fox, Paramount, Universal, and Metro (the company that would become the first "M" of MGM)—are still household words. Other Fort Lee studios—Solax, Eclair, Victor, and Lincoln—are known only to hardcore film buffs and historians.

The scope of the moviemaking that went on in Fort Lee during its five-year heyday is astounding. For epics like Fox's 1918 *Les Misérables,* nineteenth-century Paris was recreated on some sixty acres of nearby farmland, and most of the townspeople were recruited for the film's cast of five thousand extras. It's also interesting to note that many famous films, which the world automatically assumes were produced in Hollywood, were actually done in Fort

Fort Lee romance: Tallulah Bankhead and Tom Moore in Thirty a Week, *1918*

A popular actors' hangout in Fort Lee's studio days, Rambo's Hotel is now a private home

assumes were produced in Hollywood, were actually done in Fort Lee. An example is Fox's *A Fool There Was* (1915), the vehicle that launched a Cincinnati tailor's daughter named Theodosia Goodman as the country's sultriest siren. (Wisely, Fox changed her name to Theda Bara.) It was also in Fort Lee, not Hollywood, that Mack Sennett made several entries in his Fatty (Arbuckle) and Mabel (Normand) series.

Alas, for all that went on in Fort Lee (some historians have calculated that Fort Lee in its heyday was responsible for 50 percent of all the feature films produced in the U.S.), the end came quickly. With the country's involvement in World War I, the government made it difficult for Eastern movie studios to secure the coal they needed to heat their plants and, as a result, many companies headed to the warm West. A postwar economic slump further enhanced Southern California's hold on the film industry, since budget-conscious companies realized that it was just too expensive to have bicoastal production operations. Forced to choose between coasts, producers went with winter-free Southern California, and Fort Lee was finished.

Even sadder than Fort Lee's sudden demise as a film capital is the fact that almost nothing remains to remind the world of the city's glorious moviemaking years. Other than the print shop on Fifth Street that once was the city's first film studio, intrepid movie lovers will have to search hard for any tangible evidence of Fort Lee's movie history. The blue-and-white clapboard house over at 2423 First Street, for example, gives no clue that it was once an establishment called Rambo's Hotel. A popular hangout for film folk who ferried over from Manhattan to work in Fort Lee back in the 1910s, Rambo's also furnished an exterior for many made-in-Fort Lee features. Another vestige of that same era is the big Victorian house a block away at 2405 Hammet Avenue, which once belonged to America's most famous theatrical family, the "Fabulous Barrymores." All three Barrymore children—Ethel, John, and Lionel—worked in silent films on the East Coast, and some of those were made at Fort Lee.

The majority of Fort Lee's studios lined Main Street, which was known briefly as "Studio Row." Today, only one of these studio buildings survives. Located at 530 Main Street, it was originally part of Carl Laemmle's Universal empire. Ironically, the company that now occupies the old Universal site (Nova Industries) is in the business of storing videotapes and film. In fact, if you look very hard at the old Universal building, you will see cans of film through its leaded windows. Take a long hard look at those cans of film; along with some photos at the Fort Lee Public Library, they are the only visible reminders of a lost era when a small New Jersey town played a major role in the history of the American motion-picture industry.

8.   ALAN ALDA HOUSE
18 Glenwood Avenue, Leonia

Back in the mid-1970s, while at the height of his fame as Hawkeye Pierce, the ultracool surgeon of the "M★A★S★H" TV show, Alan Alda became one of the country's best-known bicoastals. Refusing to go Hollywood, the New York-born actor commuted between Los Angeles and this unprepossessing frame house in suburban New Jersey, which he had bought in the early 1960s when he was starring on Broadway in *The Owl and the Pussycat.*

The consummate family man, Alda had been married to the same woman—Arlene Stein, a professional musician and photographer—for some sixteen years when he landed his role in "M★A★S★H." He also had three teenaged daughters and, as Alda said at the time, "My wife and I felt it was better to have our home intact in the place it had always been than to uproot ourselves. . . . I'd loved that town and the people in it. We'd gone to a lot of trouble to make a home there. We had a sense of community and none of us wanted to leave it." A nightmare of logistics, Alda's commute cost a fortune in airfares and phone bills. In addition, he maintained a home in L.A., where his family would join him during the summer when "M★A★S★H" was shooting.

Today, years after "M★A★S★H," the Aldas still reside part of the year in the same house (a tennis court has been squeezed into the backyard) in the same New Jersey town (population 9,000) where as a family they celebrate Christian (he's Catholic) and Jewish (she's not) holidays, where the neighbors respect their privacy, and where reportedly one of Alan Alda's greatest joys in life is wandering around the downtown square.

9.   "PEARL WHITE MEMORIAL CLIFF"
Palisades Interstate Park, Coytesville

To today's television audiences, the term "cliff-hanger" is synonymous with the season's suspenseful final episode of a prime-time soap opera like "Dynasty" or "Dallas." Who shot J.R.? Which

Top: High drama: Pearl White atop the Palisades for The House of Hate, *1918. Bottom: Pearl White's cliff-hanger location today*

characters will survive the fire at La Mirage? Will anyone escape the terrorist attack at the palace of Moldavia? To the moviegoers of the early twentieth century, however, the word cliff-hanger was more likely to bring up the image of a hero or heroine confronting some life-threatening situation—from being tied to the railroad tracks with the train approaching to actually hanging from a cliff— at the end of an episode of one of the numerous serial films that swept the country between 1910 and World War I.

Of all the serial sirens who hung from cliffs in silent film days, the actress who reigned as Queen of the Cliff-hangers was Pearl White. She starred not only in the legendary *Perils of Pauline* but also in a string of other serials with such titles as *The Exploits of*

Elaine, The Iron Claw, The Fatal Ring, The House of Hate, and *Black Secret.* Most of Pearl's films were produced by Jersey City-based Pathé Studios with the financial backing of newspaper magnate William Randolph Hearst who bolstered the circulation of his papers by running the serial in print at the same time as it appeared on screen.

When Pearl White needed a cliff to hang from, Coytesville's Palisades provided some of the steepest of any on the East Coast, with one that was a particular favorite of early moviemakers. Large and flat enough to accommodate several actors as well as a cameraman, it also jutted out a good two hundred and fifty feet above the Hudson River in an especially dramatic—and photogenic—fashion. Today, this cliff of cliffs is unchanged, except that the George Washington Bridge now looms to the south. The site should interest not only movie lovers, but etymologists, since it may well be the exact spot at which the word "cliff-hanger" began.

NOTE: *Pearl White's cliff is not easy to find and should be visited only by the most intrepid of movie lovers. To reach the site, drive (a car is a must) north from the George Washington Bridge along the Palisades Interstate Parkway about two miles to the first gas station on the right. Pull in, park, and then backtrack south by foot for about ten minutes along the path until you reach a large clearing in the park. Continue walking south beyond the clearing for another hundred feet or so. Off to the left, you'll find a grass-covered step that leads to the cliff, as well as to a glorious view of the George Washington Bridge, the Hudson River, and Upper Manhattan. Be very careful, however, because it's very steep, very dangerous!*

10. GEORGE WASHINGTON BRIDGE
Fort Lee

Almost a mile long, this sleek silver suspension bridge spanning the Hudson River between Fort Lee and Upper Manhattan was considered the "most beautiful bridge in the world" by the Swiss architect Le Corbusier. Since the George Washington Bridge is a relative newcomer on the New York City bridge scene (it was completed in 1931), it has never had the same landmark appeal to film makers as, say, the Brooklyn Bridge, which is almost half a century older. Still, the George Washington Bridge has been featured in a number of famous films, and for some reason, it has often spelled trouble!

A classic case in point is *Ball of Fire,* the 1942 comedy from Samuel Goldwyn that has Barbara Stanwyck, a gangster's moll named Sugarpuss O'Shèa, hiding from the police in a Manhattan mansion inhabited by eight unmarried professors who've been cooped up together for nine years revising an encyclopedia. When one of them, the ultra-shy Bertram Potts (played by Gary Cooper), falls for, and instantly proposes to, Sugarpuss Stanwyck, she agrees to a marriage in New Jersey as a ploy to get her out of Manhattan and safely into the arms of her underworld boyfriend. Cut to: Stanwyck and the now top-hatted professors gliding across the George Washington Bridge in a glamorous touring car en route to the bogus wedding. Warned by her boyfriend that the bridge will be "swarming with cops," Stanwyck has a very close call when the professor driving the car (he's the worst driver on earth!) rear-ends another vehicle at the toll booth. After a very dicey couple of moments, Stanwyck charms her way through the police, only to encounter real trouble later when she realizes that she's in love with Professor Potts ("He looks like a giraffe and I love 'im") and not her mobster man.

In *How to Marry a Millionaire* (1953), Fred Clark and Betty Grable also have some tense moments crossing the George Washington Bridge when returning from what the very married Mr. Clark had hoped to be an amorous adventure at his lodge in Maine with the very available Miss Grable. The Maine odyssey has turned out to be a disaster for Clark, however. Not only did Grable wind up catching the measles, she also fell for a handsome forest ranger. Despite the fact that Clark has struck out with Grable, he still takes great pains to keep the trip secret from his wife and business associates. In fact, he boasts to Betty of his cleverness in returning to the city via New Jersey ("On this side of the river, no one knows me"). It's therefore quite a surprise when his '53 Lincoln is met by sirens, police, and ultimately congratulations as he crosses the George Washington Bridge. It is, it seems, "George Washington Bridge Week," and Clark's car is the fifty-millionth vehicle to cross the span.

On a decidedly darker note, the 1948 made-in-New York *film noir, Force of Evil,* also features a George Washington Bridge sequence. A depressing tale of the New York numbers game, the film stars John Garfield as a lawyer trying to get the numbers legalized, while his brother is hopelessly caught up in the illegal side of the racket. At the end of the film, Garfield finds his murdered brother's body ("like some dirty rag that nobody wants") floating by the rocks alongside the Little Red Lighthouse under the George Washington Bridge. Not a pretty picture—but then, *films noirs* were never noted for their happy endings.

On the other hand, television sitcoms *are,* and who can forget that memorable moment when the Ricardos and the Mertzes cross the George Washington Bridge in Ricky's brand-new 1955 Pontiac convertible at the beginning of their legendary journey to California?

11. LAMBERT'S CASTLE
Valley Road, Paterson

With its thick stone walls and its crenelated turrets and towers, Lambert's Castle (originally called Belle Vista) was the fantasy residence of nineteenth-century industrialist Catholina Lambert, the town's most important silk manufacturer. Built in 1892 and furnished lavishly with an eclectic mix of European and Oriental antiques, the castle was an exercise in the *nouveau riche* ostentation typical of the times.

The visual power of the place was not lost on early film makers, and the Edison Manufacturing Company (Thomas Edison was a close friend of Lambert) is reported to have used the castle as a background for some of its productions. D. W. Griffith also used the castle as a location and, in 1910, shot a medieval adventure there titled *The Call to Arms,* starring a young actor named Mack Sennett. Sennett, of course, would soon become a director/producer and achieve world fame with his Keystone comedies.

Today, Lambert's Castle is the headquarters of the Passaic County Historical Society and is open to the public as a museum. Besides exploring this strange structure with its Victorian Gothic interior of ornate twisted columns and sculpted plaster of Paris walls, there is an additional reason for movie lovers to visit this site. Just below the castle, on the flat grassy area between Route 80 and the hillside on which the property stands, the tracks of the Lackawanna Railroad once ran. Although there is still some debate among film historians on the subject, it is believed that many of the train sequences of the landmark 1903 film, *The Great Train Robbery,* were shot right down there. Important as the first American film to tell a dramatic story in a sophisticated, cinematic way— with cross cuts, multiple locations, carefully choreographed action and chase scenes, and a large cast of actors and extras—*The Great Train Robbery* was also the first western.

NOTE: *Lambert's Castle is open Wednesday through Sunday from 1 P.M. to 4 P.M. The $1.00 admission fee for adults includes a docent-guided tour. For information: (201) 881–2761.*

Lambert's Castle, Paterson

Great Falls, Paterson

12. GREAT FALLS
McBride Avenue, Paterson

One of the little-known wonders of northern New Jersey, Paterson's Great Falls are a thundering miniversion of Niagara. First exploited by our country's original Secretary of the Treasury, Alexander Hamilton, the Falls were harnessed to provide water power for the budding industrial city Hamilton helped establish at Paterson in 1791.

Toward the end of the nineteenth century, the Falls were exploited in a different way by a pair of early film makers named Albert E. Smith and J. Stuart Blackton. Both English immigrants, the two were part of a vaudeville act called The International Novelty Company. The novelty was that they had an Edison projector and showed films as part of their routine. Quickly realizing that it would be both cheaper and more satisfying to produce their own films rather than to buy them from Edison, Smith and Blackton figured out how to convert their projector into a camera, and they were off and running as moviemakers. At first they shot street life, parades, prizefights—literally anything that moved. By 1897, they were ready to take on something really big, and decided to capture the power and majesty of Niagara Falls on film. But when they discovered that there were some pretty spectacular falls just twenty miles away in New Jersey, Smith and Blackton saved both time and money by hopping over to Paterson, where they shot the Great Falls and passed them off to the world as Niagara. According to Smith's autobiography, the film was shown all over the eastern United States and no one ever challenged its authenticity. The "Vitagraph Hoax" of 1897 may well have been the birth of serious special effects.

Today, Paterson's Great Falls form the centerpiece of the town's National Historic Landmark District, a fascinating area of museums, shops, and restored nineteenth-century mills and factories. There are several vantage points which provide dramatic close-up views of the Falls. Indeed, from these, it's easy to see how movie lovers back in 1897 got tricked into thinking they were witnessing Niagara.

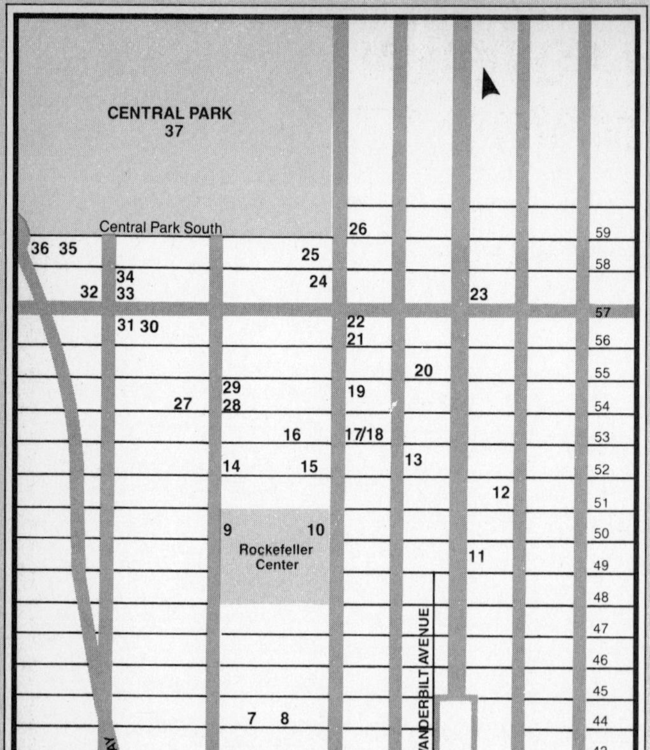

CENTRAL PARK
37

Central Park South

36 35
32
34
33
31 30

26
25
24

23

59
58
57
56
55
54
53
52
51
50
49
48
47
46
45
44
43
42
4 5

27

29
28

22
21
20
19
17/18
13

16
14   15

9   10
Rockefeller
Center

12

11

7   8

BRYANT
PARK

3

6

SEVENTH AVENUE

BROADWAY

AVENUE OF THE AMERICAS

FIFTH AVENUE

MADISON AVENUE

VANDERBILT AVENUE

PARK AVENUE

LEXINGTON AVENUE

THIRD AVENUE

1

2

34

MIDTOWN
MANHATTAN

Archetypal NYC

*Margot Kidder/Lois Lane in the Daily News/
Daily Planet lobby for* Superman, 1978

THE movie lover's midtown Manhattan represents New York at its busiest, its most intense, its most exciting. This is the New York of landmark skyscrapers, legendary department stores, historic grand hotels, glamorous restaurants and nightclubs. Possibly the only place on earth with so much power, energy, and screen appeal concentrated in such a small space, midtown is ultimately the hunk of New York that many people think of as "New York." One of the reasons that the images of midtown are so powerfully implanted in our collective consciousness may well be because the area has been immortalized by so many films—especially films made in Hollywood, which needed only the right music and a couple of dramatic process shots of the Empire State Building or Rockefeller Center to establish their New York settings. Herewith, then, a look at this awesome part of town—focusing both on its screen presence over the years as well as on the dynamic (and occasionally scandalous!) roles that many of its famed hotels, restaurants, clubs, and office towers have played in the lives of the movers and shakers of the motion picture business. For the movie lover, indeed for the rest of the world, midtown is not only archetypal New York, it's the center of the earth.

1. MACY'S
Herald Square

"The world's largest store" boasts over two million square feet of floor space and reportedly employs up to ten thousand sales people! For the movie lover, the significance of Macy's has less to do with retailing statistics than with a very important event that took place almost a century ago in the building that once stood on the mammoth department store's Herald Square site. That building—demolished at the beginning of the century to make way for Macy's—was a theater called Koster and Bials Music Hall, and it

The first picture show: Koster and Bials Music Hall, 1890s

Natalie Wood, John Payne, and Macy's Thanksgiving Day Parade in Miracle on 34th Street, *1947*

was there that, on April 23, 1896, Thomas Edison publicly unveiled the Vitascope, a magical machine that *projected* lifelike moving images on a twenty-foot screen set in a huge gilded frame. There were many oohs and aahs at Koster and Bials that famous evening as the audience saw a group of seconds-long snippets of such things as a prizefight, dancing girls, and "Venice, showing gondolas." One of these little films, titled "Sea Waves," depicted rough surf and crashing breakers and is said to have caused a bit of a stir among the spectators in the front rows. The magic, and ultimately the power, of motion pictures was clear right from the start.

About ten years after the debut of motion pictures on the Macy's site, Edison's top director, Edwin S. Porter, shot an important early story film using the newly erected department store as a location. The film, titled *Kleptomaniacs,* told the parallel stories of two women, one rich, the other poor, who get caught shoplifting at a big department store—and pointed out the disparities between the ways society treats the rich and the poor. The wealthy woman is let off and considered an unfortunate victim of kleptomania, whereas the other woman is arrested and ruthlessly hauled off to jail. Clearly, the movies had come a long way in ten years.

Forty years after *Kleptomaniacs,* Macy's had come a long way, too, when it was given a starring role in Twentieth Century–Fox's 1947 Christmas classic, *Miracle on 34th Street,* which pits an eccentric Macy's Santa Claus against a bah-humbug toy-department head. Besides a number of exteriors shot at Macy's, the film also includes footage of the store's famed once-a-year media event, the Macy's Thanksgiving Day Parade. Other films that have featured Macy's in decidedly lesser roles are *Auntie Mame,* which finds Rosalind Russell, as the madcap Mame, trying to sell roller skates at

Macy's at Christmastime; *The Group,* in which Kay Strong, played by Joanna Pettet, rises up the retail ladder as a Macy's executive, only to find that corporate success doesn't necessarily mean happiness; and, more recently, Woody Allen's *Radio Days.*

2. EMPIRE STATE BUILDING
350 Fifth Avenue

Of all New York's landmarks, none is as closely associated in the popular imagination with one single film as is the Empire State Building with the legendary monster movie, *King Kong.* When RKO released the picture in 1933, the Empire State Building was barely two years old, but it had already made history as the world's tallest building. Soaring 1,250 feet into the air, this sleek sandstone-and-steel structure stunned the world with its 102 stories, 87 elevators, 2 observation decks, and special mooring for airships. Despite the impressiveness of its statistics, the Empire State Building bombed when it first opened—the Depression was in full swing and few firms were able to rent its offices.

King Kong, on the other hand, was a big box-office success and helped fill RKO's coffers for decades. In 1981, however, the tables were turned when the now booming Empire State Building decided to celebrate the great ape's fiftieth birthday by flying an eight-story-

Metropolitan monsters: King Kong and the Empire State Building

tall nylon balloon version of King Kong from its observation tower. Alas, the aging superstar had a rather rough time of it. No one could get him blown up properly; he kept springing leaks; and finally he had to be taken down when high winds threatened to blow away his half-inflated hulk. The whole fiasco became the subject of ridicule in the newspapers and on the radio. The real *King Kong,* by the way, was an eighteen-inch-tall, fur-covered jointed metal skeleton designed by a pioneer in puppet animation techniques named Willis O'Brien.

NOTE: *Movie lovers wishing to visit the Empire State Building can do so any day of the week between 9:30 A.M. and midnight. Admission is $2.50 for adults, $1.35 for children under twelve, and provides access to both the open-air observation deck on the 86th floor (which has been immortalized in such films as* The Clock, On the Town, The Moon Is Blue, Love Affair *and its remake,* An Affair to Remember*), and to the circular, glassed-in observatory on the 102nd story.*

3. GRAND CENTRAL TERMINAL
89 East 42nd Street

Back in the glory days of Hollywood, during the 1930s and 1940s, if you were heading from New York to the West Coast, chances were Grand Central Terminal is where you would have begun your journey. And the train that you would have taken was the legendary *Twentieth Century Limited,* which traveled overnight to Chicago where passengers would then board the *Super Chief* for the rest of their westward trek. The *Twentieth Century* left Grand Central every evening at around six o'clock from track 34 where a red carpet would be rolled out for departing passengers. Making their way down that carpet might have been Marlene Dietrich or Joan Crawford, with two or three redcaps in tow to handle their voluminous baggage. Both stars, according to former Grand Central redcap Oswald S. Throne, were good tippers, as was Mae West, who not only traveled with lots of luggage, but with five or six male "escorts" as well!

Alas, times and travel styles have changed. The *Twentieth Century* bit the dust in the mid-1960s, and Grand Central, which once was home to a number of other glamorous, long-distance trains, caters mostly to commuters these days. Still, Grand Central's glorious 1913 Beaux Arts terminal building—with its massive marble staircase, seventy-five-foot-high windows, and twinkling-star-studded ceiling—remains one of New York City's most dramatic public spaces. Grand Central is also a triumph of preservation: A decade ago it narrowly escaped "radical alterations" planned by developers who wanted to build a high-rise office building on top of it. Thanks to the commitment of concerned citizens who organized a grass-roots campaign to ensure its landmark status, this didn't happen.

Over the years, Grand Central (or Hollywood facsimiles thereof) has appeared in many movies. In 1934, the landmark station was the final location for *Twentieth Century,* the Columbia Pictures comedy about a Broadway producer (John Barrymore) and his protégée (Carole Lombard), much of which takes place aboard the train of the same name, and all of which was shot in Hollywood. Meanwhile, old-movie lovers can spot MGM's version of Grand Central in *Going Hollywood* (1933) and *The Thin Man Goes Home* (1944). In the latter, Asta breaks loose in the terminal at rush hour and a very hung-over Nick Charles (William Powell) has one hell of a time retrieving the pooch.

By the 1950s, however, going on location had become the rage. Thus, when Cary Grant needed to make a fast escape from New York City aboard The *Twentieth Century,* in *North by Northwest,* director Alfred Hitchcock shot the sequence at night inside the real station. Recent New York–made films that have also used the real Grand Central include the 1982 thriller *A Stranger Is Watching,* in which a psychopath holds a mother and child captive in a secret Grand Central cavern; Francis Ford Coppola's 1984 *The Cotton Club,* where Richard Gere gets the gangster's girlfriend at the end of the film and the two of them take off for Hollywood aboard The *Twentieth Century;* and Peter Yates's *The House on Carroll Street* (1988), which lensed its suspenseful climax on location at the station. (Those spectacular scenes of arch-villain Lex Luthor's fantastic

NYC super station: Grand Central

subterranean Grand Central palazzo in *Superman* (1978) were all done on a sound stage at a London movie studio, however.)

Besides serving as an important movie location, Grand Central once had a CBS television studio on one of its upper stories, and the early dramatic series "Man Against Crime," starring Ralph Bellamy, was broadcast live from here between 1949 and 1952. Sponsored by Camel cigarettes, the program always showed the good guys smoking, and never allowed its bad guys a single puff! Today, the old CBS studio is now a posh tennis club.

NOTE: *Movie lovers who want to see Grand Central Terminal close up—the building is loaded with intriguing nooks, crannies, and catwalks—can take the walking tour sponsored by the Municipal Art Society that is given every Wednesday at 12:30 P.M. The tour meets under the massive Kodak billboard on the Main Concourse— and it's free. All aboard!*

4. HORN & HARDART
200 East 42nd Street

In the days before there were McDonald's, Burger Kings, and Wendy's on practically every other block of New York City, another type of fast-food operation was frequented by the hungry masses: the Automat. A chain of self-service restaurants which were surprisingly glamorous, with marble counters and often Art Deco ornamentation, the Automats purveyed their dishes—piping-hot chicken pot pies, franks and beans, baked apples—from a wall of locked, glass-windowed boxes, each of which could be magically opened by inserting a few nickels and turning a knob.

The brains behind the Automats belonged to a team of restaurateurs from Philadelphia named Joseph V. Horn and Frank

Hollywood Automat: Jean Arthur and Ray Milland on the set of Easy Living, *1937*

Hardart, who first installed an automatic food-dispensing system, which they had imported from Germany, in one of their Philadelphia restaurants in 1902. Over the next thirty years, Automats became the rage of both Philadelphia and New York, but somehow Horn and Hardart never expanded beyond these two East Coast cities. Nonetheless, the rest of the country knew all about these state-of-the-art food palaces; and, supposedly, when Jean Harlow arrived in Manhattan for the first time in 1930 for the premiere of *Hell's Angels,* the one place that Hollywood's blonde bombshell wanted to visit in the Big Apple was the Automat.

One of the ways that Automats became famous was through the movies, since many directors featured these unique eating establishments in their films. In the 1925 silent picture *The Beautiful City,* for example, the plot revolves around a man who has been stealing nickels from an Automat. And in the 1930s, screenwriter/ director Preston Sturges perked up his screenplays for *The Thirty Day Princess* (1934) and *Easy Living* (1937) with Automat sequences. In the first, Cary Grant meets Sylvia Sidney—an actress posing as a princess—at the Automat; and in the second, Jean Arthur is a hungry typist trying to beg an Automat meal from a detective. In 1950, *The Sleeping City* also featured an Automat setting, which heightened the stark realism of this made-in-New York *film noir.* On the other hand, Doris Day plays it for laughs in *That Touch of Mink* (1962), when she is so broke that she has to sneak free Automat lunches from her girlfriend, Audrey Meadows, who works on the other side of the little glass boxes.

Sidney Lumet wasn't interested in laughs when he shot a scene for *The Group* at a Manhattan Automat in 1965; he was interested in a place that would evoke period (in this case, late-1920s) New York City. Today, Lumet would have a hard time doing an Automat sequence on location in New York. Of the three dozen that once operated here, the sole survivor stands at Third Avenue and 42nd Street and it does a brisker business with its salad bar than with its slot boxes, which these days accept only special tokens that must be purchased from a cashier. The last Automat also manages to survive through being rented out for private parties, where older guests wax nostalgic and younger ones joke over this odd way that New Yorkers once dined. Besides this 42nd Street holdout (which Woody Allen used in his 1986 *Radio Days*), the only other way to see an authentic Automat is to visit the Smithsonian's National Museum of American History in Washington, where part of the original Philadelphia Automat is on permanent display. For movie lovers who can't make it to New York or Washington, there's always the late show.

5. DAILY NEWS BUILDING
220 East 42nd Street

"Look, down in the street, it's Christopher Reeve and Margot Kidder coming out of the Daily News Building!" Which is a cry you might have heard back in 1977 during the filming of *Superman.* In this big-budget movie version of the famous comic strip, the landmark 1930 office building of a great metropolitan newspaper, the *Daily News,* doubled as the headquarters for the legendary *Daily Planet.* Especially striking, both in the *Superman* film and in real life, is the twelve-foot globe that revolves under a spectacular black-glass cupola in the lobby of the Daily News Building. Movie lovers will undoubtedly remember the thrilling helicopter crash that supposedly took place on the roof of the Daily Planet/Daily News Building, leaving Lois Lane/Margot Kidder dangling from the side of the structure. Those sequences were a triumph of special effects—not location shooting.

6. CHRYSLER BUILDING
405 Lexington Avenue

It must be one of New York City movie director Sidney Lumet's favorite skyscrapers because in *The Wiz,* when Diana Ross and Michael Jackson ease on down the road into Lumet's fantasy version of Manhattan as the Emerald City of Oz, no less than five Chrysler Buildings pop up on the horizon—and not one Empire State Building! Woody Allen, who once said, "There are very few modern skyscrapers that I like," nevertheless includes the Chrysler Building on the itinerary of the architectural tour of Manhattan that Sam Waterston gives in Allen's *Hannah and Her Sisters*—whereas the Empire State Building is noticeably absent. And when Dustin Hoffman points out major Manhattan landmarks to his son in Robert

*Glamor in the skies: the
Chrysler Building*

Benton's *Kramer vs. Kramer,* the Chrysler Building tops the list. And when Ridley Scott wants to symbolize Manhattan at its most glamorous in *Someone to Watch Over Me,* he dazzles us with nighttime views of this glorious 1930s high-rise. What is it about the Chrysler Building that's so appealing? Its six-story Art Deco spire? Its huge chrome gargoyles that were designed to look like 1931 Chrysler hood ornaments? Or simply the fact that there will never be another building quite like this one?

Unfortunately, the Chrysler Building's meatiest film role to date has been in a dreadful made-in-Manhattan monster movie called *Q,* about a gigantic mythological bird that comes to life and flies about zapping hardhats, window washers, penthouse sunbathers, and various other high-level New Yorkers. The creature's nest? You guessed it . . . the spire of the Chrysler Building. Despite its inane plot and equally absurd performances by Michael Moriarty, David Carradine, Candy Clarke, and Richard Roundtree, *Q* is a treat for architecture lovers because it features lots of shots of the Chrysler Building's sleek lobby of Moroccan marble and stainless steel, and it also provides rare close-up glimpses of the skyscraper's distinctive spire from every conceivable angle. For movie lovers, *Q* just might be a treat, too—it's one of those films that is so unbelievably bad, it's almost good. Almost.

7. ALGONQUIN HOTEL
59 West 44th Street

A hotel that is a literary landmark, the Algonquin will always be linked to an irreverent group of Manhattan intellectuals, known as the Round Table, who hung out in its Oak Room and later in its Rose Room in the 1920s and 1930s. The crew included critics Alexander Woollcott and Robert Benchley, playwright George S. Kaufman, essayist and short-story writer Dorothy Parker, humorist Ring Lardner, actress Tallulah Bankhead, and *New Yorker* editor Harold Ross (who is said to have put together the magazine at the hotel rather than in its offices across the street). Although most of the Round Table held the movies, and especially Hollywood, in disdain, many of them eventually developed pretty strong ties with the film industry when the studios offered one of the best sources of employment for writers during the Depression. Of the elite Algonquin group, Dorothy Parker wound up spending the most time in Hollywood, where she worked on the screenplays for such classic films as David O. Selznick's 1937 *A Star Is Born* (for which she shared an Oscar with her coauthor husband Alan Campbell) and Hitchcock's 1944 espionage thriller *Saboteur.*

It was also in 1944 that Hollywood immortalized the Algonquin's Rose Room with Otto Preminger's quirky murder mystery *Laura,* featuring a scene set in the historic dining room where the Round Table held forth. *Laura*'s Rose Room, of course, was a facsimile created on a sound stage at Twentieth Century–Fox. But when MGM decided to use the Algonquin as a principal location

The Algonquin Hotel's legendary Rose Room

for *Rich and Famous* in 1982, film-making techniques had changed considerably from those of the 1940s, and practically all of the hotel scenes were done on location. A particularly amusing sequence in the film shows Jacqueline Bisset as a neurotic writer giving a tour of the Algonquin, along with a history of the Round Table, to the much younger man she has just picked up and is about to escort up to her room.

Speaking of amorous goings-on, it was in the Algonquin's lobby—a cozy clutter of Victorian armchairs, sofas, and coffee tables—that Douglas Fairbanks first wooed Mary Pickford back in the 1910s. Fairbanks, who kept a suite at the Algonquin from 1907 to 1915, was the first of many film stars who thought of the Algonquin as home. These days, the tradition is carried on by Audrey Hepburn, Billy Wilder, Julie Christie, Sir Laurence Olivier, Jeremy Irons, Yves Montand, Francis Ford Coppola, Jules Dassin, Melina Mercouri, and Peter Ustinov—all of whom like the Algonquin for its proximity to the theater district, its lobby that is perfect for cocktails and/or a proper British tea, its chandelier-hung dining room that serves old-fashioned hotel food like chicken pot pie and calves liver with bacon, its mascot (a cat named Hamlet), and, most of all, its history.

P.S. In mid-1987, the Algonquin was sold to Caesar Park Hotels, a division of a Japanese corporation that operates luxury hotels in Brazil and the Far East. The company has said that it is "committed to maintaining the atmosphere, decor, and traditions that have made the Algonquin a beloved meeting place for New Yorkers and a long-time favorite of visitors to this city." Algonquin aficionados hope that the hotel's new owners will be true to their word.

8. HOTEL IROQUOIS
49 West 44th Street

Not nearly as historic or fashionable as its next-door neighbor, the Algonquin, the Iroquois can nonetheless claim a young actor named James Dean as a former resident. This was during the dawn of his New York career back in the early 1950s, when the only "acting" job he could manage to find was as a guinea pig testing out the wacky stunts for the producers of the popular TV game show, "Beat the Clock." At the Iroquois, Dean occupied room number 802, which he shared with fellow actor (recently a producer of "The Colbys") William Bast. In those days, both guys, if they were meeting someone they deemed important, would arrange to see them next door in the lobby of the Algonquin. Today, the same ploy is still used by cagey Iroquois guests wishing to pass themselves off as Algonquinites!

9. RADIO CITY MUSIC HALL
1260 Avenue of the Americas

It advertised 6,200 seats, but the total has always been closer to 5,960. Still, when Radio City Music Hall opened in 1932 as part of New York's futuristic Rockefeller Center complex, it was the largest theater in the world. And today, depending on whether you consider a 9,000-seat auditorium in the People's Republic of China a theater (we don't), it still is. Everything about Radio City Music

Divine Deco: Radio City Music Hall's Grand Foyer

Postcard view of Radio City Music Hall stage

Hall is outsized—from its sixty-foot-high foyer to its two-ton chandeliers (the largest in the world) to its Wurlitzer organ (the mightiest on earth, with fifty-six separate sets of pipes).

While many people assume that this great Art Deco theater started out as a movie palace, Radio City Music Hall was actually planned for spectacular stage shows, whereas the now defunct Center Theater on the next block was to have been Rockefeller Center's main venue for films. When the Music Hall's six-hour opening-night program bombed, however, the enormous theater quickly turned to the formula that would spell its success for the next three decades: a thirty-minute stage show combined with a first-run family movie. More than just a commercial success, Radio City Music Hall—with its high-kicking Rockettes, spectacular Christmas and Easter pageants, and top-notch movies—became an entertainment landmark of New York City, a must on every visitor's list of things to see and do.

Not only has it played a role as an important site for the New York premieres of films like *Mr. Smith Goes to Washington, Singin' in the Rain,* and *An American in Paris,* the Hall has also wound up being featured in a number of films including *Annie, The Godfather, Radio Days,* and Alfred Hitchcock's *Saboteur,* in which Robert Cummings runs across a Hollywood mock-up of the Radio City stage while a film is being shown. Since a gunfight is taking place on screen, the audience at first doesn't realize that a real gun is being fired at Cummings in the theater.

Radio City's glory days ended in the 1960s. For one thing, the studios had started mass-releasing films by then, making it next to impossible for Radio City still to boast first runs. Also, America's tastes had changed. Family films were out of fashion in the 1960s and 1970s, and the Rockettes kicking up their heels were considered high camp, not mass entertainment. By 1978, the Music Hall was losing millions of dollars a year, and the Rockefeller Group, its parent company, decided to close it down. A white elephant, the grand Art Deco entertainment palace was earmarked for demolition. Happily, a citizens' group stepped in and managed to get the interior of the Music Hall declared a historic landmark. (TV fans may remember the 1979 special, starring former Rockette Ann-Margret, that celebrated the glories of the endangered Music Hall.) Around the same time, the Rockefeller Group committed itself to refurbishing its newly designated landmark and to trying to make it a viable financial proposition. This involved the creation of Radio City Music Hall Productions, whose purpose was to find new uses for the mega-auditorium. And so, these days, Radio City Music Hall hosts everyone and everything from rock and pop stars (Madonna, the Grateful Dead, Bette Midler, Bill Cosby) to trade shows to TV specials ("Night of 100 Stars, Part II") to its own classic Christmas and Easter extravaganzas. To make a long story short, for the first time in several decades, the Radio City Music Hall actually showed a profit in 1985. And, while movies no longer play a major role in the Music Hall's life, special screenings still go on here from time to time, such as the New York premiere (in July 1983) of the restored version of the Judy Garland/James Mason *A Star Is Born*, which featured the "lost" twenty-four minutes that had been cut from the film by Jack Warner back in 1954. Although the celebrity-studded audience included James Mason, Liza Minnelli, Lorna Luft, and Sid Luft, for many of the die-hard Garland fans who attended the premiere, the most exciting part of the evening was seeing Judy on the Radio City Music Hall's mammoth screen. The Music Hall is also where Francis Ford Coppola first unveiled his reconstructed version of Abel Gance's 1927 silent-screen epic, *Napoleon,* before New York audiences.

NOTE: *Movie lovers can experience the splendor of the Radio City Music Hall either by attending a performance or by taking an hour-long backstage tour of the place. Tours are given daily at frequent intervals; they depart from the Main Lobby. Tickets currently cost $5.00. Call: (212) 541-9436; ask for the Tour Desk.*

10. ROCKEFELLER CENTER
(48th to 52nd Streets between Fifth and Sixth Avenues)

It makes for one hell of an establishing shot: a long pan down the seventy stories of the RCA Building to the gigantic gilded statue of Prometheus backed by a row of fluttering flags and spurting jets of water. Hold on the statue, then pull back and angle down to reveal a huge outdoor café—or, if it's winter, an ice-skating rink. Pull back further to include a long courtyard studded with a series of lavishly planted minigardens. Or do the whole sequence the other way around. Rockefeller Center, which the American Institute of Architects' *AIA Guide to New York City* calls "an island of architectural excellence . . . the greatest urban complex of the twentieth century," is so beautifully laid out, so well proportioned, so *perfect* that it's hard to make it look anything less than extraordinary, no matter how you shoot it. Used in the movies, a shot of Rockefeller Center—as in *Nothing Sacred* (1937), *How to Marry a Millionaire* (1953), or *Manhattan* (1979)—*establishes* New York at its best: a perfectly balanced combination of power, glamour, and humanity.

Conceived and founded by John D. Rockefeller, the twelve high-, middle-, and low-rise buildings that comprised the original Rockefeller Center were built between 1930 and 1940. The centerpiece of the complex is the seventy-story RCA Building. When Rockefeller first envisioned his urban center in the 1920s, his plan was to provide a new home for the Metropolitan Opera House (it was on Broadway at 38th Street at the time) to be surrounded by office, retail, entertainment, and dining facilities. When the Depression hit in 1929, the Met decided that it couldn't afford to move, so Rockefeller and his advisers decided to build an office tower instead of an opera house. At the same time, the Radio Corporation of America and its subsidiary, the National Broadcasting Company, were among the few companies in the country that were prospering despite the Depression. Looking for a corporate headquarters to suit their growing needs and power, RCA/NBC found a classy home at Rockefeller Center and became the principal tenant of the handsome skyscraper at 30 Rockefeller Plaza which opened in 1933 bearing the RCA name.

For the radio and television lover, the RCA Building—which

On the Town *at Rockefeller Center: Frank Sinatra, Jules Munshin, Gene Kelly, 1949*

still houses NBC's principal New York radio and TV studios—is one of the most historic sites in the country connected with these media. Television literally came of age at 30 Rock where, beginning in 1935, the network started broadcasting two programs a week from studio 3H. These first telecasts consisted of plays, comedians, scenes from opera, cooking demonstrations (limited to salads because the intense heat from the then-necessary ultra-high-powered TV lights made stove-top cooking unthinkable), and even live transmissions from the streets of New York thanks to a mobile unit that went into operation in 1937. Despite these experiments, it wasn't until after World War II that TV really got off the ground. Then, too, NBC was at the forefront of the medium with such programs as "Kraft Television Theatre" (1947), "Howdy Doody" (1947), the John Cameron Swayze–anchored "Camel News Caravan" (1947), "Meet the Press" (1947), and Milton Berle's "Texaco Star Theatre" (1948)—most of which were televised from Radio City.

In 1952, NBC took a bold step in early-morning programming by introducing a two-hour show that mixed news, interviews, and entertainment features. The host of NBC's new "Today Show" was a laid-back gentleman named Dave Garroway and one of his sidekicks was a chimpanzee named J. Fred Muggs. Instead of using a studio in 30 Rockefeller Plaza, however, the "Today Show" was done live from a spacious Rockefeller Center showroom with street-to-ceiling picture windows on the south side of West 49th Street just west of Rockefeller Plaza. Passers-by pressed their noses up

Dave Garroway hosts the first "Today" show, January 14, 1952

Window on the world: the "Today" show's 49th Street studio, 1955

against the glass to watch the live TV production going on inside, and at various times each morning the camera was turned on the gawkers. Soon "Today" not only became a hit television show, it became a major New York City tourist attraction. Today, those same huge 49th Street windows, once showcases for the antics of Dave Garroway and J. Fred Muggs, now look in on the clerks and tellers of the Bank Hapoalim.

Besides checking out the original venue of the "Today Show," TV lovers who visit Rockefeller Center can see the show's current studio (3B) by taking the fifty-five-minute NBC Studio Tour. Among the other attractions of this behind-the-scenes look at Radio City are studio 8H, the "Saturday Night Live" auditorium (formerly home to Arturo Toscanini's NBC Symphony Orchestra) as well as the site of such classic early TV shows as "Your Hit Parade," "What's My Line," and the "Kraft Television Theatre." The tour also takes television lovers onto a replica of the set of "The Tonight Show" starring Johnny Carson, which originally was broadcast from New York. Here, visitors can participate in "Tonight Show" skits as well as see demonstrations of some of the more technical aspects of television broadcasting. And, if they're lucky, NBC Studio Tour guests might also catch glimpses of current NBC celebrities such as David Letterman, Jane Pauley, Bryant Gumbel, or Tom Brokaw, who all work in the building.

NOTE: *The NBC Studio Tour is currently given Mondays through Saturdays at fifteen-minute intervals between 9:30 A.M. and 4:30 P.M. Tours leave from the NBC Tour Desk on the main floor of 30 Rockefeller Plaza; admission is currently $5.50.*

11. WALDORF-ASTORIA HOTEL
301 Park Avenue

One of the world's grandest Art Deco structures, Park Avenue's monumental Waldorf-Astoria went up in 1931 as a replacement for the original Waldorf-Astoria, which had been at 34th Street and Fifth Avenue and was demolished to make way for the Empire State Building. With 2,200 rooms when it opened (the number has since been reduced to 1,800), the new Waldorf was the largest hotel in the world, and over the years it would host practically every major VIP on earth—from heads of state to heads of studios. The hotel's presidential suite is world famous and, unlike the "presidential suites" of many hotels, has actually put up every U.S. president since Franklin D. Roosevelt.

Of all the Waldorf's accommodations, by far the most fashionable for non-chief executives are the 113 apartments that comprise the legendary Waldorf Towers. Literally a hotel within a hotel, the Towers has its own private entrance on East 50th Street, its own concierges, its own discreet style. Among the Towers' most celebrated long-term tenants have been the Duke and Duchess of Windsor, Richard Nixon, Henry Kissinger, Cole Porter, Gregory Peck, Frank Sinatra, and Marilyn Monroe, who had a four-room apartment here in 1955 after she fled Hollywood stardom for the life of an acting student in New York.

While the Waldorf, with its twin Deco towers and its sleek *moderne* lines, is extremely impressive from the outside, the interior of the hotel is the real showstopper. The lavish lobby is a dream of mahogany-paneled walls, marble floors and columns, monumental urns, streamlined sconces and chandeliers. Stepping inside this dramatic space is like walking into a glamorous 1930s Hollywood movie. Hardcore movie lovers and late-show devotees may, in fact, remember a 1940s film from MGM that took advantage of the Waldorf's Deco dazzle. A postwar take on the studio's classic early

MGM goes to the Waldorf: Tony Sarg Oasis set for Weekend at the Waldorf, *1945*

The last word in posh: the Waldorf Towers

talkie, *Grand Hotel,* MGM's *Weekend at the Waldorf* (1945) had
an incredible lineup of stars that included Ginger Rogers, Lana
Turner, Walter Pidgeon, Van Johnson, Keenan Wynn, Robert
Benchley, even Xavier Cugat. Although the film received mixed
reviews, most critics cited the fine performance turned in by the
Waldorf. Indeed, if the film does little else, it provides a fascinating
behind-the-scenes glimpse at the workings of a great hotel, with
second-unit sequences filmed in such rarely visited areas as the
garage, the massive telephone switchboard, the in-hotel police station, the secretarial pool, and the kennels. *Weekend at the Waldorf*
is also a triumph of MGM art direction, because it is practically
impossible to tell which scenes have been shot by the second-unit
crew on location and which were done at the MGM studios in
Culver City, where much of the Waldorf's splendor was painstak-
ingly recreated.

In more recent years, the grand ballrooms and luxurious suites
of the Waldorf have been featured in such films as *The Out of
Towners* (the Waldorf is where Sandy Dennis and Jack Lemmon
should have stayed in the wacky 1970 Neil Simon story about all
the things that can go wrong on a visit to the Big Apple); *Rich and
Famous* (a 1981 George Cukor film in which rich-and-famous bestselling novelist Candice Bergen rents a whole floor); plus *The Great
Gatsby* (1974), *My Favorite Year* (1982), *Six Weeks* (1982), *Broadway Danny Rose* (1983), *Hannah and Her Sisters* (1986), and the
1985 TV mini-series "Kane and Able." Recently, too, the Waldorf
completed a $100 million-plus restoration, which will assure future
guests and future moviemakers that its Art Deco splendor will keep
shining for many years to come.

12. TRANS LUX THEATER SITE
Lexington Avenue at 52nd Street

The Trans Lux was a neighborhood movie house that stood at 586 Lexington Avenue from 1940 until the late 1970s. One hot September evening in 1954, Hollywood director Billy Wilder brought a film crew to the Trans Lux to shoot an exterior for *The Seven Year Itch.* More important, Wilder also unleashed the film's superstar, Marilyn Monroe, on the streets of Manhattan. Alerted to the event by studio publicity people, the press was on hand en masse to document the filming, and they were joined by a couple thousand spectators. In the scene, Marilyn and her downstairs neighbor, Tom Ewell, are coming out of the Trans Lux, having just seen *The Creature from the Black Lagoon.* Marilyn liked the film, but "just felt so sorry for the Creature at the end." Then, along comes the Lexington Avenue IRT and up goes Marilyn's white billowy skirt. "Oh, do you feel the breeze from the subway?" she coos to her co-star. "Isn't it delicious?"

Meanwhile, the crowd cheered and shouted, "Higher, higher!" as the country's number-one sex goddess showed her panties—and more—to all of Lexington Avenue. One visitor definitely not

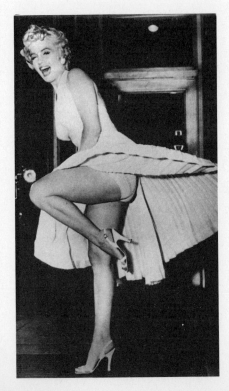

Street theater: Marilyn filming The Seven Year Itch, *1954*

amused by the proceedings, however, was Joe DiMaggio, Marilyn's husband of barely nine months. Having already found life with a superstar to be no picnic, DiMaggio viewed Marilyn's Lexington Avenue antics as the final straw. Back in Hollywood, less than a month after the incident in New York, the DiMaggios filed for divorce. Ironically, much of the scene that wrecked the marriage had to be reshot on the Twentieth Century–Fox lot.

Today, movie lovers will find a gigantic office building on the northwest corner of Lexington Avenue and 52nd Street, where the Trans Lux once stood; but the Marilyn Monroe memorial subway grating remains. Ladies, hold on to your skirts!

13. CBS BUILDING
485 Madison Avenue

In the beginning there was NBC . . . and only NBC. Then, in 1927, a new radio network called the Columbia Phonograph Broadcasting System came along to challenge the National Broadcasting Corporation's monopoly of the airwaves. The new network had a rough go of it initially, and when its owners, the Columbia Phonograph Record Company, backed out, a young cigar magnate named William S. Paley stepped in, shortened the network's name to the Columbia Broadcasting System, and perked up its credit rating by getting powerful Paramount Pictures to come in on the deal. Thus it was with great pride and much fanfare that, in the autumn of 1929, Mr. Paley cut the ribbon for CBS's headquarters in the brand-new Columbia Broadcasting Building at the corner of Madison Avenue and 52nd Street.

CBS occupied the top five floors of the impressive new twenty-four-story structure, and had fifteen studios on the premises; these ranged from tiny chambers to an auditorium large enough to hold 250 performers. Some of the studios were equipped with glassed-off, soundproof balconies to accommodate spectators for early radio shows, and one studio was set up for what everyone knew was coming sooner or later: television. Indeed, many important early experiments in television took place in the CBS Building in the 1930s. New York radio personality Guy Lebow remembers the bleak CBS TV studio back in those days, the garish makeup that performers had to wear, and the primitive camera, with its high-powered spotlight that gave actors "eye bends" after even a couple of seconds in front of it.

But it was radio that was responsible for CBS's great success in the 1930s and 1940s. As the country's number-two network, CBS devoted most of its energies to its radio programming in order to catch up with top-ranked NBC. Meanwhile, NBC was so convinced that television was just around the corner that it let its radio division slide as it moved full speed ahead on the development of TV. Thus, by the end of the 1930s, CBS—with a strong news division that included pros like Edward R. Murrow and Eric Sevareid, and equally impressive dramatic programming that featured the talents of Orson Welles and Archibald MacLeish—was a force to be reckoned with. When World War II erupted to further delay the coming of television, CBS's position in the industry was made even stronger.

CBS and Mr. Paley stayed at 485 Madison Avenue for thirty-six years. When the network moved into its present headquarters at 52nd Street and the Avenue of the Americas in 1965, it was Mr. Paley who, in the tradition of ships' captains, was the last person to leave 485 Madison Avenue.

14. "BLACK ROCK"
51 West 52nd Street

Known as "Black Rock," this thirty-eight-story skyscraper of Canadian black granite has been the corporate headquarters of CBS since 1965. The subject of many headlines in the mid-1980s, Black Rock was a prime target for various corporate takeover schemes, engineered by everyone from cable-TV czar Ted Turner to a right-wing syndicate headed by North Carolina's ultraconservative Senator Jesse Helms. In late summer 1986, however, CBS founder William Paley surprised the entertainment community and Wall Street by coming out of retirement to reorganize the company and, it was hoped, save the legendary broadcasting network from being gobbled up by outsiders.

15. THE 21 CLUB
21 West 52nd Street

When Karen Richards, wife of playwright Lloyd Richards, has a lunch date with Margo Channing, Broadway's reigning leading lady, in *All About Eve,* the setting is naturally the 21 Club. And when Karen arrives at "21," whom should she bump into but Addison DeWitt, the all-powerful newspaper columnist, who just happens to have the up-and-coming Broadway actress Eve Harrington in tow!

In the days of *All About Eve* (the early 1950s), "21" was one of *the* places in New York for the rich and the famous to break bread together. Cut to "21" in the late 1980s where, on any given day, you're likely to find a cast of characters that might include Frank Sinatra, Elizabeth Taylor, Johnny Carson, Ginger Rogers, producer Ray Stark, superagent Irving "Swifty" Lazar, major mogul Marvin Davis, real estate baron Donald Trump, former president Richard Nixon, book editor Jacqueline Onassis, or designer Bill Blass. You may not find critic Rex Reed at "21," however, since he was once barred from the dining room for not having a tie. "But this is Bill Blass," Reed is reported to have protested, referring to his dapper sports coat. Still, he flunked the stringent "21" dress test and was refused entry.

In a city that is constantly changing, "21" adheres to its traditions—from dress codes to not tolerating customers who insult waiters to ejecting patrons who've had too much to drink (allowing them to return the next day if they're sober) to not "selling" choice tables. Indeed, for many "21" has served as a "club," a place where they could go anytime and always count on finding a warm welcome and no surprises. It was no doubt this strong sense of continuity that attracted Humphrey Bogart to "21," and today his table—number 30 in the downstairs bar—is still known as "Bogie's Corner," indicated by a sign hanging nearby. In the same room, actor Robert Benchley once held court at table number 3—"Benchley's Corner." It was near this table that, in the mid-1960s, Swifty Lazar threw a glass at director Otto Preminger's bald head in an argument over the film rights to Truman Capote's *In Cold Blood.* Upstairs, in the main dining room, Joan Crawford always had the table just to the left of the entrance.

It may come as a surprise to some that this bastion of Manhattan luxury started out as an expensive speakeasy. Founded in 1930 by Jack Kriendler and Charlie Berns, "21" was then equipped with an elaborate security/screening system, secret cellars that concealed some five thousand cases of liquor, and a James Bond-like bar that could automatically dispose of all the booze on the premises in the event of an unexpected visit by the feds. In those days, the block of 52nd Street between Fifth and Sixth Avenues was one of the city's liveliest spots, noted for its speakeasys, restaurants, and nightclubs. Today, the same block is wall-to-wall office towers. The sole survivor from the street's glory days is the cluster of three brownstone townhouses that together form "21." With its wrought-iron grill, old-fashioned lanterns, two American flags, and row of

Top table at 21: Burt Lancaster and Tony Curtis in The Sweet Smell of Success, *1957*

cast-iron jockey statues out front, "21"—which recently changed its owners but not its style—remains a monument to a glamorous New York that once was and that, inside "21" at least, lives on.

16. MUSEUM OF MODERN ART
11 West 53rd Street

In addition to its trove of Van Goghs, Picassos, Monets, and Mondrians, the Museum of Modern Art counts among its treasures important works by De Mille, Chaplin, Griffith, Porter, Stiller, and Méliès. In fact, MoMA has some 10,000 films in its archives that span the medium's history from late-nineteenth-century silents to late-twentieth-century video art.

Believing that film was "the only great art peculiar to the twentieth century," former MoMA director Alfred H. Barr, Jr., established the Department of Film at the Museum of Modern Art in 1935, and immediately sent curator Iris Barry on a special mission to Hollywood to drum up support for his innovative undertaking. There, at a party given by Mary Pickford and Douglas Fairbanks at Pickfair, their lavish Beverly Hills estate, Miss Barry met industry heavyweights like Samuel Goldwyn, Harold Lloyd, Harry Warner, Harry Cohn, Ernst Lubitsch, Mervyn LeRoy, Walt Disney, Jesse Lasky, and Mack Sennett. Returning to New York with what the *Los Angeles Times* reported to be "more than a million feet" of film, Miss Barry had the beginnings of MoMA's collection. But one old-timer who was not so forthcoming as many of his Hollywood colleagues was D. W. Griffith, who refused to donate his own films to the museum, reportedly saying that nothing could convince him that films had anything to do with art. Ultimately MoMA enlisted the aid of Griffith's friend and former star actress, Lillian Gish, who eventually persuaded him to hand over to history his collection of films, music, still photographs, and papers. It seems, however, that it was the lure of the tax write-off that was really responsible for Griffith's change of heart.

For the movie lover, the best thing about MoMA's film collection is that it is constantly on view. The museum has two theaters—one with 460 seats, the other with 217—which together are used to present some two dozen screenings a week. In addition to showing films, the Film Department maintains a library of film books, screenplays, reviews, publicity material, and four million stills that is an important research center for students, authors, and historians.

By far the most important activity of the MoMA Film Department is its work in film preservation. A frightening fact is that, of all the feature films made before 1952, half have disappeared entirely; of those produced before 1930, only a quarter survive, since the nitrate stock on which they were shot eventually self-destructs. Newer motion pictures, especially those shot on color-negative film during the period between the 1950s and the 1970s, are endangered too because the dyes in their negatives are unstable.

As a result, many important classics from these decades—*Rebel without a Cause* (1955); *Tom Jones* (1963)—have faded or are fading fast. The good news is that Kodak has come up with a new color film that promises to remain stable for at least a century. The bad news is that tremendous amounts of money are needed to transfer older movies onto this new stock. Still, MoMA perseveres in its noble goal of preserving the art form unique to our century.

NOTE: *Screenings by the Film Department of the Museum of Modern Art are presented free to MoMA members, and are open to the general public for a museum admission fee of $5.00. For information, call: (212) 708–9490.*

17. MUSEUM OF BROADCASTING
1 East 53rd Street

The brainchild of CBS founding father, William S. Paley, the Museum of Broadcasting is the only facility of its kind anywhere. Dedicated exclusively to the preservation, cataloguing, and showcasing of radio and television *art,* this little museum is housed in a skinny building that was once part of the fabled Stork Club, which stood next door. Since its debut in 1976, the museum has accumulated over ten thousand television programs and an equal number of radio shows in its archives. Open to media scholars and fans alike, the museum provides twenty-three custom-built private viewing consoles where individuals can screen the cassettes they have requested. Currently the most frequently asked-for TV program is the 1964 Ed Sullivan show on which the Beatles made their live U.S. television debut. After that, in order of popularity, come "Amos 'n Andy," "Classic TV Commercials," "My Name Is Barbra," and Elvis Presley's 1956 Ed Sullivan appearance.

While the Museum of Broadcasting has many examples of the best of radio and television history in its ever-growing collection, it is constantly on the lookout for more material. In fact, it publishes a "Most Wanted Programs" list periodically in its efforts to find such long-lost video treasures as the opening of the 1939 World's Fair in New York, which is believed to have been the first commercial television broadcast in history. Another artifact high on the Museum of Broadcasting's wish list is the never-broadcast 1951 pilot for "I Love Lucy," whose plot was incorporated into the sixth episode of the first season's lineup.

Besides providing an opportunity for individuals to explore radio/TV history firsthand, the MB has a sixty-three-seat video theater for major "exhibits." These can be anything from an examination of James Dean's career in early television to screenings of "lost" episodes of "The Honeymooners." Special showings from the museum's collection also take place in its two forty-seat video-thèques. And coming sometime in 1989 is a brand-new home for the MB at 23 West 52nd Street, which will have additional space, many more video viewers, and *two* theaters, one with two hundred seats and another with seventy-five.

NOTE: *The Museum of Broadcasting is open on Tuesdays from 12:00 noon to 8:00 P.M., and Wednesdays through Saturdays from 12:00 noon to 5:00 P.M. Suggested contributions: $3.00 for adults; $2.00 for students; $1.50 for senior citizens and children under thirteen. Phone: (212) 752–7684.*

18. SAMUEL PALEY PLAZA
3 East 53rd Street

Built in 1967 by CBS founder William S. Paley in honor of his father, Samuel Paley Plaza is a pleasant little park with tables, chairs, trees, and a waterfall. A popular place in warm weather for Manhattanites and tourists to have light lunches or snacks, the park stands on the site of what was once one of New York City's most fashionable watering-holes: Sherman Billingsley's famous Stork Club. Always crammed with celebrities, the Stork Club was the favorite hangout of columnist Walter Winchell, who kept the rest of the country informed of its glamorous goings-on.

The most exclusive place to be seated at the Stork Club was in the small Cub Room, which owner Billingsley reserved for stars (many of whose portraits graced the walls) and socialites. The rest of the world had to make do with a table in the main dining room, which had a large dance floor and nonstop music. In both rooms, and at the long bar, Billingsley ran a tight ship. His strictly enforced house rules included refusing admittance to unescorted women at night, although they could turn up for lunch or at cocktail hour; also, any customer who started a fight was permanently barred from the premises.

So great was the fame of the Stork Club that Billingsley was

Stork Club stars: Henry Fonda, Joan Crawford, Ruth Warrick, Peggy Ann Garner, Walter Winchell, and Dana Andrews in Daisy Kenyon, *1947*

contracted by the *Encyclopaedia Britannica* to write its first entry on nightclubs. In addition, the club was immortalized in the movies, notably in Hitchcock's made-in-New York *The Wrong Man* (1957), with star Henry Fonda in the role of a Stork Club bass player; and in Otto Preminger's *Daisy Kenyon* (1947), where columnists Walter Winchell and Leonard Lyons play themselves in a dramatic Stork Club sequence toward the end of the film. The club closed in 1965, made a brief comeback on Central Park South in the 1970s, and now lives on on the late show.

19. ST. REGIS HOTEL
2 East 55th Street

Built by Colonel John Jacob Astor, this was the tallest (eighteen stories) and most luxurious hotel New York had ever seen when it went up in 1904. Public rooms were decorated with the finest European furnishings; china was by Royal Worcester, Royal Minton, and Sèvres. There was marble everywhere—in stairways, corridors, even in the basement engine and boiler rooms! Many guest rooms came with their own Steinway pianos, and all were equipped with such then unheard-of innovations as automatic vacuum-cleaning systems and individual thermostats to control the temperature and humidity of room air.

With all its amenities, the St. Regis attracted quite a few glamorous guests over the years—from Humphrey Bogart (it was Bogie's favorite Manhattan hotel) to Marilyn Monroe, who stayed at 2 East 55th Street when she came to town in 1954 to do location shooting for *The Seven Year Itch.* Her marriage to Joe DiMaggio was in serious trouble at the time, but matters got a lot worse the

The St. Regis

evening she shot the infamous scene on Lexington Avenue in which her skirt gets blown up by the air from a passing subway train. Supposedly, the fight that followed between Monroe and DiMaggio in their St. Regis suite was so intense that it woke up the whole floor.

Three decades later, the characters played by Michael Caine and Barbara Hershey in *Hannah and Her Sisters* get along much better in their St. Regis room, which they use as a trysting place in the 1986 Woody Allen film. Hotel sources point out that only the hotel's handsome Beaux Arts façade was used in the film, and that the interior of the suite shown on screen was decidedly less grand than a real St. Regis room. Woody made up for the slight when he returned to the hotel the next year to shoot *Radio Days,* which featured the St. Regis's King Cole dining room as the elegant 1940s nightclub where a blond Mia Farrow works as a cigarette girl. Movie lovers can also spot the St. Regis in *Taxi Driver,* where the landmark provides one of the few beautiful images in Martin Scorsese's otherwise relentlessly depressing view of Manhattan at its worst.

20. FRIARS CLUB
57 East 55th Street

This enchanting English Renaissance townhouse in midtown Manhattan has, since 1956, served as headquarters for one of the most famous private clubs in America—the Friars. Among its top officers are: Frank Sinatra, Head Abbot; Milton Berle, Abbot Emeritus; Sammy Davis, Jr., Bard; Tom Jones, Knight; Paul Anka, Herald; Alan King, Monitor; Howard Cosell, Historian; Henny Youngman, Squire. Founded in 1904 by a group of New York theatrical press agents in order to separate the legitimate members of their profession from the numerous frauds who misrepresented themselves to producers in order to gain free admittance to the theater, the Friars eventually evolved simply into a club for members of the theatrical profession. If movie lovers can wangle an invitation to the Friars' 55th Street "monastery," they will find a dining room and "Round the World Bar" (named for former Abbot Mike Todd's 1956 film, *Around the World in Eighty Days*) on the first floor, the Milton Berle Room and Joe E. Lewis Bar on the second, the Ed Sullivan Reading Room and Frank Sinatra TV-viewing Room on the third, a billiard room and barber shop on the fourth, a health club on the fifth, and a solarium and golf practice net on the roof.

World famous for their celebrity "roasts," the Friars over the years have so honored Jack Benny, Bob Hope, George Jessel, Dean Martin and Jerry Lewis, Ed Sullivan, Perry Como, Dinah Shore, Garry Moore, Johnny Carson, Burt Reynolds, Barbra Streisand, Tom Jones, Carol Burnett, Cary Grant, Elizabeth Taylor, George Burns, George Raft, Lucille Ball, and Sid Caesar. Often these roasts are stag affairs, and the jokes and language go beyond being X-rated. In 1983, comedienne Phyllis Diller made show-business history when, disguised as a man, she crashed a Friars roast for Sid

*Midtown monastery:
the Friars Club*

Caesar. Phyllis, who even used the men's room at the Sheraton
Centre Hotel on Seventh Avenue, where the event was held, managed to get through the whole affair without being discovered. Said
Phyllis of the proceedings: "It was the funniest, dirtiest thing I ever
heard in my life. Of course, I had already heard this language before,
because I once ran into a truck."

21. COLUMBIA PICTURES
711 Fifth Avenue

Whereas the sign on the outside once identified this Fifth Avenue office tower as the Columbia Pictures building, it now reads
"The Coca-Cola Company," acknowledging the soft-drink conglomerate that beefed up its portfolio in 1982 by purchasing—for
a mere $700 or $800 million—the motion picture studio that Harry
Cohn founded back in 1924. Despite the new name on the door,
711 is still Columbia's New York City headquarters.

In 1977–1978, the Oscar-lined eleventh-floor board room of
711 saw quite a bit of high drama as Columbia executives, darting
back and forth between coasts and between expensive meals at
nearby La Grenouille and La Côte Basque, tried to contain an ever-
growing corporate crisis that started when it was discovered that
their president, David Begelman, had forged some $75,000 worth
of checks. The "Begelman Affair," as it came to be known in the

headlines and on Rona Barrett's dramatic TV broadcasts, resulted in the rolling of a number of Columbia heads and may go down as one of the studio's lowest moments. Today, Columbia is seeing if things go better with Coke.

22. TIFFANY & COMPANY
727 Fifth Avenue

"Don't you just love it? Nothing bad can ever happen to you in a place like this." Thus spoke Audrey Hepburn as Holly Golightly, the ultimate Manhattan free spirit, in the 1961 Paramount version of Truman Capote's bestselling novella *Breakfast at Tiffany's.* For the film, which was directed by Blake Edwards, at the time known mainly as the creator of the "Peter Gunn" and "Mr. Lucky" TV series, a number of New York City locations were used, including exteriors and interiors of the legendary Tiffany & Company jewelers.

Tracing its roots back to 1837 (and its present Fifth Avenue location to 1940), Tiffany made certain that the Sunday shooting of the film went smoothly by stationing forty of its own security guards and salespeople around the store to keep an eye on the millions and millions of dollars' worth of sparkling merchandise. In the scene that was done inside the store, Audrey Hepburn and George Peppard shock an uppity Tiffany's salesman by asking to see something in the $10 range. (Says Audrey/Holly: "I think it's

Columbia Pictures/
Coca-Cola Building

Window shopping:
Audrey Hepburn at
Tiffany's in Breakfast at
Tiffany's, *1961*

tacky to wear diamonds before I'm forty.") The salesman winds up showing the pair a sterling silver telephone dialer for $6.75—which they decline.

23. RITZ TOWERS
Park Avenue at 57th Street

Among William Randolph Hearst's many real estate holdings in Manhattan was the posh Ritz Towers apartment hotel, a beautiful 1920s building exotically ornamented with cornices, balustrades, finials, and obelisks. It was here that Hearst and his movie-star mistress Marion Davies kept a lavish suite which they often used when they were in New York in the 1930s. While most people these days think of Miss Davies' film career as having been little more than a plaything for Hearst, the truth of the matter is that Marion was an extremely successful film comedienne who made quite a lot of money from her pictures and through her own shrewd investments. In fact, in 1937 she saved Hearst from bankruptcy by coming up with a cool million of her own money. The two were staying at the Ritz Towers at the time, and Marion spent a full day selling off her jewelry and mortgaging her real estate to produce the cash to bail out her buddy.

A decade later, another movie celebrity who resided at the Ritz Towers was Greta Garbo. Her quarters were not nearly so grand as those of her landlords, Davies and Hearst, however. Designer Cecil Beaton, who claims to have had a love affair with Garbo in the late 1940s, writes in his autobiography, *Memoirs of the 40s* (McGraw-Hill, 1972), that Garbo at the Ritz "lived like a monk with little except a toothbrush, a piece of soap, and a jar of face cream." The affair ended when Beaton had to return to work in England. He wanted Garbo to accompany him, but the great star refused his offer, saying, "You see how difficult and neurotic I am. I am impossible to get on with." Nevertheless, the two remained friends—until, of course, Beaton published his book in 1973.

24. BERGDORF GOODMAN
754 Fifth Avenue

She was queen of the thrift shops, a kooky creature of vintage feather boas and antique *schmatas.* It made good copy for a while, but once twenty-two-year-old Barbra Streisand was well on the road to superstardom via *Funny Girl* on Broadway, platinum record albums, and a $5 million TV deal, it was time to clean up the act. Which is just what La Streisand did in the spring of 1965 on network TV in an elaborate nine-minute musical production number of "Second Hand Rose" in which she donned hundreds of thousands of dollars worth of glamorous high-fashion ensembles as part of her "My Name Is Barbra" special. The setting for this extraordinary media event was nothing less than New York City's most exclusive department store, Bergdorf Goodman; and, besides furnishing the location, Bergdorf's also supplied the outfits, including fabulous furs by the store's famous resident fur designer, Emeric Partos, and hats by its not-so-well-known (yet!) in-house milliner, a young Southern gent named Halston. Not to be outdone by all the clothes and designers, Miss Streisand offered her own fashion tips to readers of the *New York Times* in a special on-the-set interview. Proving just how far she had come in the fashion department, Streisand had this to say on (1) boas: "A boa can be a great look if it's kept simple, like with grey flannel and a hairdo very tight and slim. Curls and boas don't go." (2) furs: "I used to hate mink but now I appreciate it for its solidity. . . . Lynx sheds. . . . I have Russian broadtail—it's the most beautiful fur—but terribly perishable and I can hardly wear it because it's so cold. . . . I'm mad for fisher." (3) fashion philosophy: "I like simple elegance, neat. I'd rather change my jewelry and have a few things and wear them all the time. A person is more important than clothes. A dress should fade out of sight, but greatly." One wonders if that's what she had in mind when she turned up at the 1969 Academy Awards in a see-through pants suit.

Besides appearing in the Streisand TV special (now available on videocassette) Bergdorf's is also featured in the 1979 Ali MacGraw–Alan King film *Just Tell Me What You Want,* in a scene where the two stars get into a violent argument that spills out onto the street. Look for the store, too, in *Someone to Watch Over Me* (1987).

25. PLAZA HOTEL
Fifth Avenue at 59th Street

When it opened in 1907, it billed itself as nothing less than "the world's most luxurious hotel." A monumental eighteen-story French château, the Plaza was designed by Henry J. Hardenbergh, the architect who had been responsible for New York City's fabled Dakota apartment building on Central Park West some twenty-three years earlier.

Of all Manhattan's hotels, the Plaza is the city's undisputed superstar as far as movies are concerned, and it's no wonder since, in addition to being one of New York City's most historic and handsome buildings, the Plaza enjoys an eminently photogenic setting. Not only does it have a fabulous fountain in its front yard, it has Central Park across the street and an ever-present lineup of horse-drawn carriages nearby to complete the postcard-pretty picture. The list of films, television shows, commercials, and print ads that have used the Plaza as a background is enormous. Among the more recent features are *Big Business* (1988), *Crocodile Dundee* (1986), *Brewster's Millions* (1985), *The Cotton Club* (1984), *Annie* (1983), *Arthur* (1981), *Prince of the City* (1980), *King of the Gypsies* (1978), *Love at First Bite* (1978), *The Rose* (1978), *Network* (1976), *The Front* (1976), *The Great Gatsby* (1974), *The Way We Were* (1973), *Forty Carats* (1973), *Puzzle of a Downfall Child* (1970), and *Funny Girl* (1968).

And then, of course, there's *Plaza Suite,* the 1971 film version of the 1960s Neil Simon play that's set entirely in Suite 719 of the hotel. Further back in time, Hitchcock's classic *North by Northwest* (1959) features a dramatic Plaza sequence in which Cary Grant is kidnapped from the hotel's lobby. Before that, Twentieth Century–Fox books Plaza rooms for the three star out-of-town couples vying for a plum New York City job in *Women's World* (1954) and, when *Ma and Pa Kettle Go to Town* in Universal's 1950 film, guess where they stay?

In 1930, an early New York–made talkie called *No Limit* starred the famous silent screen actress Clara Bow, and also featured the Plaza. A decade before that, Norma Talmadge's *By Right of Passage* had a major sequence done on location at an actual charity ball being held at the Plaza. Playing a small role in this film was an actress friend of Miss Talmadge's who later became a major Hollywood columnist: Hedda Hopper. The script for *By Right of Passage* was by Anita Loos, and the Plaza party that the film documented was hosted by the famed Elsa Maxwell.

Speaking of Plaza parties, one of the most spectacular ever to be staged at the hotel took place on Monday, November 28, 1966. The event was a gala "Black and White Ball" hosted by writer Truman Capote for *Washington Post/Newsweek* publisher Katharine Graham. The cream of Hollywood, Broadway, Washington, and New York City society turned up, and among the movie people on the guest list were Frank Sinatra and his then wife Mia Farrow

Superstar hotel:
The Plaza

(who twisted the night away with Bennett Cerf's son, Christopher), Claudette Colbert (who sat at an "exceedingly popular" table, according to the *New York Times*), Candice Bergen, the Sammy Davis, Jrs., Marlene Dietrich (a no-show), Greta Garbo (also a no-show), the Henry Fondas, the Walter Matthaus, the Vincente Minnellis, the Gregory Pecks, Jennifer Jones, the Billy Wilders, and Darryl Zanuck. Men wore black dinner jackets and black masks, women turned up in black or white dresses and white masks. During the evening, Mr. Capote, whose *Breakfast at Tiffany's* and *In Cold Blood* were turned into major movies, and who appeared in Neil Simon's 1979 film, *Murder by Death,* spent a lot of time alone at the back of the ballroom just watching and delighting in his creation. At the time, Capote said that the black-and-white theme for his evening was inspired by Cecil Beaton's costumes for the Ascot scenes in *My Fair Lady.* But movie lovers may wonder if Mr. Capote wasn't also influenced by party-guest Vincente Minnelli's spectacular black-and-white ball sequence in *An American in Paris?* Asked why he chose the Plaza for his gala, his answer was simple: "I think it's the only really beautiful ballroom left in the United States."

Besides being in the movies, the Plaza has hosted practically every movie star in the business at some time or other during its long career. In the late 1940s, Hollywood's hottest couple, Rita Hayworth and Prince Aly Khan, made headlines when they stayed at the Plaza and then sailed off to Europe before either party's divorce from their respective spouses was final. A few years later, after she and the Aly Khan had married, had a daughter, and split, Rita was back at the Plaza so broke that her agents had to advance her the money to pay her bill. It was in the late-1940s, too, that Marlene Dietrich made the Plaza her Manhattan base, before settling down into a Park Avenue apartment.

Dashing Cary Grant dashes through Plaza lobby in North by Northwest, *1959*

The Plaza's most famous resident, however, was not a movie star but a precocious six-year-old girl named Eloise who drove her tricycle relentlessly up and down the corridors, poured water down the mail chutes, and made room service crazy with orders for peanut butter and jelly sandwiches. Created first as a character for a night-club act and later mass-marketed through a series of charming books, Eloise was the brainchild of actress/entertainer/MGM musical coach Kay Thompson. By the late-1950s, Eloise had become so popular that the little girl and her Plaza Hotel home were immortalized by a television special that starred Mildred Natwick, Monty Woolley, Charles Ruggles, and Ethel Barrymore. Today, the Plaza remembers Eloise with a portrait that hangs on a marble wall just beyond the Palm Court.

Alas, there is nothing at the hotel to remind guests today of the glory that was the Persian Room. Opened on the heels of the repeal of Prohibition, this landmark supper club featured exotic Middle Eastern decor by movie art director and Ziegfeld Follies set designer Joseph Urban, and saw many famous show-business names perform here, among them the aforementioned Kay Thompson, who appeared with the Williams Brothers (one of whom happened to be Andy), Lena Horne, Julie Wilson, Lisa Kirk, Marge and Gower Champion, Dorothy Loudon, Carol Channing, Diahann Carroll, Dinah Shore, Robert Goulet, and the Persian Room's own resident superstar chanteuse, the "incomparable" Hildegarde. In the early 1960s, when supper clubs went out of fashion, the Persian Room became Plaza 9–, a setting for satirical revues; and when revues fell from favor in the 1970s, Plaza 9– became Cinema 3, a tiny movie theater. Ironically, in 1986 the theater featured the New York first run of *Marlene,* Maximilian Schell's documentary on the life of former Plaza resident, Marlene Dietrich.

26. SHERRY-NETHERLAND HOTEL
781 Fifth Avenue

According to columnist Earl Wilson, the late Spencer Tracy reportedly once shocked the residents of this discreet hotel by turning up in the lobby smashed and stark naked, in search of a drink. Better-behaved Hollywood residents of the Sherry-Netherland have included Diana Ross, Pia Zadora, and Danny Kaye, all of whom have owned luxurious Towers apartments. Besides celebrity residents, the hotel also is home to the exclusive private club Doubles.

27. ZIEGFELD THEATER
141 West 54th Street

The way things are going—what with the home-video explosion and the rise of pint-sized multiplex theaters—the Ziegfeld may well be the last major movie house built in New York. Architecturally uninspired, the exterior of the Ziegfeld is a gigantic 1960s white-brick box that sits on West 54th Street across from the Burlington Industries Building, which occupies the site of the old Ziegfeld Theater, built in 1927 to showcase the lavish spectacles of Florenz Ziegfeld.

The new Ziegfeld made its debut in 1969 with the New York opening of the space odyssey, *Marooned.* It was an appropriate first film for the new house, which prided itself on its own "space age" gadgetry. For the movie lover, this meant that the Ziegfeld had one of the best projection and multiphonic sound systems in town. Today the 1200-seat theater (the city's second-largest single-screen movie house after the 1500-seat Loew's Astor Plaza at 44th Street and Broadway) is still one of the best places in New York to see—and hear—spectacle films like *Cabaret, Barry Lyndon, Death on the Nile, Raiders of the Lost Ark, Gandhi,* and *Apocalypse Now.*

28. WARWICK HOTEL
65 West 54th Street

The money behind this thirty-three-story Sixth Avenue hotel, built in 1926, was that of newspaper heavyweight and sometime film producer William Randolph Hearst. When Hearst and his Hollywood-star mistress, Marion Davies, came to Manhattan in the late-1920s, they often called the Warwick home. In 1927, Marion, who was known for her unpretentious personality and her lavish Hollywood parties, played havoc with the New York social scene when Charles Lindbergh—who had just returned from his triumphant solo flight across the Atlantic—chose to attend a bash at Marion's Warwick suite over a much more prestigious party at the Vanderbilt mansion on Fifth Avenue. According to her autobiography, *The Times We Had* (Bobbs-Merrill, 1975), Mayor Jimmy Walker sent a special emissary to try to convince Marion to call off her party. She refused, however, and left the decision of which party he wanted to attend up to Mr. Lindbergh, who passed on the Vanderbilt affair and spent most of the evening sitting on the floor of Marion's Warwick suite playing the guitar. Of her social coup, Marion simply said: "It was a nice intimate little party."

One of the guests at Marion's Lindbergh party was Carole Lombard, who is said to have returned to the Warwick a decade later in the company of Clark Gable. Although they were not married (to each other) at the time, they soon would be. In the 1960s, the Warwick's most famous celebrity guests were four young men from England called The Beatles who were in New York to make their live U.S. TV debut on "The Ed Sullivan Show," broadcast from a CBS studio just a few blocks away. In the 1970s and 1980s, Cary Grant was a frequent guest at the lavish Warwick suite maintained by the Fabergé cosmetic empire, which was headquartered across the street at 1345 Avenue of the Americas and for whom Grant was a celebrity spokesman.

29. MGM BUILDING
1350 Avenue of the Americas

When Leo the Lion makes himself heard on the East Coast, it is in this glass and white-marble skyscraper that he most likely will be found roaring. The New York headquarters of MGM since the late 1960s, this Avenue of the Americas address is also home to a couple of other entertainment biggies, notably the American Federation of Television and Radio Artists (AFTRA), which is the trade union for TV and radio performers, and the William Morris Agency, the company that represents some of the biggest stars in show business.

In 1976, 1350 Avenue of the Americas played the role of UBS, the fictional United Broadcasting System in *Network,* Paddy Chayefsky's hard-hitting send-up of network television. The TV-studio sequences had to be shot in Canada, however, since supposedly no network in New York would allow its facilities to be used for the project, once they had read Chayefsky's script.

30. RUSSIAN TEA ROOM
150 West 57th Street

Practically next door to Carnegie Hall, this glitzy Russian restaurant is a high-visibility lunch spot for show-business agents, stars, and studio executives, who talk deals while noshing on blinis, blintzes, and borscht. Remember the scene in *Tootsie* (1980) when Dustin Hoffman shocks his agent (played by the film's director, Sidney Pollack) by turning up for their Russian Tea Room lunch in drag? And remember how, in the same scene, a producer just happens to drop by the table to say hello? That's the way it is at the Russian Tea Room. In *Manhattan* (1980), Woody Allen lets movie audiences see another side of the Russian Tea Room, when he takes his son to lunch there, only to have the maître-d' request that he put on a house jacket over his T-shirt before he can be seated.

Phone: (212) 265–0947. Don't leave home without your jacket.

31. CARNEGIE HALL
57th Street and Seventh Avenue

Although most people think of it as a cathedral of classical music, for Judy Garland fans Carnegie Hall will always bring to mind the historic evening of April 23, 1961, when Judy once again rose from near oblivion and dazzled New Yorkers and the New York critics with her incredible performing prowess. The evening turned out to be a milestone in Miss Garland's recording and concert careers since the two-record album of the performance, "Judy at Carnegie Hall," was the most successful she ever made.

Judy's Carnegie Hall triumph came almost seventy years to the day after the legendary concert hall opened its doors. Built by industrialist Andrew Carnegie in 1891, this great Victorian structure on West 57th Street has presented practically every major musician of the twentieth century at some time or other. A tough survivor, Carnegie Hall was slated for demolition in the late 1950s and was to have been replaced by a garish red-porcelain-faced office building. Led by violinist Isaac Stern, New Yorkers fought hard to save the historic concert hall and ultimately were triumphant when the City of New York bought the place for $5 million, and in turn leased it to the newly formed Carnegie Hall Corporation, which was committed to its musical future. In 1986, a $50 million renovation of Carnegie Hall further assured its continued presence on the city's cultural scene.

Throughout its history, Carnegie Hall has not only provided a stage for great talents, it has provided homes for some of them

Carnegie Hall, ca. 1910

Career high: Judy Garland at Carnegie Hall, 1961

too. Built over and around the concert hall are the Carnegie Hall Studios, 140 apartments that have housed such names as Leonard Bernstein, Isadora Duncan, John Barrymore, Paddy Chayefsky, Bobby Short, and Marlon Brando. Back in the 1920s, a Spaniard named Angel Cansino gave dance classes at his Carnegie Hall studio. One of his students was his brother's daughter, Rita, who would become one of Hollywood's biggest stars two decades later as Rita Hayworth.

Over the years, too, Carnegie Hall has turned up in more than a few films set in New York—from both the 1948 and the 1982 versions of *Unfaithfully Yours* (the first starring Rex Harrison, the second with Dudley Moore, in the role of a conductor who suspects his wife of cheating on him) to 1964's *The World of Henry Orient* (in which a pretentious concert pianist played by Peter Sellers is the object of the obsessive adoration of two teenaged girls). Carnegie Hall's most famous screen appearance, however, was its title role in the 1947 film *Carnegie Hall,* which brought together world-class musicians like Lily Pons, Risë Stevens, Artur Rubinstein, Jan Peerce, Ezio Pinza, Jascha Heifetz, Fritz Reiner, Leopold Stokowski, the New York Philharmonic Orchestra, and even jazz trumpeter Harry James in a dreadful story about a cleaning woman who becomes a concert promoter. Despite the plot, the musical numbers sound great. In addition to its movie appearances, Carnegie Hall has also been the site of numerous TV specials such as "Leonard Bernstein's New York Philharmonic Young People's Concerts" and the legendary "Carol Burnett and Julie Andrews at Carnegie Hall."

32. THE OSBORNE APARTMENTS
205 West 57th Street

Completed in 1885, some six years before its neighbor (Carnegie Hall) went up across the street, the Osborne is one of Manhattan's oldest apartment buildings. In contrast to its serious, brownstone

*The Osborne
Apartments*

exterior, the eleven-story structure boasts a lobby of extraordinary fantasy with matched marble floors, sculpted ceilings, gold-accented mosaics, and all sorts of carved columns and intriguing niches. The apartments at the Osborne are pretty fantastic too, and feature rooms with fifteen-foot ceilings, big bay windows, and tiny secret staircases that lead up or down to cozy bed/sitting rooms. Among the many celebrities who live or who have lived at the Osborne are café-society singer/pianist Bobby Short (featured in Woody Allen's *Hannah and Her Sisters*), fashion designer Fernando Sanchez, humorist Fran Lebowitz, actresses Imogene Coca, Shirley Booth, and Lynn Redgrave, and actors Clifton Webb and Gig Young.

Mr. Young's time at the Osborne ended in tragic headlines on October 19, 1978, when police discovered the bodies of the Oscar-winning (*They Shoot Horses, Don't They?*) movie star and his wife of three weeks, German-born Kim Schmidt, inside the couple's Osborne apartment. According to the police, the sixty-year-old Young—who had a history of alcoholism and who had made only five pictures in the ten years since his Oscar win—had shot his thirty-one-year-old wife and then turned the gun on himself. Young's last film, released posthumously, was titled *The Game of Death.*

33. ANITA LOOS APARTMENT BUILDING
171 West 57th Street

She got her start in the movies in 1912 when, as a teenager in San Diego, she sent an unsolicited scenario to D. W. Griffith at the Biograph Studios in New York. Griffith bought the story for $25,

*The Alwyn Court
Apartments*

turned it into a movie called *The New York Hat* with Mary Pickford and Lionel Barrymore, and encouraged the young woman to keep the scenarios coming. The rise of Anita Loos as one of silent films' top scenarists and title writers was practically a story out of one of her own movies. Loos's greatest success came in 1925; it was not through a screenplay, however, but with her novel *Gentlemen Prefer Blondes,* which has since been adapted and readapted for both stage and screen. The most famous screen adaptation was Twentieth Century–Fox's lavish 1953 musical starring Marilyn Monroe as Loos's loveable blonde gold digger Lorelei Lee, but the performer who has gotten the most mileage out of *Gentlemen Prefer Blondes* is Carol Channing, who has toured in two musical-comedy versions of Loos's story for decades—the original and *Lorelei,* specially adapted to accommodate Miss Channing's post-ingenue years.

From the 1940s until her death in 1980 at the age of ninety-three, Anita Loos lived on the corner of Seventh Avenue and 57th Street. Among her neighbors was Earl Blackwell, a man who has had an impressive career running an only-in-New York (or perhaps L.A.) enterprise called Celebrity Service. Those who subscribe to Blackwell's "service" receive a daily "Celebrity Bulletin" that lists the comings, goings, and press contacts of some of the world's most famous personalities. Blackwell's sixteen-room 57th Street penthouse is a rooftop replica of an eighteenth-century French château, complete with ornate white-and-gold ballroom and formal gardens. Needless to say, this movie-set-glamorous spot is often the site of celebrity-studded Manhattan parties and receptions.

34. ALWYN COURT APARTMENTS
180 West 58th Street

While the Dakota on Central Park West is the New York building that got the starring role in *Rosemary's Baby* back in 1968, it was really the Alwyn Court on Seventh Avenue at 58th Street that inspired former resident Ira Levin's novel of witchcraft in modern Manhattan. One of the city's most handsome apartment buildings, the Alwyn Court—with its intricately sculpted terra cotta and limestone façade—was also one of the most luxurious when it went up in 1908. At the time, the great twelve-story structure offered wealthy New Yorkers apartments with private wine cellars and as many as thirty-four rooms! Decidedly less grand was the little building that stood next door at 909 Seventh Avenue. Here, in 1916, the vice squad raided the apartment of a Mrs. Georgia Thym, arresting her along with a male visitor named Rodolfo Guglielmi. The charges involved white slavery and blackmail and, although Mr. Guglielmi insisted that he had been framed, he spent three days in jail. Little was made of the incident at the time, but when Mr. Guglielmi became Rudolph Valentino a few years later, a scandal-hungry press uncovered the story and had a field day. Today all that remains of 909 Seventh Avenue is a stone archway and an iron gate.

Meanwhile, back at the Alwyn Court, another show-business name—actor Darren McGavin—also ran into trouble with the law and was ordered to pay a $20,000 fine in 1984 after admitting that he had lied to the New York City Rent Control Board in order to keep his under-$500-a-month apartment in the building. Evidently McGavin had claimed the Alwyn Court as his principal residence whereas, in reality, he lived in Beverly Hills. Besides the fine, McGavin also lost his lease. Now a cooperative-apartment building and extensively renovated and beautifully restored, the Alwyn Court is the current address of actress Rita Gam.

35. GAINSBOROUGH STUDIOS
222 Central Park South

Wedged between modern high-rise apartment buildings, the Gainsborough—with its mosaic brick façade, its elaborate second-story frieze, and its bust of the painter Gainsborough—is a class act on an often architecturally bland block. The 1907 building was originally designed to house artists. Today its top tenants are film star Candice Bergen, who has lived here since her single days in the 1970s, her husband, French film director Louis Malle, and the couple's young daughter Chloe. Talk about class acts!

36. "SUPERMAN" BUILDING
240 Central Park South

What do reporter Lois Lane and actress Sylvia Miles have in common? The same Central Park South address. In the movie *Su-*

perman, Ms. Lane somehow manages—on her *Daily Planet* salary—to live in an enormous penthouse atop this classy 1941 brick highrise. In real life, Ms. Miles *does* live here, in an apartment that she says is so small that she's reduced her whole life to "a wardrobe trunk with a view."

37. CENTRAL PARK

The city's own great outdoors, this 840-acre preserve of hills, meadows, fields, and lakes was designed in the 1850s by the noted team of Frederick Law Olmsted and Calvert Vaux and has attracted film makers from D. W. Griffith to Woody Allen. In the early days of silent pictures, the park was less often used as a New York City landmark than simply as a convenient place to shoot sequences that called for rural settings. In some instances, too, it was called on to double for an exotic "foreign" location. D. W. Griffith, for example, cleverly turned the area around Central Park's ornate Bethesda Fountain into an Italian piazza for a photoplay that supposedly took place in Florence. As film making became more sophisticated, and as stories set in New York became a staple of the industry, Central Park—with its unique vistas of pastoral countryside juxtaposed with a dramatic backdrop of metropolitan highrises—became a staple of the New York film.

More than just a pretty background, Central Park is often used by directors when the plot or mood of the film calls for a romantic, away-from-the-harsh-world-of-the-city interlude. In *Eyewitness* (1981), for example, the growing attraction between a janitor (played by William Hurt) and a sophisticated newscaster (Sigourney Weaver) heats up when the two characters are alone with each other alongside the Central Park Lake. The same is true in Joan Micklin Silver's 1978 film about turn-of-the-century Jewish immigrants, *Hester Street,* when at a picnic in Central Park's Rambles, a shy Old World bachelor becomes fully aware of his amorous feelings for the wife of his "Americanized" Lower East Side neighbor. And in what more romantic, indeed other-worldly setting than Central Park could Joseph Cotton encounter the elusive Jennie (Jennifer Jones) in David O. Selznick's *Portrait of Jennie* (1948)?

Aside from pure romance, film makers often use the park to express the fun and freedom of New York City at its best. There are wonderful park scenes in *The World of Henry Orient* (1964), where its two schoolgirl heroines celebrate their newfound friendship by romping across rocks and bridges. In *Annie Hall* (1977), Woody Allen and Diane Keaton have a blissful time people-watching at the Bethesda Fountain. And in the spectacular opening production number of MGM's *On the Town* (1949), Frank Sinatra, Gene Kelly, and Jules Munshin, as three sailors with a day in the city, spend part of that day cycling in Central Park.

Hands down, the film that made the most extensive and creative use of Central Park as a location was the 1980 movie version of the famous 1960s Broadway musical *Hair.* Turning the park into

Close encounter in Central Park: Joseph Cotton and Jennifer Jones in Portrait of Jennie, *1948*

a fantasy world inhabited by 1960s love children, director Milos Forman creates an idyllic place, totally devoid of muggers, where friendly policemen ride dancing horses and where people swim nude in the lake as casually as they would on a secluded Greek island. An even more fantastic vision of the park turns up in MGM's 1953 musical extravaganza *The Band Wagon,* in which director Vincente Minnelli calls on the park's fountains, rocks, and a horse-drawn carriage to provide the backgrounds for the "Dancing in the Dark" production number with Fred Astaire and Cyd Charisse. In this instance, however, it's Central Park according to Cedric Gibbons, the famed MGM art director. Gibbons also recreated the park, specifically the seal tank at its zoo, for Judy Garland and Robert Walker as the young lovers in Vincente Minnelli's *The Clock* (1945). And while on the subject of Hollywood studio versions of the park, does anyone remember Universal's 1948 *Up in Central Park,* one of Deanna Durbin's last films?

Although the majority of Central Park's screen appearances show it off as one of New York's prettiest locations, occasionally the park proves to be a dangerous place—as when Jack Lemmon and Sandy Dennis spend the night in it in *The Out of Towners* (1970); and in *Marathon Man* (1976), where Dustin Hoffman meets his nemesis, a sadistic Nazi played by Sir Laurence Olivier, on a catwalk above the Central Park reservoir; and in *Still of the Night* (1979), with a kinky killer out to trap Meryl Streep amid the Rambles.

The park's connections with show business go beyond its importance as a film location. With its Delacorte outdoor theater under the direction of New York Shakespeare Festival producer Joseph Papp, the park is the site of live theatrical productions each summer, some of which, like *The Pirates of Penzance* and *The Mystery of Edwin Drood,* have become smash Broadway hits. At the same time, the theater's neighbor, the ninety-acre Great Lawn, is often used for outdoor concerts that can attract huge audiences.

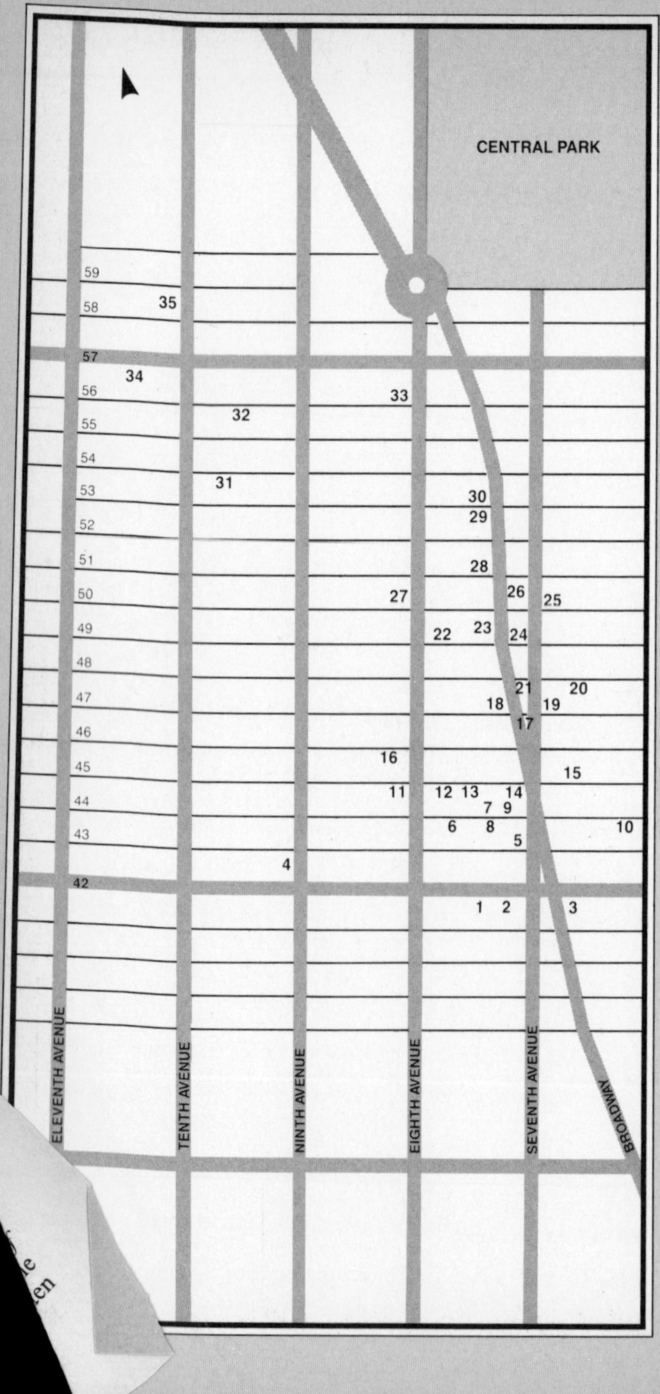

CENTRAL PARK

59
58   35
57
56   34
55   32
54
53   31
52
51
50
49
48
47
46
45
44
43
42

33

30
29
28
27   26   25
22   23   24
21   20
18   19
17
16
11   12 13   14
7 9
6   8
5
4   10

1 2   3

ELEVENTH AVENUE
TENTH AVENUE
NINTH AVENUE
EIGHTH AVENUE
SEVENTH AVENUE
BROADWAY

BROADWAY

That's Entertainment!

3

Paramount Theater, 1927

TIMES SQUARE, 42nd Street, Broadway—just the mention of these magical names elicits images of glittering marquees, glamorous opening nights, show-stopping musical numbers. The entertainment capital of the world, New York's Broadway theater district is hallowed ground for movie lovers. First of all, it was on Broadway stages that the careers of some of our greatest film stars—Mary Pickford, Bette Davis, Joan Crawford, Rudolph Valentino, Barbra Streisand, Robert Redford—were launched. It was also on and off Broadway that the glorious age of the movie palace flourished in New York during the 1920s, 1930s, and 1940s. But, alas, while movie lovers can still attend many of Broadway's legitimate theaters, the sad reality is that most of its historic "cathedrals of the motion picture"—such as the Roxy, the Paramount, Loew's State, the Strand, the Rivoli, and the Capitol—are gone.

On a happier note, movie lovers exploring the theater district can discover here an often-overlooked world of sound stages, recording studios, and production offices that is centered in the 40s and 50s west of Eighth Avenue. In this thriving area, film making has gone on since the days of silent pictures, and while many of the historic studios in this part of town are no longer affiliated with Twentieth Century–Fox, Warner Bros., or Paramount, as they once were, they are still turning out features, television series, and commercials. This is where Hollywood on the Hudson gets down to business.

1. LIBERTY THEATER
234 West 42nd Street

The Liberty played a major role in the history of motion pictures on March 3, 1915. The occasion was the official East Coast opening of a movie that represented a milestone in the art of film making. Indeed, so much money, effort, and time had gone into this epic production that a full-fledged Broadway theater was leased for its premiere and its promoters charged the then unheard-of price of $2.00 for a reserved ticket. The film was D. W. Griffith's *The Birth of a Nation,* and it ran for eleven months at the Liberty. Highly controversial owing to its decidedly racist look at the post-Civil War South, the film was protested by the NAACP as well as by a number of other groups who tried to block its exhibition. The fact that Griffith's film aroused so much feeling was ultimately one of the reasons for its landmark status in film-history books, for *The Birth of a Nation* proved just how powerful the medium of film could be if used to its full potential.

The Birth of a Nation also proved that movies could make really big money—especially at $2.00 a head. One of those who profited greatly from *The Birth of a Nation* was a former junk dealer from Massachusetts named Louis B. Mayer. Having gone from junk to running movie theaters, Mayer managed to tie up the New England distribution rights to Griffith's landmark film and made a fortune on the deal. Writing in her memoir, *The Movies, Mr. Grif-*

Liberty Theater, 1986

fith, and Me (Prentice Hall, 1969), the legendary Lillian Gish, who was one of the stars of *The Birth of a Nation,* tells of meeting L. B. Mayer in Hollywood in the 1920s. According to Gish, Mayer thanked her for starting him on the road to success. When she asked what he meant, he replied: "Well, in 1915, when *The Birth of a Nation* was released, I was running a group of theaters in Haverhill, Massachusetts, where I'd started out with a nickelodeon. When *The Birth of a Nation* came along, I pawned everything I owned—my house, my insurance, even my wife's wedding ring— just to get the New England states' rights. Since then, everything's been very pleasant. If it hadn't been for D. W. Griffith, *The Birth,* and you, I'd still be in Haverhill."

Two years after he had used the Liberty Theater for *The Birth of a Nation,* D. W. Griffith again rented the place for the New York run of *Intolerance,* his epic follow-up to (and some say apology for) his Civil War blockbuster. *Intolerance* dealt with much less controversial stuff—man's inhumanity to man—and despite good reviews, it lost money.

Today the Liberty—which is currently big on porno and action flicks—is scheduled for restoration and a return to legit use as part of the city's proposed 42nd Street Development Project.

2.   NEW AMSTERDAM THEATER
214 West 42nd Street

Originally built for vaudeville producers Klaw and Erlanger in 1903, the beautiful Art Nouveau New Amsterdam was taken over in 1913 by the great Florenz Ziegfeld as a site for his famous Follies. Practically every one of the next fourteen years, Ziegfeld came out with a new edition of his spectacular stage show at the

New Amsterdam, and he would unleash on the world talents like Fanny Brice, Eddie Cantor, Will Rogers, W. C. Fields, Marilyn Miller, Paulette Goddard, Mae Murray, and Marion Davies.

While Ziegfeld's Follies flourished downstairs at the New Amsterdam, its rooftop nightclub—the New Amsterdam Roof—pulled in *la crème de la crème* of New York society, who came to see Ziegfeld stars in a glamorous cabaret setting. Later, when Prohibition killed the New Amsterdam Roof, the place led a varied life as a conventional theater, radio studio, rehearsal hall, and TV studio. Radio buffs may remember it as home of the WOR Mutual Theater in the late 1930s/early 1940s, when it was broadcasting the chilling series, "The Shadow," which once starred Orson Welles.

Ziegfeld departed from the New Amsterdam's main theater in 1927. It spent the next ten years as a Broadway house, was converted into a movie palace in 1937, and continued to show films until 1983. At that time it was purchased by the Nederlander Theater organization, which announced plans to restore both of its historic theaters as part of a much-awaited 42nd Street Development Project. Those plans are up in the air, however, and today the New Amsterdam stands vacant—a symbol of a Times Square that still hasn't made a comeback worthy of its legendary past.

NOTE: *To see the New Amsterdam—and Times Square—in their heyday, the 1929 made-in-New York talkie,* Glorifying the American Girl, *has a location sequence that documents an opening night at the theater with wonderful shots of Florenz Ziegfeld, Billie Burke, financier Otto Kahn, and Mayor Jimmy Walker.*

New Amsterdam Theater, 1903

3. KNICKERBOCKER BUILDING
152 West 42nd Street

Today it's just a Times Square office building whose tenants include the New York School of Locksmithing and several TV and radio broadcast-training institutes. Still, it's a strikingly beautiful old building with its wrought-iron balconies, sculpted cornices, and elegant mansard roofs. Erected in 1902, this was Colonel John Jacob Astor's famed Knickerbocker Hotel, which for twenty years was one of Broadway's most fashionable places to stay and to play. Offering great luxury, the Knickerbocker had a glorious dining room with marble floor and a ceiling modeled after one in Napoleon's palace at Fontainebleau in France. For its mirrored café, the artist Frederic Remington provided an Indian battle scene, and for the hotel's oak-paneled barroom Astor commissioned Maxfield Parrish's "Old King Cole and His Fiddlers Three," which today hangs in the King Cole Bar of another of Astor's hotels, the St. Regis at Fifth Avenue and 55th Street.

The services at the Knickerbocker more than matched its lavish decor. For business people who arrived without baggage, the hotel provided pajamas, combs, and brushes at no extra charge. And if a guest had an unexpected formal function to attend, the Knickerbocker had a full array of tuxedos and accessories in a wide range of sizes. Again, there was no charge.

Knickerbocker Hotel building today

One of the hotel's most famous erstwhile residents was the great showman, George M. Cohan. Known more as a vaudevillian, playwright, and songwriter, Cohan constantly appeared in films from the late 1910s through the early 1930s, including many that were adaptations of his own plays, such as *Gambling* (1934). During this same period, Cohan also saw a number of his plays become films in which he did not appear. Among these were *The Miracle Man,* done in 1919 as a silent and in 1932 as a talkie; *Elmer the Great* (1933); *Song and Dance Man* (1936); and *Little Nellie Kelly* (1940), which starred Judy Garland. Despite Cohan's involvement in film, he will be best remembered by movie lovers through James Cagney's portrayal of him in Warner's 1942 musical *Yankee Doodle Dandy.*

Another of the Knickerbocker's former residents was the famous opera singer, Enrico Caruso; he not only held forth on the stage of the Metropolitan Opera a few blocks away at Broadway and 38th Street, but also appeared in two films for Adolph Zukor's Famous Players company in 1918. Despite his great fame, an opera singer in a silent picture didn't make it with the public, and after Caruso's first Famous Players film, *My Cousin,* flopped at the box office, his second was never released.

One of the biggest stars of early movies happened to have been staying at the Knickerbocker hotel during a very important period in her life. The star was Mary Pickford, and it was while a guest at the Knickerbocker in 1916 that she ran into Douglas Fairbanks at a dance at the nearby Algonquin Hotel on West 44th Street. Each of the two superstars were married to another person at the time, but their meeting at the Algonquin was definitely the start of something big. In her autobiography, *Sunshine and Shadow* (Lowe and Brydone, 1956), Mary remembers it well: "I hugged the echo of his words for days, repeating them over and over again to myself. . . . I had been living in half shadows, and now a brilliant light was suddenly cast upon me, the sunlight of Douglas's approval and admiration." Four years later they became man and wife, going on to reign as the King and Queen of Hollywood from their fabulous Beverly Hills mansion, Pickfair. The Knickerbocker's fortunes were not so propitious; a year after the Doug-and-Mary nuptials, the hotel shut down and was converted into the office building that it remains today. Its demise was blamed on Prohibition.

4. MANHATTAN PLAZA
400 West 43rd Street

A unique experiment in subsidized housing, Manhattan Plaza is the first and only luxury apartment complex where the majority of residents are working show-business people who, during lean periods, are required to pay only 25 percent of their gross earnings in rent. At the same time, the building's star residents—like Helen Hayes, Angela Lansbury, Jane Alexander, writer James Kirkwood, and the late Tennessee Williams—have to come up with the same big bucks that most Manhattanites are forced to pay for the privilege of living in the Big Apple.

How did Manhattan Plaza come about? Definitely *not* through the beneficence of some stage-struck real estate developer. Originally, the building was to have been yet another high-rent high-rise. However, as Manhattan Plaza was nearing completion in 1976, the developers were having a hard time luring high-income tenants to their project's dicey Hell's Kitchen location between Ninth and Tenth Avenues. It was then that the subsidy plan was devised by the City of New York in order to salvage the money that the City had invested in the building. Today, thanks largely to Manhattan Plaza, the neighborhood around it now abounds with restaurants, shops, and Off-Broadway theaters.

5. PARAMOUNT BUILDING
1501 Broadway

Known simply as 1501 Broadway these days, this thirty-five-story Times Square pyramid crowned by a Deco clock tower and a gigantic glass globe is actually one of the greatest monuments to early moviemaking still standing in Manhattan. Erected in 1926, 1501 Broadway made its debut as the Paramount Building, the man behind it being Paramount Pictures' Adolph Zukor, the mogul who founded the Famous Players Company back in 1912 and then went on to head one of the world's most powerful studios.

Times Square trilogy (left to right): Times Building, Paramount Building, and Astor Hotel, ca. 1930

The dramatic mountain of a building that Zukor erected for his company on Times Square not only housed Paramount offices, but was also home to the glorious Paramount Theater. Designed by architects Rapp and Rapp, the Paramount had three lobbies, including a Great Hall punctuated at one end by an extraordinary marble staircase modeled after the one at the Paris Opéra, plus a myriad of special public rooms that ranged from a tea gallery to a ladies' smoking lounge to a music room where a string orchestra played chamber music for customers waiting for seats. To keep track of the theater's 3,900 seats, 150 ushers had a special electronic signal system that told of vacancies in the vast auditorium.

Throughout the years, the Paramount became just as famous for the headliners that studded its live stage shows as for the movies it presented. Of the performers associated with the Paramount, none is more legendary than Frank Sinatra, whose appearances at the theater in the early 1940s brought out the droves of squealing teen-aged girls who helped turn Sinatra into a superstar. Writer Kitty Kelley, in her "unauthorized" biography of Frank Sinatra, *His Way* (Bantam Books, 1986), has looked carefully into Sinatra's Paramount legend and has discovered that much of it may have been a carefully orchestrated publicity stunt in which a press agent not only distributed free tickets to pack the Paramount, but even coached some young audience members on how and when to squeal during the performance.

The Paramount bit the dust in the 1950s. Hollowed out rather than knocked down, the space that the theater took up in the Paramount Building was then "filled in" with offices. Today, all that remains of the legendary Paramount Theater is the building that Adolph Zukor built on top of it. Movie lovers can still get a glimpse of 1920s movie magic by stepping inside the sleek black-marble lobby of 1501 Broadway. Especially eye-grabbing are the bronze elevator doors and the gilded light fixtures. From the beauty of this lobby, one can imagine just how splendid the old Paramount Theater must have been.

6. ST. JAMES THEATER
246 West 44th Street

It was just like in the movies. The show was *The Pajama Game* at the St. James. The star dancer, Carol Haney, broke her leg not long after opening night, and the chorus girl had to fill in for her. A big movie producer—Hal Wallis—was in the audience, and he was so taken by the twenty-year-old understudy's performance that he offered her a movie contract. And that's how Shirley MacLaine went to Hollywood.

In addition to giving the world Shirley MacLaine, the St. James is the theater that, in 1943, hosted a musical no one expected to be a hit—Rodgers and Hammerstein's *Oklahoma*. Of special interest to movie lovers may be the fact that the director of this landmark musical comedy (notable because it featured songs and ballet numbers integral to the storyline) was the film director, Rouben Mamoulian, whose classic movies include *Applause,* a 1929 sound film about the world of burlesque that was made in New York; *Dr. Jekyll and Mr. Hyde* (1932) with Fredric March; *Song of Songs* (1933) starring Marlene Dietrich; Garbo's *Queen Christina* (1933); *Becky Sharp* (1935), the first feature film to use three-strip Technicolor; and *Silk Stockings* (1957) with Fred Astaire and Cyd Charisse.

Among its other important Broadway productions, the St. James also boasted *The King and I* (1951), *Li'l Abner* (1956), *Flower Drum Song* (1958), and *Hello Dolly* (1964), which, when it closed in 1970, was the longest-running musical in Broadway's history to that date. The St. James can also boast at least one former usherette who became a movie star: Lauren Bacall, who worked the theater in the early 1940s in order to make ends meet during her starving-actress days in Manhattan.

7. BROADHURST THEATER
235 West 44th Street

This is the theater that really put Humphrey Bogart on the map. Despite the fact the Bogart had acted in theater *and* films since the early 1920s, his career was, at best, mediocre when he was signed to do the part of a gangster in Robert E. Sherwood's *The Petrified Forest,* which opened at the Broadhurst on January 7, 1935. Being cast as a tough guy was something new for Bogart, who had usually played ineffectual second leads both on stage and on screen. *The Petrified Forest* was to change all that, especially when Bogart recreated his Broadway role in the Warner Bros. film version of the play. In typical Hollywood fashion, however, Bogart almost missed out on the film because Warner Bros. really wanted its resident gangster, Edward G. Robinson, to do the part. Ultimately they wanted *The Petrified Forest*'s other star, Leslie Howard, even more than Robinson, because Howard told the studio that he wouldn't do his role unless Bogart was cast. Bogie got the part, and quickly became the toughest guy on the Warner lot.

Another Hollywood legend of the 1940s got a big career boost via the Broadhurst stage. The show was a 1939 revue, *The Streets of Paris,* that featured comics Bud Abbott and Lou Costello, dancers Gower (Champion) and Jeanne, and a host of other performers. The real star of the show, however, was a Latin bombshell named Carmen Miranda, who went on to parade her fruit-laden headdresses and her fiery temperament through a string of Twentieth Century–Fox films with Latin locales and titles such as *Down Argentine Way* (1940), *That Night in Rio* (1941), and *Weekend in Havana* (1941). Appropriately, Miss Miranda's Portuguese father ran a wholesale fruit operation in Brazil!

The Broadhurst also saw Rosalind Russell triumph as *Auntie Mame* from 1956 to 1958, before she did the same thing in the Warner Bros. film version in 1959. It was also this theater where

Bogart at the Broadhurst: The Petrified Forest, *1935*

Woody Allen's *Play It Again, Sam* ran; the 1969 comedy starred Mr. Allen as well as the actress who would go on to be a major leading lady in both his on- and off-screen life: Diane Keaton. Finally, it's not everyday that Superman meets superstar on stage, but it happened at the Broadhurst in 1976, when Christopher Reeve and Katharine Hepburn co-starred in the comedy, *A Matter of Gravity.*

8. SARDI'S
234 West 44th Street

What Hollywood's old Brown Derby restaurant on Vine Street was to the movie industry, Sardi's on West 44th Street continues to be for the Broadway theater in Manhattan. Once described as "the club, mess hall, lounge, post office, saloon, and market place of the people of the theater," Sardi's was founded in 1921 by Vincent Sardi, an Italian immigrant who started his New York restaurant career as a waiter. In 1921, Sardi and his wife opened their original restaurant at 248 West 44th Street, several doors away from its present location, to which it moved in 1927 to make way for the St. James Theater. From the start, the warm, family atmosphere that the Sardis brought to the theater district appealed to show folk. What also appealed was the generosity that Vincent Sardi showed toward many performers during their lean periods "between engagements." Supposedly, James Cagney, in his struggling days, frequently dined at Sardi's on credit. By the same token, Sardi's became known as a place where the famous could go and be assured that their privacy would be respected. In the 1940s, when she had left

Hollywood, and every journalist on earth wanted to interview her, Greta Garbo could dine at Sardi's in relative seclusion.

Today Sardi's no longer provides handouts to out-of-work actors, but it is still a place where some of New York's most celebrated theater and movie people gather. Usually Sardi's is a celebrity-spotter's dream; but even when there are no heavyweights in the place, movie lovers will still find themselves surrounded by some of the biggest names in show business, because their autographed caricatures hang on every available inch of wall space. Don't ask who did the sketches, however; the identity of Sardi's artists has always been a closely guarded secret.

9. SHUBERT THEATER
225 West 44th Street

She had been branded "box-office poison" in 1938 by the president of the Independent Theater Owners of America because her pictures didn't make money. She wanted desperately to play Scarlett O'Hara in *Gone with the Wind,* but David O. Selznick wouldn't give it to her. When asked why, the famous Hollywood producer told Katharine Hepburn, "Because, my dear, I can't see Rhett Butler chasing you for twelve years." And so, when playwright Philip Barry approached her about a play he was writing with her in mind for the lead, Miss Hepburn, fed up with Hollywood, consented to do the role of headstrong heiress Tracy Lord in *The Philadelphia Story.* In addition, together with her good pal at the time, millionaire aviator/movie mogul Howard Hughes, she put up half of the money needed to produce Barry's play. It was a wise move on Kate's part. *The Philadelphia Story* opened at the Shubert Theater on March 28, 1939, and was a critical and financial smash hit. It not only bolstered Hepburn's sagging career, it made her a wealthy woman—especially after she and Hughes sold the screen rights to MGM, a deal that gave her the starring role in the picture as well as a lucrative long-term contract with the studio.

Movie lovers may also be interested in knowing that it was at the Shubert Theater that Barbara (she hadn't yet dropped the second "a") Streisand made her Broadway debut (and stole the show) in *I Can Get It for You Wholesale* in 1962. Playing the role of a secretary named Miss Marmelstein, Barbra also stole the heart of the show's leading man, Elliott Gould, whom she married in 1964. While doing *Wholesale,* she reportedly got bored in her small role and asked various other female members of the cast to switch parts with her for a performance or two. Needless to say, the other actresses declined her offers. She also chewed gum onstage, which irked the stage manager enormously. On the gum-chewing business, Streisand had this to say in an interview: "Listen, what does gum in your mouth matter if you're doing your job?"

In 1974, the Shubert saw Patti and Maxine Andrews, the two surviving members of the Andrews Sisters, the legendary singing trio of the 1940s, headline a campy Hollywood Canteenish musical called *Over Here.* Two of the boys in the chorus of the show would go on to film fame: John Travolta and Treat Williams. The following year, the Shubert Theater welcomed producer Joseph Papp's *A Chorus Line* to its stage. Eight years later, in September of 1983, the show made show-business history when it became the longest running musical in the history of Broadway.

10. HIGH SCHOOL OF PERFORMING ARTS
120 West 44th Street

Liza Minnelli went here, as did Al Pacino, Eartha Kitt, Diahann Carroll, Michelle Lee, Dom DeLuise, and Melissa Manchester. Ultimately, however, New York City's High School of the Performing Arts will be remembered less for the famous show folk it has trained than for the famous film that it inspired: *Fame.* While *Fame* was shot entirely in New York, one city location that never saw any action during the filming was the High School of the Performing Arts! At the time (1979), the Board of Education refused to allow the school to be used because it didn't approve of the profanity, sex, or recreational-drug use called for by the script. In fact, it looked at one point as though *Fame* might have to find a high school in another city. That's when the Mayor's Office of Film, Theater, & Broadcasting stepped in and came up with the abandoned Haaren High building on Tenth Avenue and 59th Street—no longer under Board of Ed control—for the location.

Meanwhile, the real High School of Performing Arts closed down in 1984 when the Board of Education merged it with New

High School of the Performing Arts building

Fame *on West 47th Street*

York City's High School of Music and Art to become the new La Guardia High School on Amsterdam Avenue, behind Lincoln Center. Recently, Performing Arts' former West 44th Street home was turned into Liberty High School. It's gonna live forever?

11. MARTIN BECK THEATER
302 West 45th Street

She was riding high in 1933. She had received rave notices for her performance in *Morning Glory,* and her work in the not-yet-released *Little Women* was the talk of Hollywood. Indeed, at twenty-four, Katharine Hepburn could do no wrong. And so, instead of making another picture, the impetuous young actress decided to do a Broadway show. A British play called *The Lake* was chosen for her by the bright young director Jed Harris. Unfortunately, it was a terrible play—and Katharine Hepburn was dreadful in it. So dreadful that Dorothy Parker wrote of Hepburn's performance the famous, "she ran the gamut of emotions from A to B." *The Lake* played the Martin Beck Theater for about seven weeks, after which a somewhat humbled Miss Hepburn escaped to Europe. Ironically, the day she set sail, she was comforted by the news that she had just won an Academy Award for *Morning Glory.*

Practically a half century later, another legendary Hollywood star tried her luck at the Martin Beck and, much to the surprise of both audiences and critics, Elizabeth Taylor turned in a creditable performance in her Broadway debut in the role of Regina Giddens in the 1981 revival of Lillian Hellman's *The Little Foxes.* But when

Katharine Hepburn in
The Lake, *1933*

Miss Taylor returned to Broadway the following year in what the world expected to be one of the major theatrical events of the twentieth century—Elizabeth Taylor starring with her ex-husband Richard Burton in Noël Coward's *Private Lives*—she did not fare as well. *Private Lives,* which played the Lunt & Fontanne Theatre on West 46th Street, was a critical and commercial disaster. Indeed, toward the end of the run, when many of the people in the audience were there on discount tickets, Taylor's diamonds were more talked about than her performance. Liz has not been back to Broadway since.

Meanwhile back at the Martin Beck, movie lovers with good memories may recall the theater's appearance in *From Main Street to Broadway,* a 1953 film that featured Tallulah Bankhead, Mary Martin, Rex Harrison, Lionel and Ethel Barrymore, and Joshua Logan in cameo roles.

12. JOHN GOLDEN THEATER
252 West 45th Street

Does anybody remember the play *Aged in Wood,* by the famous Broadway playwright Lloyd Richards? It ran at the Golden in 1949. It starred the legendary Broadway actress Margo Channing, and it was during the run of *Aged in Wood* that Miss Channing befriended a shy young fan from San Francisco who briefly became her girl Friday. Soon, however, Eve Harrington managed not only to sabotage Margo Channing's career, but her friends and love life as well. By now, movie lovers will realize that *Aged in Wood* was not a real drama, but was the play in the film *All About Eve,* which starred Bette Davis as Margo, and Anne Baxter as Eve. Few people realize that the Golden Theater was also in the film—but if you watch carefully, and if you know your theater-district geography, it's easy to figure out that the Golden is definitely the Broadway house—with the Royale and the Booth theaters visible just up the street beyond it—that was used for *All About Eve*'s second-unit exteriors.

Now, fasten your seat belts for an even more esoteric bit of *All About Eve* trivia. What show was playing next door at the Royale Theater while *Aged in Wood* was at the Golden? Answer: *The Devil's Disciple,* starring Maurice Evans, which actually *was* playing at the Royale in 1949.

13. ROYALE THEATER
242 West 45th Street

It was a bizarre bit of casting: a blond, blue-eyed, all-American young man from Indiana in the role of a homosexual North African houseboy named Bachir. But that's the part that James Dean played in a dramatization of André Gide's novel, *The Immoralist,* which opened at the Royale Theater on February 1, 1954. After constant battles during out-of-town try-outs with the play's director, Daniel Mann, Dean further antagonized his director on opening night by lifting up his native robe and curtseying to the Royale audience during his curtain call. Mr. Mann was not amused by Jimmy's jest—nor by the fact that he announced the same night that he was leaving the show in two weeks to do a film in Hollywood. Unbeknownst to anyone, during previews of *The Immoralist,* Elia Kazan had secretly approached Jimmy and given him a screen test for *East of Eden.* Despite his abrupt departure from the cast, Dean nonetheless won a Theater World Award as a "promising newcomer" of the 1953–54 season on the basis of his stage performance at the Royale.

The following season, a British musical opened at the Royale on September 30, springing another amazingly talented newcomer onto the Broadway stage. The show was *The Boy Friend,* and its magnificent young star was Julie Andrews, who would go on to dazzle New York audiences as Eliza Doolittle in *My Fair Lady* before achieving superstardom in Hollywood. Another Royale production of interest to movie lovers is the 1961 debut of Tennessee Williams's *The Night of the Iguana,* which brought Bette Davis back to the Broadway stage just before the *What Ever Happened to Baby Jane?* (1962) phase of her film career.

14. SCREEN ACTORS GUILD
1515 Broadway

Like many professionals, movie actors have a labor union. The 44th floor of the Minskoff Building is headquarters for the New York City offices of the Screen Actors Guild (SAG). Out of a total of 70,000 members nationwide, some 23,500 actors belong to SAG in the New York metropolitan area. For a day's work in a theatrical film, the 1988 SAG minimum base rate is $398 for a day (featured) player and $91 for an extra. But before you think of rushing into the film business, be advised that 80 percent of SAG's New York members make under $5000 a year from their screen appearances.

15. LYCEUM THEATER
149 West 45th Street

New York's oldest surviving theater that is still being used for legitimate productions, the Lyceum, with its ornate façade of sculpted limestone punctuated by five fat fluted columns and three huge arched windows, is also one of the city's most handsome houses. Built in 1903 by a then famous theatrical producer, Daniel Frohman, the Lyceum contained Frohman's living quarters above the second balcony, and he frequently made use of a special secret window that looked down on the stage to phone directions to his cast and crews! Today Frohman's former Lyceum apartment houses the archives of the Shubert Theater organization.

On July 12, 1912, the Lyceum hosted a very important event in motion-picture history, when a private screening was held there of a revolutionary European film version of *Queen Elizabeth* starring the great French actress, Sarah Bernhardt. The film was revolutionary because it lasted for a then unheard-of fifty minutes, and

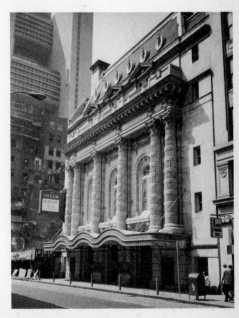

Lyceum Theater

because it featured a major actress instead of one of the anonymous beauties that populated most early movies. The American rights to *Queen Elizabeth* had just been purchased by a little man named Adolph Zukor, who planned both to market *Queen Elizabeth* in America and to set up a company that would film famous stage stars in famous plays. Which is where the Lyceum comes into the story: Its producer, Daniel Frohman, was one of the partners that Zukor had recruited for his bold venture. Frohman would be particularly valuable to the new Famous Players Film Company (one of the companies that eventually formed Paramount Pictures) because he would supply the stars, the plays, and the theatrical clout to get Famous Players' pictures off the ground.

Soon, through films like *His Neighbor's Wife* with Lillie Langtry, James K. Hackett in *The Prisoner of Zenda,* and James O'Neill (Eugene O'Neill's father) in *The Count of Monte Cristo,* the new Famous Players Company primed the public's taste for their trademark "Bigger and Better Pictures." And when this happened, not only did appearing on screen lose its stigma for stage stars, but other American producers jumped on the bandwagon and began coming out with longer films. In a matter of months, short films, which had been the staple of the American motion-picture industry for the first fifteen years of its existence, went out of fashion, and the "feature craze" began. For film historians, it began at the Lyceum.

Another beginning at the Lyceum was that of the film career of Bette Davis, who was discovered in 1930 by an executive from Universal while she was in a play there called *The Solid South.* Davis went directly from the Lyceum stage to Hollywood to appear

*Bette Davis
on Broadway—with
Duncan Penwarden in*
Broken Dishes, *1929*

Sarah Bernhardt on screen: Queen Elizabeth, *1912*

in *Bad Sister* (1931), in which she played the "good" sister. Actually this was not the first time that Bette had been discovered on Broadway. The year before she had been seen in a play called *Broken Dishes* at the Ritz Theater and was given a screen test by the Samuel Goldwyn Company in New York. When Sam Goldwyn saw Bette's test, he is quoted as having said: "Who did this to me?"

P.S. The Lyceum lobby was featured in *A Double Life,* 1947.

16. JOE ALLEN
326 West 46th Street

When Elizabeth Taylor made her Broadway debut in *The Little Foxes* in 1981, this is where you could usually find her after the show. It's where you can usually find a lot of theater/movie people—from gypsies to superstars—and if you don't see your favorite celebs at the long bar or brick-walled dining room of Joe Allen's New York establishment, you may run into them at one of the restaurant's clones in London, Paris, L.A., or Toronto. Founded by a former actor named Joe Allen, the restaurant features simple, very American fare like chili (Liz's favorite in her pre–Betty Ford days), barbequed ribs, calves liver, steak, and pan-fried chicken. These are all served in a room plastered with posters of Broadway flop shows—from *Moose Murders,* which brought 1940s movie/1950s TV star Eve Arden to Broadway for about ten minutes in 1983, to *Frankenstein,* a 1981 turkey starring John Carradine and several-million-dollars'-worth of special effects, which closed on opening night.

Judy's Palace portrait

17. PALACE THEATER
1564 Broadway

The gold plaque backstage reads: "This was the dressing room of Judy Garland who set the all-time long-run record October 16, 1951, to February 24, 1952, at the RKO–Palace Theatre." (Judy was also remembered with a portrait which hung for many years in the Palace's opulent French Renaissance–style lobby and which is now at the Museum of the City of New York.) For Garland fans, the Palace is not just where Judy started her concert career in the U.S., it is the sacred spot where she proved that her talent was far greater than anyone had previously imagined. Fed by a live audience, Garland in person went beyond anything she had ever done on film. Ultimately, the legend of Judy Garland was not born on the MGM soundstages, but on the stage of the Palace Theater.

The idea of having Judy play the Palace was that of producer Sid Luft, who eventually became her third husband. Down on her luck, Judy had been suspended by MGM in June of 1950 for not showing up for the shooting of *The Barclays of Broadway.* Then, two days later, there had been a much publicized suicide attempt in which she tried to slash her throat. As far as Hollywood studio executives were concerned, Judy Garland was no longer bankable. Unable to work in America, Judy wound up doing a series of concerts in England in 1951. They were highly successful, but on her return to America the only jobs her agents were able to line up for her were some radio guest shots. Clearly, drastic measures needed to be taken in order to show Hollywood—and America—the talent that had taken England by storm. And for Sid Luft, the Palace was the ticket.

Judy at the Palace was very much a case of being at the right place at the right time. In 1951, the great Temple of Vaudeville, which opened in 1913, and which had seen headliners like Sophie Tucker, Eddie Cantor, the Marx Brothers, Kate Smith, Fred Astaire, W. C. Fields, Fanny Brice, and Ethel Merman in its halcyon days, was a tattered remnant of its former self. Vaudeville was finished and the theater had gone from a policy of stage-show-plus-movie to just showing films—and not first runs. Luft's plan was to get RKO (which owned the theater) to refurbish the historic house for what would be not just Judy's U.S. concert debut, but the return of "two-a-day" vaudeville to the Palace. And so it came to pass that Judy Garland, backed up by comedian Alan King, acrobats, and various other variety acts, did two shows a day at the Palace for nineteen weeks in 1951–1952.

Of her opening night, her biographer Gerold Frank writes in *Judy* (Harper & Row, 1975) that it "was the biggest night Times Square had known since D-Day." Of her performance, in which she not only sang but recreated several classic production numbers from her films ("Get Happy" from *Summer Stock*, "A Couple of Swells" from *Easter Parade*), one reviewer called it "the most fantastic one-hour solo performance in theater history." For her fans, seeing her on the Palace stage represented her triumph over Hollywood, over the suicide attempts, the bad press, the drugs, and the bad times. But the euphoria didn't last long. Three weeks into the run, Judy collapsed on stage and had to be taken to a hospital. Diagnosed as suffering from "nervous exhaustion," she returned to the Palace five nights later and was welcomed back with practically as much enthusiasm and acclaim as on opening night. Only Judy could make a "comeback" within a comeback. It was the first of many many more. The pattern, like the legend, was born at the Palace.

Judy was followed at the Palace by more Hollywood names: Betty Hutton, Danny Kaye, Jerry Lewis, then Judy herself returned in 1956—again to rave reviews. Sadly, the following summer the theater in which she had single-handedly brought about the revival of vaudeville reverted to showing movies once again. But in 1965 the Nederlander theater organization took over the place, refurbished it once more, and turned it into a legit house. Its first production was Bob Fosse's *Sweet Charity,* which opened in early 1966 starring Gwen Verdon. Its second production was—guess who?—Judy Garland, this time with her three children—Liza Minnelli, Lorna and Joey Luft—as part of the act.

Besides Judy Garland, another Hollywood great who has had more than just a casual association with the Palace is Lauren Bacall. In 1970 she starred at the Palace in *Applause,* the musical version of *All About Eve,* and won a Tony Award for her performance. (In a clever bit of replacement casting, Anne Baxter, who had played the role of Eve Harrington in the film *All About Eve,* took over the role of Margo Channing in *Applause* when Bacall left to do the show in London.) In 1981, Bacall returned to the Palace as the star

of *Woman of the Year,* the Broadway musical version of the classic
Spencer Tracy–Katharine Hepburn film. Again, Bacall won a Tony
for her performance in a Broadway show based on a Hollywood
dramatic film. And in another clever bit of replacement casting,
Raquel Welch took over the role when Bacall went on vacation for
a couple of weeks toward the end of the run. Raquel, to everyone's
surprise, got wonderful reviews from the New York critics. Supposedly, the person least pleased with Raquel's notices was Miss
Bacall who, when she returned to the Palace, is reported to have
sulked in her dressing room. Was she possibly feeling a bit like an
older Margo Channing threatened by the younger Eve Harrington?
Welcome to the theater!

18. STRAND THEATER SITE
1585 Broadway

Broadway lost a great movie house when they tore down the
old Strand theater in 1987. Erected in 1914 and designed by Thomas
W. Lamb, New York's dean of theater architects, the Strand (which
had been hacked up into two houses and was known as the Warner
Twin at the time of its demise) was one of the most historic movie
houses in New York City because it was the first major theater on
Broadway conceived for the primary purpose of exhibiting motion
pictures. In other words, it was Broadway's first true movie palace.
At the helm of the Strand was S. L. Rothapfel, who went by the
name of "Roxy" and who was noted for creating the spectacular
stage shows that were the expected accompaniments of feature film
presentations in the early days of movie palaces. Having just worked
wonders at New York's first real movie palace, the Regent on 116th
Street, Roxy pulled out all the stops at the Strand. Besides the patriotic *tableaux vivants,* the operatic interludes, and the dancing
fountains, the theater's opening night featured "The Strand Topical
Review," an early form of the newsreel that amazed audiences with
scenes of a baseball game that had taken place that same day! Then
there was the feature itself, a western from the Selig Company called
The Spoilers, which at nine reels (almost two hours) set a new record
for its length. In order to change reels with no interruptions, the
theater boasted four projectors.

The Strand was perhaps most notable for the crowd that came
out on opening night. Writing in the *New York Times,* drama critic
Victor Watson described the evening as follows:

> Going to the new Strand Theatre last night was very much like
> going to a Presidential reception, a first night at the opera or
> the opening of the horse show. It seemed like everyone in town
> had simultaneously arrived at the conclusion that a visit to the
> magnificent new movie playhouse was necessary. . . . I must
> confess that when I saw the wonderful audience last night in
> all its costly togs, the one thought that came to my mind was
> that if anyone had told me two years ago that the time would

come when the finest-looking people in town would be going to the biggest and newest theatre on Broadway for the purpose of seeing motion pictures I would have sent them down to visit my friend, Dr. Minas Gregory at Bellevue Hospital. The doctor runs the city's bughouse, you know.

Over the years, a commonly held misassumption about the Strand was that it was the theater where Al Jolson changed the course of motion picture history by uttering those famous words, "You ain't heard nothing yet," in *The Jazz Singer* back in 1927. Although it is often thought—and sometimes written—that *The Jazz Singer* premiered here, the historic sound film actually debuted four blocks up the street, at Broadway between 51st and 52nd Streets, in a theater that had been called the Piccadilly but whose name was changed to the Warner in 1926, when Warner Brothers took it over to screen its first commercial sound film. To continue to set the record straight, Warner's first commercial Vitaphone film was not *The Jazz Singer* but rather *Don Juan,* which featured synchronized musical accompaniment by the New York Philharmonic Orchestra but was essentially still a silent film with no singing or spoken dialogue. Then came *The Jazz Singer,* which brought singing and a few lines of synchronized dialogue to the screen in 1927. Finally, the first truly "all-talking" picture was *The Lights of New York,* which was released by Warner Bros. later in 1927 and which also premiered at the former Piccadilly, at 1664 Broadway. That historic theater, which played such an important role in the birth of the talkies, is gone, too. It was torn down in 1953.

Strand Theater, 1947

I. Miller Building

19. I. MILLER BUILDING
Northeast corner of 47th Street and Broadway

"The Show Folks Shoe Shop Dedicated to Beauty in Footwear."
So says the inscription on the 47th Street side of this little two-story
building on Broadway, which was once a branch of the I. Miller
Shoe Company that specialized in dance and theater footwear. Today, Times Square denizens eat pizza where they used to try on
shoes, but if movie lovers look up when they pass the old I. Miller
building along West 47th Street, they will be treated to a wonderful
gallery of statues immortalizing famous women in show business.
Fashioned by A. Stirling Calder—father of mobile-maven, Alexander Calder—the star statues include Mary Pickford, Ethel Barrymore, diva Rosa Ponselle, and Ziegfeld Follies queen, Marilyn
Miller. While movie lovers may not realize that Miss Miller appeared
in a few early sound films, they will remember the 1949 Warner
Bros. film version of her life, *Look for the Silver Lining,* which
starred June Haver. They may also remember Judy Garland's cameo
performance as Miss Miller in MGM's 1946 film version of Jerome
Kern's life, *Till the Clouds Roll By,* in which Judy sang "Who?"
and "Look for the Silver Lining."

20. CORT THEATER
138 West 48th Street

Known as a "lucky house" because of the many long runs that
played here early in its history, the Cort opened in 1912 with Lau-
rette Taylor starring in *Peg o' My Heart,* which ran for two years.
One of its medium runs was *The Jazz Singer,* which played 315

*Grace Kelly with
Mady Christians in*
The Father, *1949*

performances between 1925–1926, starred George Jessel, and was
quickly turned into the world's first commercially successful motion
picture with sound (starring Al Jolson—not George Jessel).

Other Cort productions of interest to movie lovers may be the
1949 revival of Swedish playwright August Strindberg's *The Father,*
which featured the Broadway debut of a beautiful young actress
from Philadelphia named Grace Kelly; and the three-night run of
a play called *See the Jaguar* in 1952, which put James Dean on a
Broadway stage for the first time.

In 1955, a teenager from Brooklyn made her way across the
East River to Manhattan and the Cort Theater to see *The Diary of
Anne Frank,* which was a big hit at the time. It was Barbra Streisand's
first time in a Broadway theater . . . but not her last.

Between 1969 and 1973, the Cort had a stint as a TV studio,
during which time "The Merv Griffin Show" was the theater's principal tenant.

21. LATIN QUARTER
200 West 48th Street

Chorus girls, comics, acrobats, headliners, and more chorus
girls—that was the secret of the Latin Quarter's long-time supper-
club success. Founded in 1942 by nightclub mogul Lew Walters
(newsgal Barbara Walters's dad), the Latin Quarter occupied the
same underground space that once housed the downtown branch
of Harlem's famed Cotton Club. Today the Latin Quarter, after
many changes of management and format, endures as a Times
Square disco.

22. ST. MALACHY'S CHURCH AND ACTORS CHAPEL
239 West 49th Street

In the heart of the theater district, St. Malachy's is a Roman Catholic church with a separate "Actors Chapel" where show folk can escape the crazy world of making rounds and/or actually working in theater and films in New York.

In August of 1926, St. Malachy's was the scene of the world's most famous show-business funeral—that of Rudolph Valentino. It began with his untimely death from a bleeding ulcer and peritonitis at New York Polyclinic Hospital on Monday, August 23. It continued for a full week at Frank Campbell's Funeral Church, which at the time was on Broadway at 66th Street. At Campbell's, there were mobs of mourners, special police patrols, and all sorts of rumors. These ranged from speculation that Valentino had been murdered, to stories that a wax dummy and not Valentino's body was on display at Campbell's, in case someone in the unruly crowd tried to desecrate the corpse.

Amidst all the rumors and pandemonium, one thing was certain: United Artists, the studio behind his most recent pictures, was going to make the most of the situation. Hollywood had learned from the premature deaths of other 1920s superstars like Barbara La Marr and Wallace Reid that the public forgot quickly. So this time, they would do things right. Valentino's would be the most carefully orchestrated—and well-publicized—star funeral in the history of the movie business.

Plans called for the body to lie in state at Campbell's for a full week, after which a funeral Mass would be said at St. Malachy's on Monday, August 30. This posed one small problem, however, because Valentino had been twice divorced and therefore, in the eyes of the Catholic Church, which doesn't recognize divorce, was not entitled to a Catholic burial. But where there's a will, there's a way—both in Hollywood *and* in Rome—and it was later decided that since both of Valentino's marriages had been contracted in civil courts, and not in Catholic churches, both were invalid. Thus, the "bachelor" star was entitled to a full High Requiem send-off.

The St. Malachy's funeral was quite a spectacle. Shopkeepers and apartment dwellers on 49th Street charged outsiders to view the proceedings from their fire escapes and rooftops. Indeed, it seemed more like a premiere than a funeral as cheers from the crowds greeted arriving stars like Gloria Swanson, Douglas Fairbanks, George Jessel, Hope Hampton, and Marilyn Miller. The featured attraction, naturally, was Valentino, whose rose-bedecked coffin was followed by such close friends as Norma and Constance Talmadge, Mary Pickford, and Pola Negri, the Polish-born star who claimed to be Valentino's last lover and whose dramatic performance as mourner extraordinaire—complete with frequent faintings and designer widow's weeds—was the subject of much publicity.

After the church services, it was back to Frank Campbell's

Rudolph Valentino

again, where the body remained for another two days (special permission had to be obtained from the Commissioner of Health for the body to stay above ground for so long) in order for Valentino's brother, who was en route from Italy, to pay his last respects. With the arrival of the actor's brother, the show continued with a five-day train journey to Los Angeles, where there was yet another star-studded funeral at the Church of the Good Shepherd in Beverly Hills. Finally, a good two weeks after his death, Valentino was laid to rest in crypt number 1205 of the Cathedral Mausoleum at the Hollywood Memorial Park Cemetery.

The two-week funeral festival was a great success, by the way. United Artists couldn't make enough prints of Valentino's two latest films, *The Eagle* and *The Son of the Sheik,* to satisfy the demands of exhibitors. In fact, much to the studio's delight, Valentino was raking in more money in death than he had in life. Which just goes to prove that with the right publicity campaign, a dead legend can be worth more than a live superstar.

P.S. It was at St. Malachy's that, on June 3, 1929, Joan Crawford married Douglas Fairbanks, Jr.

23. BRILL BUILDING
1141 Broadway

Welcome to Tin Pan Alley. New York's historic headquarters for music publicists, arrangers, and booking agents, the Brill Building was once the nerve center of the nation's songwriting business. Today, aside from a few exceptions like Chapel Music and Paul Simon, who have offices here, the building is no longer the exclusive domain

Brill Building

of the music industry in New York, just as New York is no longer the force it once was in the music business. Indeed the days when songwriters made the rounds of the Brill's offices and hung out in The Turf restaurant (now the Colony music store) on its ground floor are gone. On the other hand, the Brill Building has remained in show business and today boasts a pretty impressive tenant roster: Rastar (Ray Stark) Productions, Judith (Mrs. John) Belushi, Lorne ("Saturday Night Live") Michaels, screenwriter/producer Paul Schrader (*Taxi Driver; Light of Day*), film maker Frank Perry (*Last Summer, Diary of a Mad Housewife, Compromising Positions*), and the production company for Universal's New York-based TV series, "The Equalizer."

The Brill Building—with its gleaming-brass entrance and lobby of more brass, plus mirrors and marble—has been featured in two famous made-in-New York motion pictures: *The House on 92nd Street* (1945) and *The Sweet Smell of Success* (1957). In the first, the Brill doubled as a talent agency; in the second, it was supposedly Burt Lancaster's apartment house. The building also pops up in Woody Allen's *Broadway Danny Rose* (1983). It gets its name, by the way, not from anybody in show business, but from the Brill Brothers, who were the haberdashers who originally built and occupied the place, then just two stories, in 1929. In 1933, major alterations brought more stories and more-glamorous tenants.

24. RIVOLI THEATER SITE
1620 Broadway

Designed by the famous theater architect Thomas W. Lamb in the style of a great Greek temple, the Rivoli (most recently known as the UA Twin) was heralded as "The Triumph of the

Motion Picture" when it debuted on December 28, 1917, with a bill that featured Douglas Fairbanks in *A Modern Musketeer* along with a spectacular stage show of singers, dancers, and patriotic tableaux—all backed up by a full orchestra and the biggest Wurlitzer organ ever to be installed in any theater.

The man behind the magic was S. L. "Roxy" Rothapfel, who had established himself as a master manager of movie palaces with his successful steering of the Regent on 116th Street as well as the Strand and the Rialto theaters on Broadway. Rothapfel, whose personal tastes were as extravagant as his movie houses, had a lavish suite of offices at the Rivoli, complete with a Japanese manservant who did everything from place bets at the racetrack to fry hot dogs for his colorful boss. Roxy also made a brief foray into the production end of the movie business during his Rivoli tenure. His plan was to film his lavish stage shows and to distribute them to smaller theaters. After one episode—and any number of horrendous reviews—of the Rothapfel Unit Programme, Roxy dropped the project and stuck to producing live shows to accompany the feature films that ran at his theaters.

Over the years the Rivoli had been an important Broadway movie house with one of the street's best sound systems; in fact, modern stereophonic sound debuted at the Rivoli in 1948 with the dramatic storm sequence at the end of David O. Selznick's *Portrait of Jennie.* The first-run home of such big-screen spectaculars as *Samson and Delilah, Around the World in Eighty Days, The Sound of Music, Lawrence of Arabia,* and the *Superman*s, Broadway's Parthenon of a movie palace was hacked into two theaters in 1981, and several years later it mysteriously lost the handsome classical frieze that had adorned its façade. Without the frieze, the Rivoli could not be declared a landmark, and without landmark status, in 1987, the "Triumph of the Motion Picture" went down in defeat.

"The Triumph of the Motion Picture": the Rivoli, 1930

Roxy Theater, ca. 1935

25. ROXY THEATER SITE
Northeast corner of 50th Street
and Seventh Avenue

It was the "Cathedral of the Motion Picture," the ultimate movie palace—the one and only Roxy Theater. When it opened on March 11, 1927, the publicity blurbs boasted: "We cannot find adjectives and superlatives strong enough to describe the thousand-and-one wonders and innovations of the Roxy, truly the most sumptuous and stupendous theater ever erected." And that it was, with 5,920 seats, six box offices, a five-story grand foyer and rotunda, ushers in black tie, dazzling Baroque decor, lounges, smoking rooms, hospital rooms, plus three organ consoles, twenty-one-bell cathedral chimes, a resident symphony orchestra of 110 musicians and four conductors, a chorus of one hundred voices, and a ballet company of fifty dancers.

The Roxy not only marked the apogee of the Age of the Movie Palace, it represented the high point in the career of S. L. Rothapfel, the famous theater entrepreneur whose nickname, Roxy, was immortalized by this great new entertainment establishment. The premier attraction at the Roxy was *The Love of Sunya,* a made-in-New York film that had been produced by, and also starred, La Marquise de la Falaise de la Coudraye; to millions of movie lovers La Marquise was better known as good old Gloria Swanson. Swanson, in her autobiography, *Swanson on Swanson* (Random House, 1980) had this to say of the glamorous 1927 premiere of the Roxy and of her film:

When we pulled up under the marquee and got out of the car, a tremendous roar went up. In the blinding glare of a double row of klieg lights trained on the shiny new building, I turned and waved, and before I could turn back again and enter the theater, an unstoppable wave of people surged forward and almost knocked us over. In spite of the efforts of the police, we had to fight our way into the lobby in order not to be crushed against the closed doors and walls.

Inside the monumental foyer, in front of an inclined bank of red and white carnations that spelled out his name, Roxy stood with his family, being photographed with celebrities. Henri [Swanson's husband, the marquis] and I joined them to kiss and shake hands with the people we knew in a steady blaze of flash powder. Roxy had pulled out all the stops. The parade of notables included four U.S. senators, three U.S. generals, three consul generals, two borough presidents, the governor of New Jersey, and the minister of Lithuania, as well as Adolph Ochs, Mrs. Otto Kahn, and Mr. and Mrs. Jimmy Walker. The crowd almost broke down the doors when Charlie Chaplin tried to sneak in unnoticed, and they went wild again when they recognized Harold Lloyd and his wife. We stood there for twenty minutes and greeted an endless stream of people with engraved invitations: the Shuberts, Irving Berlin, Lois Wilson, Sport Ward, Hope Hampton, Tommy Meighan, Joe Schenck, Walter Wanger, Will Hays—even Jesse Lasky. Then we all took our seats down front in the great auditorium, and the show began.

The show at the Roxy would go on for over three decades, and Swanson would be on hand for the theater's demolition in 1960, just as she had been for its gala opening in 1927. For the sad event, Gloria turned up in a black evening sheath and a feather boa to bid farewell not only to a theater, but to an era. Today, an electronics store as well as the glass-and-marble American Management Association Building occupy the famous corner where the Roxy once stood. There ought to be a plaque—but there isn't. Movie lovers can, however, get a glimpse of the Roxy in the film, *The Naked City* (1948), which uses the theater's foyer for several sequences.

26. WINTER GARDEN THEATER
1634 Broadway

Although it seems as though *Cats* has been running practically forever at the Winter Garden, the theater has a rich history that goes back long before Andrew Lloyd Webber's feline fantasy took over (and totally reconfigured) the place in 1982. In 1911, the year it opened, the Winter Garden featured Al Jolson, the actor who would revolutionize the motion-picture industry with his sound success in *The Jazz Singer* some fifteen years later, in a musical called *Vera Violetta*. Also in the cast was a comedienne who would go on to be a major force in the movies with her sexually explicit screen antics in the 1930s. Her name was Mae West.

Another major Hollywood name to appear on the Winter Garden stage early in his career was an Italian immigrant who made up half of a dance team called Glass and Di Valentina. At the time, the dancer had already changed his last name from Guglielmi to Di Valentina, but things wouldn't really click for him until he settled on Rudolph Valentino. An equally famous Hollywood name-change also played the Winter Garden before heading to California. The show was a lavish revue called *The Passing Show of 1924* and one of the gals in the chorus was a sexy lady from San Antonio named Lucille Le Sueur. When MGM spotted her on Broadway and signed her to a contract, the studio conducted a nationwide contest to find a suitable name for their new starlet. The winning name: Joan Crawford.

Speaking of Hollywood, in 1928 Warner Bros. took over the Winter Garden and made it a showplace for the company's new Vitaphone talking pictures, which held forth at the theater through 1933—when it was featured in Warner's *Gold Diggers of 1933*. The place subsequently went legit again and from 1935 to 1940 employed Vincente Minnelli as its "revue master," during a period when the theater specialized in producing dazzling musical extravaganzas in memory of the late Florenz Ziegfeld. Besides directing these spectacles, Minnelli, who had previously been art director at Radio City Music Hall, also designed the sets and costumes. Some of the future film stars who appeared in Minnelli's Winter Garden productions were Eve Arden, Ethel Waters, Eleanor Powell, and Bob Hope.

Besides serving as a springboard for Hollywood talent, the Winter Garden has also been a place for film stars to stage their Broadway comebacks. Two cases in point: Rosalind Russell, who brought new life to her career when she took Broadway by storm in *Wonderful Town* in 1953; and Angela Lansbury, whose film roles had dwindled to playing the world's bitchiest women (as in *The Manchurian Candidate* and *The World of Henry Orient*), became a talent to reckon with after she scored a knockout on the Winter Garden stage in 1966 with *Mame*.

Last but not least, there is Barbra Streisand, who starred at the Winter Garden as Fanny Brice—the legendary comedienne who had frequently played that theater in her heyday—in *Funny Girl*. As the world knows, Streisand went direct from the Winter Garden to Hollywood to star in, and win an Oscar for, the film version of *Funny Girl*. Since then, she has never returned to Broadway.

27. ADONIS THEATER
839 Eighth Avenue

Once upon a time, back in those hot muggy days of New York summers without air conditioning, movie houses often showed films on their rooftops between June and September. The Adonis Theater, a small (951 seats) house on Eighth Avenue, which opened as the Tivoli in 1921, provides an interesting glimpse of the past because vestiges of its old, open-air roof theater (screen, projection booth, ornamental urns, and elevator) survive and can be seen from 50th Street and Eighth Avenue. Surprisingly, it wasn't air conditioning that ultimately killed rooftop theaters in New York, it was sound.

When pictures began to talk, they had too much competition from street noises—especially on Eighth Avenue! Today, the former Tivoli, with its attractive columned façade and the unusual fixtures on its roof—specializes in gay porn films.

28. MARK HELLINGER THEATER
237 West 51st Street

Opened in 1930 as a Warner Bros. movie palace, the Mark Hellinger was originally called the Hollywood. The theater's architect/designer was the noted Thomas W. Lamb and his spectacular interior of sweeping staircases, ornate columns, and exotic balconies is still one of the most flamboyant of any legit house on Broadway. For the first two decades of its life, the Hollywood kept changing its name as well as its format, switching back and forth from films to stage shows to films. During one of its legit periods, the 1939 *George White's Scandals* had Ann Miller tapping on Broadway for the first time. Ironically, she would be back on the same stage forty years later in one of the theater's biggest hits, *Sugar Babies* (1979), which co-starred Mickey Rooney and ran for 1,208 performances—not one of which did Ann miss.

As successful as the *Sugar Babies* run was, it was not the Mark Hellinger's longest. That honor is still held by *My Fair Lady,* which starred Rex Harrison and Julie Andrews in the original cast and ran for 2,717 performances between 1956 and 1962. After *My Fair Lady,* the Hellinger saw two Hollywood legends grace its stage in the late 1960s: Marlene Dietrich, who in 1968 based her one-woman show, which had been a smash hit the year before at the Lunt & Fontanne on West 46th Street, at the Hellinger; and Katharine Hepburn, who made her Broadway musical-comedy debut as the

Mark Hellinger theater in its "Hollywood" days, 1935

revolutionary French fashion designer, Coco Chanel, in Alan Jay
Lerner and André Previn's 1969 *Coco.*

During a "dark" period in 1985, the Mark Hellinger was taken
over by director Richard Attenborough and turned into a movie
studio. The project was the long-awaited film version of the super-
smash Broadway hit, *A Chorus Line,* which was shot entirely at the
Mark Hellinger. A critical disaster, the film quickly faded from
view, while the Broadway show just kept rolling along.

29. BROADWAY THEATER
1681 Broadway

Opened in 1924 with Douglas Fairbanks starring in *The Thief
of Baghdad,* this 1,765-seat theater spent the first years of its life as
a motion picture/vaudeville palace known as the Colony. For movie
lovers, a premiere of monumental importance took place at the
Colony on November 18, 1928. The film ran barely eight minutes,
but its impact is still being felt around the world and its star is
probably the most famous of any screen personality in history. The
title of the little movie was *Steamboat Willie,* and it unleashed a
mouse named Mickey upon the world. Also in the cast were Minnie
Mouse and a villain named Pete. While it was Mickey Mouse that
brought fame and fortune to Walt Disney, this was not Disney's
first cartoon character or cartoon series. In 1924, in partnership
with his brother Roy, Disney came out with the *Alice in Cartoonland*
shorts, which were followed by *Oswald the Rabbit.* But neither Alice
nor Oswald were a match for the mouse that took off and soared
from the Colony movie screen back in 1928.

In 1930, the Colony changed its name to the Broadway, when
it became a legit house for a few years. Then, in the mid-1930s, it
went back to running films, went legit again in 1940, and—except
for a brief stint showing Cinerama wide-wide-wide-screen flicks in
the 1950s—has remained so ever since. Because of its vast stage
and large seating capacity, the Broadway is often used for musicals.
Among its top productions over the years have been *Gypsy* (1959),
which starred Ethel Merman; Andrew Lloyd Webber and Tim Rice's
Evita (1979), the musical based on the legendary Argentine dictator-
superstar, Eva Perón; and *Les Misérables* (1987).

30. ED SULLIVAN THEATER
1697 Broadway

The Ed Sullivan opened its arched Gothic doors in 1927 as
Hammerstein's Theater and featured a film-plus-variety-show format. Four years later, the house went legit and hosted Broadway
productions. Then in 1934, showman Billy Rose took over the place
for his lavish musical stage shows. Two years after that, CBS stepped
in and Hammerstein's became the CBS Radio Playhouse. The
theater's grandest era began in the early 1950s when CBS brought

in bright lights, built camera runways, and used what it now called Studio 50 for some of its most famous television variety shows, including the "Jackie Gleason Show," the "Garry Moore Show" (which gave Carol Burnett her prime-time boost) and, of course, the show to which the theater now owes its name, the "Ed Sullivan Show" (originally called "Ed Sullivan's Toast of the Town"). Still a vital part of NYC's TV scene, the theater has recently been used to tape the "Kate and Allie" sitcom before a live audience.

The Ed Sullivan Theater is a historic site not only because of all the stars who have appeared on its stage, but also because of the legendary acting school—Lee and Paula Strasberg's Actors Studio— that once occupied the fourteenth floor of the building. It was here that unknowns like Shelley Winters, Marlon Brando, James Dean, Eli Wallach, Rod Steiger, and Kim Stanley learned their craft. It was also here that one very well-known film star—Marilyn Monroe—came to perfect hers. Although she started off studying privately with Lee Strasberg, she eventually joined the group class. Remembering one of Marilyn's early scenes, actress Kim Stanley said, "We were taught never to clap at the Actors Studio—it was like a church—and it was the first time I'd ever heard applause there." Of Miss Monroe's talent, Lee Strasberg once observed: "I have worked with hundreds and hundreds of actors and actresses, and there are only two that stand out way above the rest. Number one is Marlon Brando, and the second is Marilyn Monroe. . . ." The Actors Studio was at 1697 Broadway between 1948 and 1955; today it is located at 432 West 44th Street.

31. FOX MOVIETONE NEWS SITE
450 West 54th Street

If you look carefully, you can just make out the faded "Movietone" sign on the side of this low brick factory building between Ninth and Tenth avenues . . . and if you listen carefully, you might be able to hear the distinctive voice of Lowell Thomas narrating what were the world's most famous newsreels. While Fox had consolidated most of its film production in Los Angeles by the mid-1930s, the company kept its Movietone News division at 450 West 54th Street in Manhattan from the 1920s through the 1970s. The Movietone name, by the way, was Fox's trademark for the sound-on-film system it developed in the late 1920s. Much more sophisticated than the sound-on-disc (Vitaphone) system that Warner Bros. used to introduce the world's first commercially successful sound films, Fox's Movietone system (or some variation of it) was the one that all of the studios—including Warner—eventually adopted.

Movie lovers who visit the Movietone site should also take a look at the large studio building that stands next door at 460 West 54th Street. Still called the "Fox Stage" by old-timers, this studio was originally part of Twentieth Century–Fox's New York operation, but from the 1950s to the 1970s it became one of the busiest rental stages in New York. Among the many features shot at 460 West 54th Street were *On the Waterfront* (1954), *Middle of the Night* (1959), *Fail Safe* (1964), *The Pawnbroker* (1964), *The Group* (1966), *The Owl and the Pussycat* (1970), *Where's Poppa?* (1970), *Shaft* (1971), and *The Exorcist* (1974). During the shooting of the last film, which dealt with a young girl's possession by the devil, all sorts of strange goings-on were reported on the old Fox Stage—from film that didn't develop properly to a fire and other hard-to-account-for accidents. Since then, some industry insiders now refer to the place as "the Exorcist studio."

In addition to feature films, 460 West 54th Street also counts "Inner Sanctum," "The Reporter," and "I Spy" among the TV series that have been filmed here. Today, as Cameramart Stages, the historic film-making facility is used mainly for television commercials.

32. WILLIAM FOX STUDIOS SITE
444 West 56th Street

Now the main branch of the John Jay College of Criminal Justice, this was where movie mogul William Fox kept watch over his impressive empire during most of the 1920s. Fox, who was brought to America as an infant by his Hungarian immigrant parents, grew up in poverty on New York City's Lower East Side. Dropping out of school at the age of eleven, he slaved in the garment industry for much of his youth. In 1903, at the age of twenty-four, he spent his life savings of $1,660 to buy a 146-seat movie theater in Brooklyn. When this venture earned him some $50,000 over the next five years, Fox reinvested the money into more movie houses and eventually got into the production side of the industry as well. At the height of his power in the late 1920s, Fox had assets valued at $300 million, which included studios in Los Angeles and New York, plus over 1,500 movie theaters across the country.

Twentieth Century–Fox soundstage, Tenth Avenue and 56th Street

But 1929 was a bad year for William Fox. On March 3 of that year, he was poised to become the most powerful man in the movie business when he finalized a deal to purchase the controlling interest in his principal competitor, Loew's Inc. This maneuver would have given Fox all of Loew's theaters as well as their production arm, MGM Studios. But Fox had gone too far, and the U.S. government stepped in and prevented the transaction from going through. Then, as Fox was fighting the government decision, he was seriously injured in an automobile accident that laid him up for three months. To make a bad situation even worse, along came the stock market crash, which had a devastating effect on the William Fox Company. One of the ways the company's other directors dealt with its serious financial troubles was to ease William Fox out of the business. In fact, by 1934, when the Fox organization had joined with Twentieth Century Pictures to form Twentieth Century–Fox, William Fox was no longer in the corporate picture.

Even without Fox, his New York offices—which also included the large building at 450 West 56th Street that's now a sound studio—stayed under Twentieth Century–Fox control until the 1970s, when John Jay College took over the property. Movie lovers who visit the site should peek inside the lavish main lobby at number 444. With its stained-glass windows and sleek Deco doors and light fixtures, the space looks as though it could have been a movie set. A Fox movie, of course.

33. HEARST MAGAZINE BUILDING
959 Eighth Avenue

His empire was vast and encompassed newspapers, motion-picture studios, hotels, real estate, and magazines. His taste was extravagant, especially when it came to architecture and design. His California homes—a fantastic castle on 50,000 acres in the north, and a 118-room beach "cottage" in the south—were playgrounds for the biggest names in Hollywood back in the 1920s and 1930s, all of whom flocked to the parties and weekends frequently staged at these fabulous places by his movie-star mistress, Marion Davies. At Eighth Avenue, between 56th and 57th streets in Manhattan, stands a smaller, but no less extravagant monument to William Randolph Hearst's sense of style: the Hearst Magazine Building, a massive fortress extravagantly decorated with columns, statues, and balustrades that reminds one of the Jugenstil buildings of turn-of-the-century Vienna.

Created to house the magazine division of Hearst's empire, this spectacular 1928 structure was the work of Joseph Urban, a man less well-known as an architect than as a set and costume designer. Urban went from decorating Florenz Ziegfeld's Follies to becoming artistic director of the Metropolitan Opera as well as a famous art director for early movies. One of Urban's landmark films was the 1921 production of *Enchantment,* which is believed to have been the first American film to use Modernist sets. Not

The art director as architect: Joseph Urban's Hearst Magazine Building

surprisingly, the producer of *Enchantment* was William Randolph Hearst, and the star of the film was Marion Davies. On designing for films, Urban had this to say to *Photoplay* in 1920: "The motion picture offers incomparably the greatest field to any creative artist of brush or blueprint today. It is the art of the twentieth century and perhaps the greatest art of modern times. It is all so young, so fresh, so untried. It is like an unknown ocean stretching out before a modern Columbus." During the 1920s, Urban would design some twenty-five films for Hearst. While many of these are lost, Urban's work can still be appreciated at 959 Eighth Avenue. (The six-story building, by the way, was originally intended to have another seven stories rise above it; they were never built.)

34. CBS BROADCAST CENTER
524 West 57th Street

Spanning most of the south side of 57th Street between Tenth and Eleventh avenues, this giant broadcasting complex has housed CBS's main radio and television studios since 1953. "60 Minutes," the "CBS Evening News," and the "CBS Morning Show" are all done here—as is the indomitable soap opera "As the World Turns." Once upon a time in the late-1960s, some eight soap operas were broadcast from CBS's West 57th Street facility, and the building reigned as the city's premier "soap factory." Productions at the time included "Search for Tomorrow," "The Secret Storm," "The Edge of Night," "The Guiding Light," and "Dark Shadows." During those heady days when West 57th Street was cranking out soaps the way Hollywood studios once cranked out pictures, Anita Loos and Helen Hayes visited the CBS Broadcast Center for their book *Twice over Lightly* (Harcourt, Brace, Jovanovich, 1972), which chronicled the two ladies' madcap sight-seeing adventures through New York. At CBS, they discovered that the main studio building had formerly been a milk processing plant and that it had inherited quite a few flies from its previous life. The flies, it seems, were especially troublesome on early soap sets, and many a scene had been stolen by an errant insect landing on an actor's nose. According to Loos and Hayes, the situation had gotten so bad that production assistants armed with fly swatters from Hammacher Schlemmer were needed to stand guard during shootings.

Today, most of the flies have abandoned West 57th Street—as have many of the soap operas, gone either to California or off the air entirely.

35. HAAREN HIGH SCHOOL SITE
899 Tenth Avenue

Robert Mitchum, its most famous former student, called it a finishing school: "If you went there, you were finished," Mitchum said of Haaren High—a tough, all-boys institution on the northern fringes of Hell's Kitchen. Originally called the De Witt Clinton High School when it opened in 1906 (De Witt Clinton moved to the Bronx in 1929), Haaren High was housed in one of the city's most beautiful school buildings—a striking seven-story "Flemish Renaissance" structure with bell-shaped gables, ornate Gothic columns, crests, and bas-relief figures.

Besides boasting Robert Mitchum as a celebrity alumnus, in 1966 Haaren could pride itself on being the principal location for the film *Up the Down Staircase*—the gritty, true-to-life portrait of a New York City high school based on the popular novel of the same name by Bel Kaufman. The film, shot during one of the hottest summers on NYC's record, took place in the winter. Especially memorable for passers-by was a snowstorm scene that had the actors bundled up in winter coats while artificial snow was falling all over Tenth Avenue on what was one of the hottest days of the year!

Ten years after its *Up the Down Staircase* success, Haaren shut down as a high school; but another major film role was still in the cards for what many had written off as an abandoned building. The year was 1979, the film was *Fame,* and, as is often the case in show business, Haaren was not the producer's first choice for the role. However, when the Board of Education refused to allow *Fame* to be shot at the place that had inspired the film—the High School of the Performing Arts—the Mayor's Office of Film, Theater, & Broadcasting fearful of losing the production to another city, proposed Haaren, which already had one film role to its credit.

While no more big film roles have come its way since *Fame,* a recently restored Haaren hopes to remain in show business as an office building for media-related enterprises.

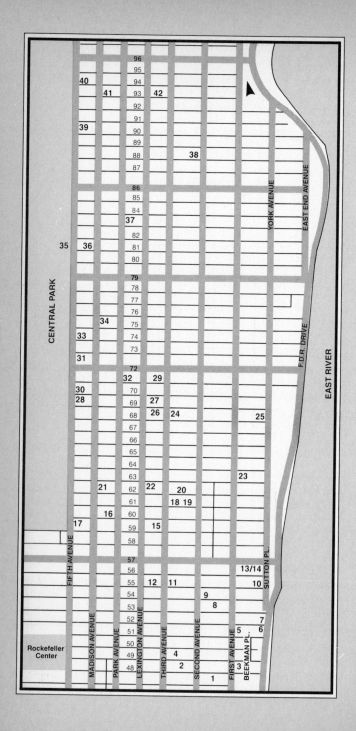

THE UPPER EAST SIDE

Beverly Hills East

Dietrich at El Morocco with Jean Gabin

WHAT becomes a legend most? Often an Upper East Side address. Throughout the twentieth century, this chic, ultra-exclusive part of Manhattan—with its solid apartment buildings, discreet hotels, and lavish townhouses—has been home to some of the biggest names in the movies. For movie lovers, a visit to the Upper East Side provides a chance to check out the Manhattan digs that legends like Garbo, Gish, Hepburn, Swanson, Dietrich, Crawford, and Monroe ultimately preferred to Southern California's sunshine. Among the numerous other delights awaiting movie lovers on the Upper East Side are Woody Allen's favorite restaurant, the Gabor family jewelry store, the secret location of *The House on 92nd Street,* and the world's most celebrated funeral parlor.

1. TWENTIETH CENTURY GARAGE
320 East 48th Street

This is no ordinary parking garage. For movie lovers, this great brick building was once the site of the Norma Talmadge Film Company. Named for one of the brightest stars in silent pictures, the studio was controlled by producer Joe Schenck, who was Miss Talmadge's husband as well as her mentor. In addition, Schenck also guided the careers of Norma's famous sister, Constance, and had comics Fatty Arbuckle and Buster Keaton under contract too. At any one time, all four of these legendary performers might be shooting films on the four floors of the Norma Talmadge Studios, which writer Anita Loos, who worked on scenarios for Schenck, described as "as lively as a Keystone farce."

By the 1930s, the Norma Talmadge Studio had become the De Forrest Photo Films Company, and both of the Talmadge sisters had retired from films. Norma, who never lost her Brooklyn accent, bombed in the couple of sound pictures that she made. Divorced from Schenck in 1927, she stayed briefly on the edge of the limelight by marrying comedian George Jessel in 1931. Constance, on the other hand, was wise enough to retire from the screen without uttering a word.

The career of Joe Schenck was another story. In 1933 he formed the Twentieth Century Picture Corporation with Darryl Zanuck. Two years later, Twentieth Century merged with William Fox to become Twentieth Century–Fox, where Schenck remained a major mogul for the next two decades and where he was especially helpful in getting the career of a beautiful young contract player named Marilyn Monroe off the ground. In 1952, the Motion Picture Academy of Arts and Sciences honored Schenck with a special Oscar "for long and distinguished service to the motion picture industry." Schenck died in Hollywood in 1961.

Today there is no Joe Schenck building to remember this influential producer's New York beginnings. There is, however, the Twentieth Century Garage, which bears the same name as one of Schenck's major ventures.

Hepburn house, Turtle Bay

2. TURTLE BAY GARDENS
48th and 49th Streets between Second and Third Avenues

A very special place to live, Turtle Bay Gardens is made up of the blocks of townhouses on 48th and 49th streets between Second and Third avenues. What makes them special is the fact that each house not only has its own private garden in back, but all share a large communal garden as well. For movie lovers, the most famous resident of this charmed Manhattan neighborhood is Katharine Hepburn, who has lived in the same four-story brownstone with the black wrought-iron gates and white-curtained windows at 244 East 49th Street for over half a century.

Over the years, Miss Hepburn has had a number of famous neighbors. Composer Stephen Sondheim lives next door at number 246 and Garson Kanin and his wife Ruth Gordon once lived on the same block. They were best of friends until Mr. Kanin wrote *Tracy and Hepburn* in 1971, a literary endeavor which the very private Kate is said not to have appreciated. As the world knows, the headstrong Miss Hepburn is not a woman to be crossed. A case in point concerns a burglar who, in the late 1930s, broke into her Turtle Bay house while she was napping, and was about to make off with a $5,000 necklace that her man-friend at the time, Howard Hughes, had given her. Waking up in the knick of time, Hepburn bellowed at the thief: "What are you doing here?" She then chased him into the street where he hopped into a getaway car—without the necklace.

3. UNITED NATIONS PLAZA APARTMENTS
860 and 870 United Nations Plaza

Around the corner from the low-rise townhouses and apartments of Beekman Place, the twin glass skyscrapers of the United Nations Plaza Apartments at 49th Street and First Avenue, just north of the United Nations, offer not only luxurious housing but extraordinary floor-to-ceiling views of the city. Built in 1966, the U.N. Plaza instantly attracted a number of celebrities to its posh pads. Among its star tenants over the last two decades have been Johnny Carson (during "The Tonight Show" 's Manhattan days), the late Truman Capote ("living on *Cold Blood* money," is the way Helen Hayes once put it), Cliff Robertson and Dina Merrill (before the split), Mickey Rooney (who sublet here during his triumphant Broadway run in *Sugar Babies*), the late producer David Susskind, tennis star Vitas Gerulaitis, photographer/film director Gordon Parks (*Shaft*), Academy Award–winning director Michael Cimino (*The Deer Hunter*), TV host Hugh Downs, TV newsman Edwin Newman, and the late Senator Robert Kennedy.

4. PAUL NEWMAN APARTMENT
230 East 50th Street

For a long time when Paul Newman wasn't racing cars, hawking salad dressing, promoting liberal causes, making movies, or spending time at his Connecticut country home, he might have been at his *pied-à-terre* in this discreet little East Side Building.

5. SHIRLEY MACLAINE APARTMENT
400 East 52nd Street

A lady of many lives, actress-author-psychic Shirley MacLaine (born Shirley MacLean Beatty) has lived one of them in this modern apartment building on the edge of Beekman Place.

6. THE CAMPANILE
450 East 52nd Street

She is the world's most public private person. Even though she has not made a film since 1941, octogenarian Greta Garbo still fascinates the press, the masses, even the precious few who are permitted to be her friends. Dressed in floppy hat, long trench coat, and trademark dark-dark glasses, she prowls about Manhattan, darting in and out of doorways, peeking at shop windows, occasionally attending a film at the Plaza Theater on East 58th Street. For years she has lived in a seven-room apartment in The Campanile, a small 1920s brick building with Gothic arches and leaded-glass windows on the *cul-de-sac* where 52nd Street meets the East River. While Garbo's neighbors over the years have included such notables as Alexander Woollcott (Dorothy Parker dubbed the

The Campanile

building "Wit's End"), Rex Harrison, Henry and Clare Booth Luce, by far her most interesting fellow tenants were the Russian couturier Valentina and her millionaire husband George Schlee. In an arrangement straight out of neighbor Noël Coward's play, *Design for Living,* Garbo had an intense personal relationship with Mr. Schlee from the mid-1940s until his death in 1964. He was not only her financial adviser, he was her escort, her confidant, and often her traveling companion. All the while, Schlee remained married to Valentina, who not only made Garbo's clothes but sometimes accompanied Schlee and the former movie actress on social outings. The whole arrangement was eminently civilized but fell apart rather abruptly when Schlee was stricken with a fatal heart attack while staying at the Crillon Hotel in Paris, where he and Garbo had adjoining suites. When Garbo discovered that Schlee was dead, she reportedly ran from the hotel and left Valentina to deal with the messy details involved with death in a foreign country. Garbo's irresponsible behavior is said to have so angered Valentina that she made it clear that she didn't want the actress to attend her husband's funeral. The two are still neighbors at 450 East 52nd Street but reportedly haven't exchanged a word in over twenty years.

7. RIVER HOUSE
435 East 52nd Street

Protected by an ornate iron gate that opens onto a formal driveway, River House is one of the fashionable East Side's most prestigious addresses. Besides great privacy and security, the building also provides its residents with such luxuries as squash and tennis courts, a swimming pool, a ballroom, and, in the days before the F. D. R. Drive skirted the East River, River House even had its own private boat dock. Like many Manhattan apartment buildings, River House is a cooperative, which means that its tenants own shares in the building and have a say in its affairs via an elected board of directors. Since the board at River House has traditionally been a conservative lot, the building is sometimes better known for the people who have been refused apartments than for those who actually reside here.

Among the former group, celebrity fashion designer (and former actress) Gloria Vanderbilt had a rough go of it at River House in 1980 when the board denied her an apartment, reportedly because her finances weren't up to River House standards. The multimillionairess then sued River House, alleging that the real reason she had been refused the apartment was because she enjoyed a close friendship with black cabaret singer Bobby Short. River House denied that racism had entered into its decision, but did acknowledge that it thought Miss Vanderbilt's high profile in Manhattan society would bring "unwelcome publicity" to the building. Little Gloria eventually dropped the suit, and was happy at last when she found friendlier digs up on Gracie Square.

Among the celebrities that *have* met River House standards are former secretary of state Henry Kissinger and his wife Nancy; actress/author/diplomat Clare Booth Luce, whose play *The Women* was turned into MGM's all-star movie of the same name in 1939; director Joshua Logan of *Mr. Roberts, Picnic, Bus Stop, Sayonara,* and *South Pacific* fame; and, reportedly, Charlie Chaplin.

8. NEIGHBORHOOD PLAYHOUSE SCHOOL OF THEATER 340 East 54th Street

In 1915 the Neighborhood Playhouse was established as an amateur theater group on Manhattan's Lower East Side. It was one of many projects in the Henry Street Settlement's fight to improve

Glorious Garbo

Cozy at El Morocco: Eddie Fisher and Elizabeth Taylor

the lot of slum dwellers. Although the Neighborhood Playhouse closed in 1928, the acting school that grew out of it has flourished ever since. Located in a handsome double townhouse on the Upper East Side since 1948, the Neighborhood Playhouse School of Theater counts among its famous former students Gregory Peck, Tyrone Power, Diane Keaton, Robert Duvall, Lorne Greene, Elizabeth Ashley, Eli Wallach, Anne Jackson, Keir Dullea, James Caan, Joanne Woodward, Jeff Goldblum, Griffin Dunne, Tammy Grimes, Efrem Zimbalist, Jr., Dabney Coleman, Brenda Vaccaro, Suzanne Pleshette, Darren McGavin, Patrick O'Neal, Pamela Bellwood, Mary Steenburgen, Lee Grant, and director Sidney Pollack.

9. EL MOROCCO
307 East 54th Street

At 154 East 54th Street from 1931 (the year of its debut) to 1961 (the year its founder John Perona died), El Morocco flourished for three decades as one of New York's most famous *boîtes*. With its white palm trees and zebra-striped banquettes, the place looked like a Hollywood movie set, and it pulled in all the Hollywood biggies—Sinatra, Bogart, Errol Flynn—whenever they were in town. (It is said that the only night the club closed down was when Flynn died in 1959.) One Hollywood personality not welcome at El Morocco, however, was Zsa Zsa Gabor. It seems that one evening in the 1950s the tempestuous Hungarian actress had a disagreement with Mr. Perona, and lashed out at him so vehemently that she was permanently banned from the premises. Supposedly, Zsa Zsa often waited outside El Morocco in her friends' limousines while they tried to talk Perona into letting her inside. He never relented.

After Perona's death in 1961, El Morocco moved further east across 54th Street to its present address, where it has had its ups and downs, its gala reopenings and quiet closings ever since. In

May 1987, after having been shuttered for some six years, the night-club—restored and revved up with $2 million—once again made a comeback, complete with its long-time maître-d', Angelo Zucotti (who once turned away Humphrey Bogart when the actor refused to check the two stuffed pandas he had in tow). Several months before El Morocco's reopening, TV viewers got a flash of the club's former glory in the mini-series, "The Two Mrs. Grenvilles," when a mock-up was used for the scene in which socialite Billy Grenville (Stephen Collins) meets the chorus girl of his dreams, who becomes his wife (Ann-Margret). In real life, the characters on whom Dominick Dunne's story was loosely based (William Woodward, Jr., and Ann Eder) met at El Morocco.

10. "HOW TO MARRY A MILLIONAIRE" APARTMENT
36 Sutton Place South

They were three of the most glamorous gold diggers ever to go prospecting in Manhattan—Lauren Bacall, Betty Grable, and Marilyn Monroe—and their ensemble aim was quite simple: Each wanted to tap into the life of the richest man she could find. To do this, they needed a base of operations that would fit their decidedly upscale aspirations. Or, as Bacall bellowed early on in the film: "To catch a mouse, you use a mousetrap . . . to catch a bear, you use a bear trap." The three beauties found the ideal bear trap in a palatial penthouse that was available for sublet on posh Sutton Place. It cost $1,000 a month—a lot of money back in 1953; but it had bedrooms and terraces for days, and it came completely furnished. The furniture, however, didn't last long as the gals started selling it off piece by piece when they discovered that *How to Marry a Millionaire* was not the easy task they had thought it to be. The luxury apartment building used as an exterior for this classic CinemaScope comedy from Twentieth Century–Fox still looks exactly as it did in the film.

Sutton Place sirens: Marilyn Monroe, Betty Grable, and Lauren Bacall with Cameron Mitchell in How to Marry a Millionaire, *1953*

11. P. J. CLARKE'S
913 Third Avenue

Third Avenue today is a busy boulevard that shows off some of Manhattan's sleekest, chic-est new skyscrapers. It's a far cry from the *old* Third Avenue with its low-rise brick tenement buildings and low-lit neighborhood pubs, all in the shadow of the overhead tracks of the famous Third Avenue "El." One of the few vestiges of the old Third Avenue is a two-story brick building on the northeast corner of 55th Street that still houses P. J. Clarke's bar. The archetypal New York neighborhood bar, P. J.'s—with its tin ceiling, beveled mirrors, and wood-paneled walls hung with sports photos— is a casual place for a business lunch or a happy-hour cocktail. For movie lovers, P. J.'s is of special interest because it served as Nat's Bar in Billy Wilder's classic 1945 film about alcoholism, *The Lost Weekend*. Or so the legend goes. In reality, none of the footage shot at the bar could be used because of the noise of the "El" running overhead, so the bar was recreated on a Paramount soundstage in Hollywood.

What Wilder couldn't duplicate in Hollywood, however, was the long sequence in *The Lost Weekend* where a desperate Ray Milland staggers up Third Avenue trying to pawn his typewriter. Shooting early in the mornings, Wilder, cameraman John Seitz, and Milland spent two weeks and covered sixty-five blocks of Third Avenue sidewalks working on this famous scene in which Milland can't find an open pawnshop, because it's Yom Kippur, the holiest day of the Jewish religious calendar. For Milland the shooting was particularly grueling, and he was reported to have been "muscle sore, chest-foundered, and swaybacked" by the time it was over. In

Third Avenue classic: P. J. Clarke's

Third Avenue man: Ray Milland shooting The Lost Weekend, *1945*

fact, when the company returned to Hollywood, Milland was in such bad shape that they had to shoot around him for three days until he got rid of the limp he had developed from pounding the Third Avenue pavements with typewriter in hand. But ultimately it was worth the pain, because Milland won an Academy Award for his performance in *The Lost Weekend.*

12. MICHAEL'S PUB
211 East 55th Street

On Monday, March 30, 1987, the world may have watched as Woody Allen's screenplay for *Hannah and Her Sisters* won an Academy Award, but one person who wasn't near a television set was Mr. Allen himself. Instead he was playing the clarinet over at Michael's Pub as part of its weekly New Orleans and Ragtime Night. A creature of habit, Mr. Allen has been a boy in the band at Michael's practically every Monday evening since the early 1970s.

NOTE: *For movie lovers who want to catch Woody's act, phone (212) 758-2272 for reservations.*

13. LILLIAN GISH APARTMENT
430 East 57th Street

For over half a century, Sutton Place has been Lillian Gish's Manhattan home. An extraordinary woman whose film career began in 1912 with D. W. Griffith's *An Unseen Enemy,* Lillian Gish appeared in such landmark silent pictures as *The Birth of a Nation* (1915), *Intolerance* (1916), *Way Down East* (1920), *Orphans of the Storm* (1922), and *The Scarlet Letter* (1925). When her film career slowed down in the 1930s, it was not, as it was for many of her contemporaries, on account of the talkies, but rather because Hollywood's taste in heroines had changed, and virtuous virgins like Miss Gish were no longer in fashion. The actress dealt with this

Lillian Gish in The
Birth of a Nation, *1915*

turn of events by concentrating on the Broadway stage, where she
had a string of successes in classical roles. Her film career was far
from over, however, for she went on to triumph as a character
actress in a number of films in the late 1940s and 1950s, from
David O. Selznick's *Duel in the Sun* (1947) and *Portrait of Jennie*
(1948) to United Artists' *Night of the Hunter* (1955). And La Gish
goes on and on. Witness her roles in *A Wedding* (1978), *Sweet
Liberty* (1986), and *The Whales of August* (1987). Honored with a
Lifetime Achievement Award by the American Film Institute in
1984, Lillian Gish is not just a legend, she is an American institution.
The ninety-plus-year-old actress likes living in the Sutton Place
area of the Upper East Side, she says, because "it is like a village
where everyone knows you."

14. MARILYN MONROE APARTMENT
444 East 57th Street

If you wanted to reach Marilyn Monroe in the late 1950s, you
had only to look in the Manhattan telephone directory under
"Marilyn Monroe Productions Inc., 444 E. 57 . . . PL 9–5353."
Marilyn moved into 444 with her third husband, playwright Arthur
Miller, in 1956; and when she died some six years later in Holly-
wood, she still held a lease on the same Sutton Place apartment.
In fact, when she made her final visit to the city in June 1962 to
sing "Happy Birthday" to President John F. Kennedy at Madison

Square Garden, she stayed at 444—although some sources reported that she spent at least part of the evening at the Carlyle Hotel, where the president was staying *without* Jackie.

Marilyn's East 57th Street apartment was on the thirteenth floor and had a lovely view of the East River. During the good times of her marriage to Miller, she played housewife and delighted in making breakfast and midmorning coffee for her writer husband. Marilyn also played decorator, and did the whole place in white. Indeed, when she flew to California to make *Some Like It Hot* in 1958, Marilyn insisted that her suite at the Bel-Air Hotel be decorated in white to match her Manhattan home.

By early 1961, however, Marilyn's New York apartment was showing the strains of her personal and professional troubles. Now divorced from Miller and a veteran of stays in several mental hospitals, Marilyn had become a semirecluse, and her secretary reported that her once-posh pad was "filthy, dirty, and depressing, with dog stains all over the carpets." According to her hairdresser, George Masters, Marilyn was "living on caviar, champagne, and hard-boiled eggs. She could let herself look like an old bag for two weeks. She'd smell sometimes, and never comb her hair for weeks. That's why it would take nine hours to get her ready and recreate Marilyn Monroe."

It was during this desperate period of her life that Marilyn is said to have come close to committing suicide by jumping out of her living room window. The reason for her extreme panic at the time was because she had read that Clark Gable's wife had blamed "the King's" recent death on the delays and tensions caused by Marilyn's erratic behavior while shooting *The Misfits*. Marilyn didn't jump, however, supposedly because she recognized a woman on the sidewalk below her. It was also around this time that Marilyn finally gave up on New York—the city that had held so much

Marilyn Monroe apartment

Marilyn in Manhattan: riding a pink elephant at a Madison Square Garden benefit, 1955

promise for her when she arrived in late 1954—and decided to go back to where she came from: Hollywood. A year later, she would give up on Hollywood, too.

15. BLOOMINGDALE'S
1000 Third Avenue

A landmark of conspicuous consumption on the Upper East Side, Bloomingdale's has naturally found its way into more than a few made-in-Manhattan movies. Notable Bloomie's on-screen shopping sprees include Diane Keaton and Michael Murphy's perfume-counter encounter in Woody Allen's *Manhattan* (1979), and the sequence in Paul Mazursky's *Moscow on the Hudson* (1984) in which the Russian musician played by Robin Williams defects to the West, smack in the middle of this bastion of capitalism.

16. CHRIST UNITED METHODIST CHURCH
Park Avenue at 60th Street

It was a fashionable affair, the marriage of socialite Frances Seymour Brokaw of 646 Park Avenue to Mr. Henry Jaynes Fonda of Hollywood, California. The ceremony took place on September 16, 1936, at Park Avenue's ultra-WASPy Christ United Methodist Church, and in his autobiography Mr. Fonda says of the event: "I don't know if I was ready for that kind of fancy dress wedding. They got me into a black coat with swallowtails, a pair of striped pants, an ascot around my neck, and a high silk hat on my head. Shit! I thought any minute the director would yell, 'Roll 'em! Action!' "

Henry Fonda had met Frances Brokaw earlier that year in

London, where he had been shooting *Wings of the Morning*. It was love at first sight, followed by a whirlwind courtship carried on in Berlin, Budapest, and Paris, and culminating in matrimony on Park Avenue. There was no honeymoon, since Fonda was scheduled to start a picture in Hollywood the next day. But while all had been idyllic in Europe and New York, the couple ran into problems in California. For one thing, Frances Fonda never really fit into the town where her husband made his living and could never settle for being just another Hollywood housewife. Despite their problems, the Brokaw-Fonda union endured and produced two children: Jane Seymour Fonda, born on December 21, 1937; and Peter Henry Fonda, February 23, 1940. As time went on, however, Mrs. Fonda's inability to cope with life in L.A. became more pronounced and she was plagued with hypochondriacal illnesses that put her out of commission for longer and longer periods of time. Even the family's move to the East Coast (when Fonda was starring in *Mr. Roberts* on Broadway in 1946) didn't help. In fact things got worse, and by 1949 Frances Fonda was spending more time in institutions than out of them. At the same time, her husband had met another woman—Susan Blanchard—and had asked his wife for a divorce. Mrs. Fonda granted this freely, even wished her husband good luck. But it was she who needed the luck. In April of 1950, Frances Seymour Fonda ended her life, cutting her throat with a razor blade that she had smuggled into the sanitarium where she had been confined for several months. The funeral, in contrast to the glittering wedding fourteen years earlier, took place at a funeral home in upstate New York with only Henry Fonda and his mother-in-law Sophie Seymour in attendance.

Christ United Methodist Church

Copacabana postcard

17. THE COPACABANA
10 East 60th Street

Immortalized in the Barry Manilow song "Lola" (about a Copa chorus girl), which later inspired the 1985 Emmy Award–winning television movie called "Copacabana," New York City's Copacabana reigned as one of the town's most glamorous night spots from its opening in 1940 until well into the 1950s. Among the star performers who headlined here were Ella Fitzgerald, Sid Caesar, Frank Sinatra, Tony Bennett, Sammy Davis, Jr., Nat King Cole, Jimmy Durante, and a couple of comics named Dean Martin and Jerry Lewis who, in 1949, broke all Copa records when they took in $68,543 in one week.

Four years before that, it took Lena Horne to break the Copa's color barrier, becoming the first black entertainer to perform in the club's posh downstairs room. It was a bittersweet achievement, however: While the Copa allowed Miss Horne to perform, they refused to let blacks in the audience. This resulted in picket lines and protests and caused much grief for the star. Although she honored her contract and completed her run, from then on she made sure that all future nightclub contracts contained a clause barring racial discrimination at the door. The next time she played the Copa, blacks were part of the audience.

Movie lovers may be interested to learn that June Allyson was once a Copa Girl, as were Joanne Dru and Janice Rule. Movie lovers may also remember a 1947 bomb of a picture called *Copacabana,* in which Groucho Marx (with neither his mustache nor his brothers) played an agent who tried to double his commission by booking his client (Carmen Miranda) into the same New York

City nightclub as two separate acts (a veiled chanteuse and a Latin spitfire)!

Well past its prime by the late 1960s, the Copa closed down in 1973, but has had various comebacks and incarnations since. It presently keeps a rather low profile on the New York night scene as a disco.

18. MONTGOMERY CLIFT TOWNHOUSE
217 East 61st Street

The star of *The Search* (1948), *Red River* (1948), *The Heiress* (1949), *A Place in the Sun* (1951), *From Here to Eternity* (1953), *Raintree County* (1957), *Suddenly Last Summer* (1959), *The Misfits* (1961), and *Freud* (1962) lived in this four-story townhouse on East 61st Street from 1960 until his death at the age of forty-five in 1966. The home—which Teddy Roosevelt had given to his daughter, Alice Longworth, as a wedding present—had a sixty-foot living room, four bedrooms, six baths, six fireplaces, and a big garden in back. Despite these sumptuous surroundings, Clift's final years were far from happy ones. In constant pain from the injuries he had sustained in a near-fatal automobile accident in Hollywood in 1957, the star was hooked on drugs as well as plagued with a host of other health problems that ranged from premature cataracts and hypothyroidism to alcoholism and insomnia. Clift was also obsessed

Montgomery Clift townhouse

with the loss of his leading-man good looks and with the knowledge that both of his co-stars in *The Misfits,* Marilyn Monroe and Clark Gable, had recently died. Believing that bad things come in threes, he spent the early 1960s waiting to be the next to go.

Sick, drugged, and drunk much of the time, Clift fell in with a sex-and-drugs crowd, and his East 61st Street abode was often the scene of some wild goings-on. Eventually when things had gotten so out of hand that Clift reportedly would try to solicit male sex partners by calling down at passers-by from his upstairs window, his family and doctor hired a full-time male companion to care for the fast-fading superstar. On July 27, 1966, the light from that star faded completely.

Soon after his death, Clift's townhouse was sold by his sister with the stipulation that the new owners put up a plaque in the front of the building to read: "Montgomery Clift lived here in 1960–1966." The buyers did as they had been asked, but became so bothered by Clift cultists hanging around the building that they planted a bush in front of the plaque to hide it. Today, movie lovers passing by the former Clift townhouse will find that the plaque has disappeared totally.

19. BILL COSBY TOWNHOUSE
243 East 61st Street

Although his "Cosby Show" TV townhouse can be found on St. Luke's Place in Greenwich Village, Mr. Cosby in private life sometimes calls the Upper East Side home. His primary residence, however, is an Early American farmhouse on a 286-acre estate near Amherst, Mass., which he purchased in 1971 when he stepped out of the limelight to pursue a doctorate in education at the University of Massachusetts.

20. TALLULAH BANKHEAD TOWNHOUSE
230 East 62nd Street

She made "Dah-ling" a fashionable form of address long before the Gabors came on the scene. She drank heavily, smoked six packs of cigarettes a day, went to bed with both men and women, was renowned for her bawdy stories, and yet, throughout it all, Tallulah Bankhead was one great lady. She moved into this handsome East 62nd Street townhouse in the late 1950s, when her longtime home in the suburban community of Bedford Village had become too difficult for her to handle. Indeed, the lush life that Tallulah had led for four decades was starting to catch up with her by the time she hit the Upper East Side. Despite face and bust lifts, her looks had gone, and her career was reduced to summer stock and occasional guest shots on TV and radio. When she was home, her favorite pastime was a game of bridge that would last into the wee hours of the morning and during which much alcohol would be consumed. She also liked baseball, and could often be found at the Polo Grounds cheering for the New York Giants.

Tallulah's townhouse

Although Tallulah Bankhead was not a movie star per se, she made films throughout her long career in show business. In fact, when she arrived in Manhattan as a stage-struck fifteen-year-old in 1918, among her very first acting jobs were roles in two silent films, *When Men Betray* and *Thirty a Week,* both shot in nearby Fort Lee, New Jersey. It wasn't until 1931, however, that Tallulah's motion-picture career began in earnest. Having become a great star of the London stage in the 1920s, the glamorous expatriate was wooed back to her native land with a lucrative movie contract from Paramount, which planned to market her as a second Marlene Dietrich. Back in New York, Tallulah quickly made three films at Paramount's Astoria studio. Although the films—*Tarnished Lady,* directed by George Cukor, and *My Sin* and *The Cheat,* both directed by George Abbott—were not terribly successful, the studio kept Tallulah under contract and the following year starred her in three Hollywood films—*Thunder Below, Make Me a Star,* and *Devil and the Deep,* the last of which featured Gary Cooper, Charles Laughton, and Cary Grant. She was also loaned out to MGM in 1932 for *Faithless.* Again, Tallulah's films were not wildly successful, and she eventually returned to New York and to the Broadway stage, where she enjoyed a busy career for the next two decades. Among her legendary stage performances were as Regina Giddens in Lillian Hellman's *The Little Foxes* in 1939 (a role that Bette Davis later played in the film version) and her portrayal of Sabina, the maid in Thornton Wilder's *The Skin of Our Teeth,* which won her a New York Drama Critics Award in 1942.

A year later, just when everyone least suspected it, the unpredictable Tallulah returned to motion pictures, and scored the coup

*Paramount pretty:
Tallulah Bankhead,
ca. 1931*

of her career in Alfred Hitchcock's *Lifeboat,* winning the New York Film Critics Award for Best Actress of 1944 for her performance as a mink-coated reporter. Despite her newfound film success, Tallulah was not so lucky with *A Royal Scandal,* which she made the following year, and once again she gave up on the medium. Ironically, she would return to the screen in 1965 as the star of the low-budget horror film *Die, Die, My Darling,* a performance which, along with two guest shots on the "Batman" TV series around the same time, turned out to be her show-business swan songs. The great lady, who was never what is usually considered a movie star, but whose first and last professional appearances were on film, died in New York in 1968. By that time, she had moved from her East 62nd Street townhouse into an apartment at 447 East 57th Street.

21. JOLIE GABOR JEWELRY STORE
699 Madison Avenue

Her daughters Zsa Zsa and Eva have been in the business of selling glamour on stage, screen, and television for years. At the same time, Jolie Gabor, thoroughly modern matriarch of the most famous Hungarian refugee family in America, has sold glamorous jewelry at this chic little Madison Avenue boutique since 1946. Extremely successful both in rearing her daughters and in minding her business, Madame Gabor has managed to score a long run on a street where shops come and go by the month. For movie lovers, besides the baubles on display in Jolie Gabor's windows, special treats are often portraits of her glamorous progeny, including her spotlight-shy—can this be?—eldest daughter, Magda. Like those of daughters Eva and Zsa Zsa, Mama Jolie's age is the subject of much conjecture. Estimates put her birthdate somewhere between 1890 and 1903.

22. BARBIZON GOLDEN TULIP HOTEL
140 East 63rd Street

Smack in the middle of the East Sixties, this was one of the world's most fashionable boarding houses when it opened in 1927 as the Barbizon Hotel for Women. Although its rooms were small and Spartan simple, the twenty-seven-story hotel provided extras like a huge swimming pool and health club, a library with a full-time librarian, plus all sorts of club and game rooms. The hotel also had a strict policy regarding the opposite sex: Men were not admitted beyond the second-floor Recital Room. The Barbizon Hotel for Women was thus a place where protective parents could send their daughters and feel relatively untroubled about their whereabouts in the big city. Judy Garland and Vincente Minnelli, for example, knew teenaged Liza was in good hands when she made the Barbizon her New York nest during the making-the-rounds period of her career. Nor did the John Kellys of Philadelphia have to worry too much about their daughter Grace falling in with the wrong crowd as long as she was at the Barbizon. Ditto for the Bergens of Beverly Hills when their sweet Candy dropped out of the University of Pennsylvania for the bright lights and big bucks of a Manhattan modeling career. The Leachmans, those lumber barons of Des Moines, could breathe easier with little Cloris based at the Barbizon when she came to New York to try her wings on Broadway after having been a runner-up in the Miss America pageant. The hotel also lists Joan Crawford as a former famous occupant, but Joan's Broadway chorus-girl career had ended before the Barbizon was built, and it is hard to imagine Joan "the movie star" as a Barbizon girl.

The Barbizon Hotel for Women flourished for close to forty years, but toward the end of the 1960s the sexual revolution as well as a decline in the hotel's physical plant caused it to lose much of

The Barbizon

its former cachet. Nonetheless, it was still a beautiful building—with its tapestry-brickwork façade, its gargoyles and columned balconies—and recently it was totally renovated and turned into a full-service hotel . . . for both sexes.

23. MYRNA LOY APARTMENT
425 East 63rd Street

Bubbly, witty, fast-talking Nora Charles of *The Thin Man* will go down in film history as one of the movies' most sophisticated New York ladies. Today, the great star who created her on screen lives—appropriately—on the Upper East Side. The surprise is that Myrna Loy was born way out West (in Montana) and grew up in Southern California. Over the years, her neighbors in this 1955 high-rise have included Eydie Gorme and Dr. Joyce Brothers.

24. BARBRA STREISAND APARTMENT
1157 Third Avenue

Early on in her journey to superstardom—and a long, long way from Malibu, where she would eventually own a vast compound of five houses near the sea—Barbra Streisand lived in an apartment above Oscar's Salt of the Sea Restaurant. The year was 1962, she was twenty-one, and this was the first apartment she'd ever had on her own. The neighborhood wasn't bad, but it seems that the apartment reeked of fish from the restaurant downstairs, and predictably, so did much of Streisand's wardrobe. Fish or no fish, Barbra eventually reeled in her *I Can Get It for You Wholesale* leading man, Elliott Gould, who wound up sharing the Third Avenue pad with the lady who would be his wife. Here the two had romantic meals that they ate off of a sewing machine in the living room because, according to Mr. Gould, "a big rat named Oscar lived in the kitchen." Although Barbra didn't seem to mind her hovel, her managers Marty Erlichman and Marty Bregman did. And when they decided that their client needed a major makeover in order to prepare her for the big-time that lay ahead, one of their top priorities was to move Barbra and Elliott to less odorific quarters.

25. MR. AND MRS. RICKY RICARDO
623 East 68th Street

He was a Cuban band leader, and she was the wackiest of wives. Together they lived in apartment 3D of a Manhattan apartment house managed by their neighbors and good friends, Fred and Ethel Mertz. When the Ricardos had a son, Little Ricky, in 1953, the family moved to a larger apartment (3B) in the same building. Later, as was true of many Manhattan couples with young children in the 1950s, the Ricardos abandoned the city and headed for the suburbs. In their case, they settled in Greenwich, Connecticut.

The Mertzes followed them and became their good neighbors in the country, just as they had been in the city. But by 1959 there were rumors that the real-life marriage behind the Ricardo TV marriage was on the rocks, and by 1960 "I Love Lucy" was off the air. Television hasn't been the same since.

P.S. The Ricardo apartment building is extremely hard to find. In fact, it's impossible to find, since the six-hundred block of East 68th Street would probably be smack in the middle of the East River! The best place, therefore, to check out the Manhattan residence of Lucy, Ricky, Fred, and Ethel is on one of the many reruns of their classic sitcom.

26. LIZA MINNELLI APARTMENT
150 East 69th Street

After years of being evicted from apartments and hotels when Mama Judy Garland couldn't pay the bill, Little Liza has handled her financial and housing situation with far greater savvy than her mother. Witness this toney East Side building complete with driveway and Japanese gardens where she maintains her New York digs.

27. "DRESSED TO KILL" OFFICE
162 East 70th Street

In Brian De Palma's bloody little 1980 horror film, *Dressed to Kill,* Michael Caine plays a mild-mannered Manhattan psychiatrist named Dr. Robert Elliot, who practices out of a posh office in the basement of this Upper East Side brownstone. Despite the fashionable address, movie lovers would do well to think twice before going into therapy with Dr. Elliot. Ask Angie Dickinson.

Dressed to Kill
office

28. JOAN CRAWFORD APARTMENT
2 East 70th Street

She was not just one of Hollywood's greatest stars, she was one of its toughest survivors. When she was dropped by MGM in 1943, Crawford quickly resurfaced at Warner Bros., with whom she won an Oscar for her performance in *Mildred Pierce* in 1945. When her career was again on the downswing in the mid-1950s, she made a brilliant move with her marriage to Pepsi-Cola tycoon Al Steele. Indeed, for the first time in her life, she had hitched up with a man who could support her, instead of the other way around. With her new husband, Joan moved from Los Angeles to New York, and quickly set to finding an apartment that would befit a movie star married to a captain of industry. Two East 70th Street was the chosen address, and here the Steeles secured not one but two (!) apartments which they then turned into a massive duplex. Joan's adopted daughter, Christina, describes the renovations in great detail in her now legendary look at her mother's life, *Mommie Dearest* (Morrow, 1978).

> This was no ordinary remodel. Where there had been sixteen rooms there would now be eight. The plans called for two master bedrooms, two master baths, a living room, library, dining room, kitchen, and maid's room. Despite the fact that between them Mr. and Mrs. Steele had five children—her four and his one son—there was no guest room. . . .
>
> At first glance, it was spectacular. The space and view were unexcelled in Manhattan. But there was something barren about it. There were none of the beautiful antiques from our California house, none of the old paintings. Everything was new and modern and plastic. Even the flowers and plants were plastic. Mother preferred them because they could be kept sparkling clean and were regularly washed in soapy water. There were plastic covers on all the upholstered furniture that crinkled and stuck to you when you sat on them. All the windows were sealed. There was no fresh air. The temperature was regulated

Joan Crawford apartment

Selling herself:
Joan with 1962
autobiography

at about sixty degrees both winter and summer so that it was always freezing cold in the apartment.

When guests came for the first time, Mother gave them the grand tour. She showed them the apartment, then she showed them all her closets. She proudly opened the rows of mirrored doors to show off floor-to-ceiling racks of clothes, each garment carefully covered with plastic. That was followed by an inspection of the hat closet, the shoe closet, and the handbag closet. I wondered if she'd gotten the idea of this closet tour from our visit to Shirley Temple's house when I was a little girl.

Upstairs, Mother's pink-and-white bedroom was the larger of the two master suites, and downstairs the white, green, and yellow rooms reflected practically nothing of Daddy except a chess set and some carved-ivory elephants in a bookcase.

The wood floors were polished to a dangerously slippery shine and, where rugs existed, they were pure white. No one was allowed to wear shoes beyond the entrance hall because Mother didn't want those white rugs soiled. Many an unsuspecting guest was unpleasantly surprised by Mother's edicts before word got out about having to go barefoot in her apartment.

Joan and Al lived lavishly on East 70th Street—but not wisely. The apartment had cost close to $1 million to redo, which Steele had financed by borrowing against his future salary at Pepsi-Cola. Thus, when Steele died unexpectedly of a heart attack in 1959, Joan was left with massive debts. Once again, her survivor's instinct kicked in. She not only moved to less-grand quarters at 150 East 69th Street, she turned her token membership on the board of directors of Pepsi-Cola into a lucrative full-time occupation. (Movie lovers will remember the scene in the Pepsi boardroom from the film of *Mommie Dearest* in which Joan (played by Faye Dunaway) delivers the famous line: "Don't fuck with me, fellas!")

Joan also made a smart move in 1961 when director Robert Aldrich approached her about doing a film version of a creepy novel called *What Ever Happened to Baby Jane?* Seeing the potential box-office appeal of the vehicle, Crawford persuaded Aldrich to cast her arch rival Bette Davis in the title role. But whereas Bette went for $60,000 up front plus 5 percent of the film's profits, crafty Crawford settled for a mere $30,000 salary against a whopping 15 percent of the gross. Needless to say, the film was a runaway hit and Joan wound up making over $1 million on the deal. This, coupled with her Pepsi-Cola cash, set her up for the rest of her life.

29. "BREAKFAST AT TIFFANY'S" APARTMENT
171 East 71st Street

Supposedly it was a tiny apartment in the East 70s, but for those who know New York, the enormous pad—complete with zebra-skin rugs on the floor—that Paramount art directors designed for Holly Golightly (Audrey Hepburn) in Truman Capote's *Breakfast at Tiffany's* could exist only in one place: on a Hollywood soundstage. When *Breakfast at Tiffany's* came to New York City to shoot exteriors, however, reality won out over fantasy, and a real East 70s townhouse was chosen to represent Holly's apartment building. Wedged between an identical (save for the striped awnings) townhouse on the left and a distinctive stone building with Gothic arches on the right, this backlot-beautiful location looks exactly the same today as it did in 1961 when it was immortalized in *Breakfast at Tiffany's.*

Breakfast at Tiffany's *block*

30. POLA NEGRI APARTMENT
907 Fifth Avenue

Once a famous silent-screen star, Pola Negri was a Polish-born actress who came to Hollywood via her fame in German movies. While her exotic on-screen persona sold tickets in the 1920s, she—and her heavy Polish accent—didn't survive the talkies, and she spent most of the 1930s in Europe, until World War II broke out.

Pola Negri's place in film history is sometimes traceable less to her films than her being the self-proclaimed last lover of Rudolph Valentino. Her "grief" at the time of Valentino's death was legendary. Director Walter Wanger supposedly said of Pola's train journey to the Valentino funeral that "she fainted all the way from Hollywood to Kansas City and then laid down on the job—but promised her press agent to come through with some really big swoons in Chicago and carry it right through to Rudy's bier in New York." Another story tells of Pola's emerging from her bungalow at the Ambassador Hotel to attend Valentino's funeral in L.A. Since photographers were present, Miss Negri had already pulled back her veil to let the cameras capture every nuance of her sorrow. And when one of the cameramen asked if she'd mind repeating her performance because he had muffed his shot, Pola went back inside the bungalow and did the whole scene a second time!

In the early 1940s, when Pola returned to the U.S. after her European sojourn, people were talking about a romantic involvement that she was rumored to have had with another famous personality—Adolph Hitler. Pola denied the allegations, but was never able to pick up her American acting career. In the 1950s, she resided in Manhattan at 907 Fifth Avenue. Neighbors reported that a great portrait of Valentino hung in a prominent place in her foyer. By the end of the decade, she had moved into the San Antonio mansion of oil heiress Margaret West. When Miss West died in 1963, she willed her jewelry and lifetime use of the Texas house to Pola. When Pola died in 1987, she was still living in Texas.

31. GLORIA SWANSON APARTMENT
920 Fifth Avenue

She was born in Chicago, made a name for herself in Hollywood, became a countess in France, but ultimately, for Gloria Swanson, New York was home. In fact, in the 1920s, when the bulk of feature-film production was deserting the East Coast for California, Swanson went from West to East, and made some of her major 1920s movies in New York City.

Actually, with the exception of her magnificent comeback as aging silent-movie star Norma Desmond in *Sunset Boulevard* (1950), Swanson virtually retired from the screen in 1934, and was involved in a variety of New York City-based ventures throughout the 1940s. These ranged from her own cosmetics company to a business that backed inventors to starring in road shows of Broadway

Straphanger Swanson: Manhandled, *1924*

plays. In 1948 Swanson broke new ground in show business when she hosted one of the world's first weekly hour-long television talk shows. Broadcast by WPIX in New York, this pioneering venture in TV programming featured a set that duplicated Swanson's Fifth Avenue apartment, and the format—a mix of celebrity interviews, public-service segments, and cooking demonstrations—was not unlike many of the morning shows that are now televised all across the country.

In 1970, at the age of seventy-two, Swanson had yet another career triumph when she replaced Eileen Heckart in *Butterflies Are Free* on Broadway. During the run of the show the indomitable Swanson drove herself to and from the theater in her own little yellow Toyota! Home then, as it had been for several decades in New York, was a spacious apartment at 920 Fifth Avenue. Married to her sixth husband, writer William Dufty, Swanson was at the same New York address when she died in 1981.

32. "MIDNIGHT COWBOY" APARTMENT
114 East 72nd Street

Movie lovers will remember how Sylvia Miles slipped John Voight past the doorman of 114 East 72nd Street after she had picked up the young Texan outside on the street in *Midnight Cowboy*. At the time of their encounter Miss Miles was walking her poodle and having a hard time getting the animal to "Do it for Mama!" Miles received an Oscar nomination for her brief appearance as the trashy, over-the-hill East Side matron in the film; Voight also got an Academy Award nomination for his work and was judged best actor of 1969 by the New York Film Critics.

33. WOODY ALLEN APARTMENT
930 Fifth Avenue

A one-man film industry, Woody Allen produces, directs, writes, and usually stars in movies that, more likely than not, are set in New York City. Prolific (he comes out with about a film a year), and acclaimed even by the Hollywood establishment (witness *Annie Hall*'s and *Hannah and Her Sisters*' Oscars), Allen reportedly likes to work in New York because he feels "serene in the knowledge that, if I want to, I can always go home and get a sweater." For many years, Woody has kept his woolies at 930 Fifth Avenue.

34. CARLYLE HOTEL
35 East 76th Street

One of Manhattan's chic-est and most discreet hotels, the Carlyle has catered to the rich and famous for decades. Among its current regulars are Elizabeth Taylor, George C. Scott, Robert Evans, Steve Martin, the Paul Newmans, and Warren Beatty (who is said to be a lousy tipper). In the early 1960s, the Carlyle was where President John F. Kennedy liked to stay, and it is reported that Marilyn Monroe was a frequent, often incognito, visitor to his suite when Mrs. Kennedy was not accompanying him.

Besides its elegant rooms, suites, and cooperative apartments, the Carlyle is also known for the glittering Cafe Carlyle, where Bobby Short sings sophisticated songs. It was here that Woody Allen had a less-than-satisfying date with Dianne Wiest in *Hannah and Her Sisters* (1986) and wound up uttering the ultimate put-down: "You don't deserve Cole Porter!"

35. METROPOLITAN MUSEUM OF ART
Fifth Avenue at 81st Street

It was one of the greatest, longest, and kinkiest seduction scenes ever: Angie Dickinson in the Metropolitan Museum of Art playing

Metropolitan Museum of Art

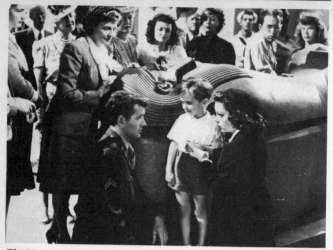

The Met according to MGM: Robert Walker and Judy Garland at the Egyptian galleries in The Clock, *1945*

cat-and-mouse with a mysterious man in dark glasses. After many minutes of cruising among the Impressionists and Post-Impressionists, the two finally make more than eye contact. The film is *Dressed to Kill,* Brian De Palma's homage to Hitchcock, and for those who haven't seen it, we won't divulge what happens. What we will divulge is that while the famous *Dressed to Kill* seduction scene seems to take place in the Metropolitan Museum of Art, the truth of the matter is that the museum would allow De Palma only to do exteriors on its property. For the interiors, therefore, the director had to head down to his hometown—Philadelphia—where the Museum of Fine Arts, that columned Greek temple that looked so sensational in the original *Rocky,* opened its doors and its galleries to the *Dressed to Kill* crew. In 1966, the Philadelphia Museum of Fine Arts had done the same thing for a long sequence in Barbra Streisand's television special, "Color Me Barbra." Again, the Met had been the producers' first choice for a location, but again the Met refused to allow a film crew—even Barbra Streisand's—to shoot among its treasures.

Back in 1944, it was a little different when Vincente Minnelli wanted to stage a sequence in the Met's Egyptian galleries for *The Clock,* which starred his wife Judy Garland and Robert Walker. All the director needed to do was to make his wishes known to MGM's art department, and, voilà, the Met was recreated for Minnelli on the soundstage. And while those exteriors of the Metropolitan in *The Clock* are authentic, Judy and Bob never had to set foot out of Culver City to appear to be on the steps of the great New York museum. It was all done through the magic of the "process shot," i.e., rear projection. Ah, Hollywood!

36. FRANK E. CAMPBELL FUNERAL HOME
1076 Madison Avenue

The setting for the final production number in the careers of many a superstar, the Frank E. Campbell funeral home has been in the business of stylish send-offs since the 1890s. Constantly in the news when it hosted Rudolph Valentino's last rites in 1926, Campbell's was then on the West Side of Manhattan at Broadway and 66th Street. In its present East Side location since 1937, Campbell's has buried such celebrities as Tommy Dorsey, Gertrude Lawrence, Ezio Pinza, John Garfield, Montgomery Clift, Judy Holliday, Joan Crawford, and James Cagney from its Madison Avenue chapel.

But the funeral to end all funerals—indeed, the only one to rival Valentino's—was the production Campbell's staged for Judy Garland's final farewell appearance in June of 1969. Some 22,000 faithful fans, many of whom had lined up at the funeral home even before the plane bearing her body from London had touched down at John F. Kennedy Airport, filed past Judy's glass-topped, blue-velvet-lined casket for over twenty-four hours. Many carried portable record and tape players which echoed Garland's greatest hits as they waited to see their idol one last time.

Since Judy's husband, Mickey Deans, the thirty-three-year-old former manager of New York's trendy Arthur discothèque, was reportedly too distraught to deal with the historic circumstances that enveloped him, Judy's daughter Liza Minnelli handled most of the funeral arrangements, with the help of her godmother, entertainer Kay Thompson. Wanting to keep everything upbeat, Liza

Kay Thompson, Lorna Luft, and Liza Minnelli leaving Judy Garland's funeral at Frank Campbell's, 1969

insisted that Campbell's be decorated with yellow (Judy's favorite color) and white flowers, and ordered everyone invited to the private funeral service to wear "anything but black." There were, of course, problems. Make-up, for one. It seems that Judy had requested in her will that Gene Hills, her old MGM make-up man, do her final face. Hills, however, was in charge of Eva Gabor's make-up for the TV series "Green Acres," and Eva refused to let him off the show. Then there was the problem of the color of the casket. Liza wanted it white but Campbell's didn't have a white one readily available. To the rescue came Kay Thompson, who suggested spray-painting the mahogany number that the funeral parlor had come up with.

The trickiest point of all had to do with cremation. Judy had requested it, and Liza wanted to adhere to her mother's wishes. But Judy's ex-husband, Sid Luft, and their two children, Lorna and Joey, were against it. In the end, the Lufts prevailed. Sid Luft also felt that Judy should be buried in Hollywood, but on this point it was Liza who won out and saw to it that her mother was laid to rest on the East Coast at Ferncliff Cemetery in New York's Westchester County. According to Liza, Judy loathed Hollywood.

The service itself brought out Mickey Rooney, Ray Bolger, Lauren Bacall, Jack Benny, Cary Grant, Katharine Hepburn, Burt Lancaster, Dean Martin, Lana Turner, Freddie Bartholomew, Otto Preminger, and comedian Alan King. King, who had warmed up audiences for Judy's triumphant run at the Palace Theater back in 1951, reportedly joked to Liza at the beginning of the service, "This is the first time that your mom was ever on time for a performance." The rites were officiated by the same Catholic priest who had married Judy and Mickey Deans (her fifth husband) in London six months earlier. The highlight of the ceremony, however, was the eulogy delivered by Judy's *A Star is Born* co-star, James Mason. (Mickey Rooney was considered for this role, but it was felt that he was too upset by Judy's passing to handle the assignment.) The final touching moment was when the whole congregation sang *The Battle Hymn of the Republic*—the song that Judy had sung on her TV show in November 1963 when the whole nation was mourning the untimely death of President John F. Kennedy. And then, amidst both laughter and tears, it was over. There was no applause, however, and no calls for more. This time Judy was not coming back for an encore.

37. MARLENE DIETRICH APARTMENT
993 Park Avenue

For close to three decades, Marlene kept, and often resided in, a four-room apartment in this serious thirteen-story Park Avenue building at 84th Street across from St. Ignatius Loyola Church. Among her many treasures here was a photo of her great friend Ernest Hemingway, which sat for years on a Sheraton table in her living room and bore the inscription: "To Marlene, if she still loves me or if she doesn't—Papa." Dietrich also had amassed an impressive art collection which was displayed throughout her apartment and included paintings by Chagall, Cézanne, Corot, Delacroix, Picasso, and Utrillo.

A *hausfrau* at heart, the ultraglamorous Marlene was frequently known to get down on her hands and knees with a wash bucket and scrub her own floors. She was also known to play telephone tricks, and often screened phone calls by pretending to be the maid. Sometimes the maid charade went even further. New York actor and die-hard Dietrich fan Martin J. Walsh recalls the time in the early 1970s that he gained admittance to 993 Park to deliver a bouquet for her birthday. After ringing the legendary lady's doorbell (apartment 12E), Walsh was told by a high-pitched voice that "Miss Deetrish" was not in. When Walsh announced his gift, the door was cracked open, a famous arm appeared and snatched the posies, and the door was closed again.

These days Marlene resides at 12 avenue Montaigne in Paris where her "maid" still screens all calls. It was this Paris apartment that Maximilian Schell re-created in a film studio for his Academy Award–winning documentary on Dietrich's life and career, *Marlene*. Marlene, who speaks throughout the film, refused to allow Schell to photograph her or her apartment for the project.

38. ELAINE'S
1703 Second Avenue

Welcome to Manhattan's ultimate celebrity hangout, an unprepossessing Second Avenue bar/restaurant that owes its superstardom to its owner/overseer Elaine Kauffman, a woman who knows how to make the famous feel like family and how to make a lot of other people (especially if they don't happen to have a reservation) feel as though maybe they had better try somewhere else for dinner. Among Elaine's regulars are Shirley MacLaine, Warren Beatty, Mike Nichols, Diana Ross, Milos Forman, Diane Keaton, Chevy Chase, and Sidney Lumet—to name a few stars of the movie crowd. Elaine's most famous table—off to the side of the busy passageway that links the restaurant's very fashionable front room with a back dining room known as "Siberia"—belongs to Woody Allen. An unwritten house rule: No one—not even the biggest celebrity in the place—approaches the famous New York film maker's table when he's occupying it. Ever.

Woody Allen not only hangs out in Elaine's, he has used it as a location, notably in *Manhattan* (1979) where Elaine's is the trendy venue of the film's opening scene. Another regular, director Sidney Lumet, has also immortalized Elaine's onscreen, although only insiders will recognize it as the bustling Manhattan bistro where TV execs Faye Dunaway and William Holden find love among the Nielsen ratings in *Network* (1976). Meanwhile, for movie lovers who think they might like to have dinner at Elaine's sometime, her phone number is (212) 534-8103. Good luck—and if you get in, stay away from Woody!

Class location: the Carnegie Mansion

39. CARNEGIE MANSION
2 East 91st Street

A survivor from the days when Fifth Avenue was noted for its grand private homes rather than its imposing apartment buildings, the 64-room Carnegie Mansion was built in 1898 by industrialist Andrew Carnegie. Home to Carnegie's widow until her death in 1946, the place was later used by Columbia University and today is the headquarters of the Cooper-Hewitt Museum, which focuses on architectural, decorative, and industrial design. Movie lovers may recall the elegant Georgian building from its many roles in features as well as in made-for-television films and mini-series: *Marathon Man* (as the Russian embassy), *The Next Man* (as the Saudi Arabian embassy), *Arthur* (as Dudley Moore's grandmother's home), and "The Two Mrs. Grenvilles" (as the Grenville mansion)—plus *Godspell, The Anderson Tapes, Jumpin' Jack Flash, 84 Charing Cross Road,* Sidney Sheldon's "Master of the House," and Judith Krantz's "I'll Take Manhattan."

40. ROBERT REDFORD APARTMENT
1125 Fifth Avenue

Until they separated in the mid-1980s, Robert and Lola Redford lived for many years in a co-op in this big brick building at Fifth Avenue and 94th Street. In 1981, the Redfords—and their apartment—wound up in the tabloids when two burglars entered their seventh-floor domain via a fire escape and an open bathroom window while Bob and Lola and their youngest daughter were sleeping. Upon entering, the thugs awakened Mrs. Redford by knocking over a flowerpot on the bathroom window sill. Realizing what was going on, Lola tiptoed to the intercom, buzzed the doorman downstairs, and got him to call the police. When the thieves heard Mrs. R. on the intercom, they fled via the same bathroom window and were ultimately apprehended on the roof by the police. *Mr.* Redford, it seems, slept through the whole incident.

41. THE HOUSE ON 92ND STREET
53 East 93rd Street

"Elsa Gowns" was the name of Elsa Gebhardt's dress shop on the north side of 92nd Street, near the corner of Madison Avenue, in Twentieth Century–Fox's landmark 1945 spy thriller, *The House on 92nd Street*. In this riveting, action-packed tale of Nazi agents operating in New York City during World War II, Elsa Gowns is actually a front for the Fifth Column-ists. Based on an actual FBI case and shot entirely on location, *The House on 92nd Street* told its dramatic story in a realistic, documentary way, a style that the film's producer, Louis de Rochemont, had perfected as creator of "The March of Time" newsreel series. Writing in the *New York Times,* film critic Bosley Crowther said at the time that *The House on 92nd Street* proved that "realism can be entertaining, too." Of course, even in the most realistic films, there's always a trick or two, and in *The House on 92nd Street,* one of the tricks was that the house used in the film was actually on *93rd* Street! Today, the famous movie mansion no longer stands, although its identical twin—the Alamo Apartments next door at 55 East 93rd—is often mistaken for it.

42. MARX BROTHERS HOME
179 East 93rd Street

Early in the twentieth century, a stage-mother named Minna Schoenberg Marx raised five sons at this address and saw to it that they all entered show business at early ages. Originally named Milton, Leonard, Adolph, Julius Henry, and Herbert, Minnie's Boys became much better known as Gummo, Chico, Harpo, Groucho, and Zeppo Marx. Their father, a tailor in the same Yorkville neighborhood, kept the guys nattily attired for auditions.

Leo G. Carroll and Signe Hasso in The House on 92nd Street, *1945*

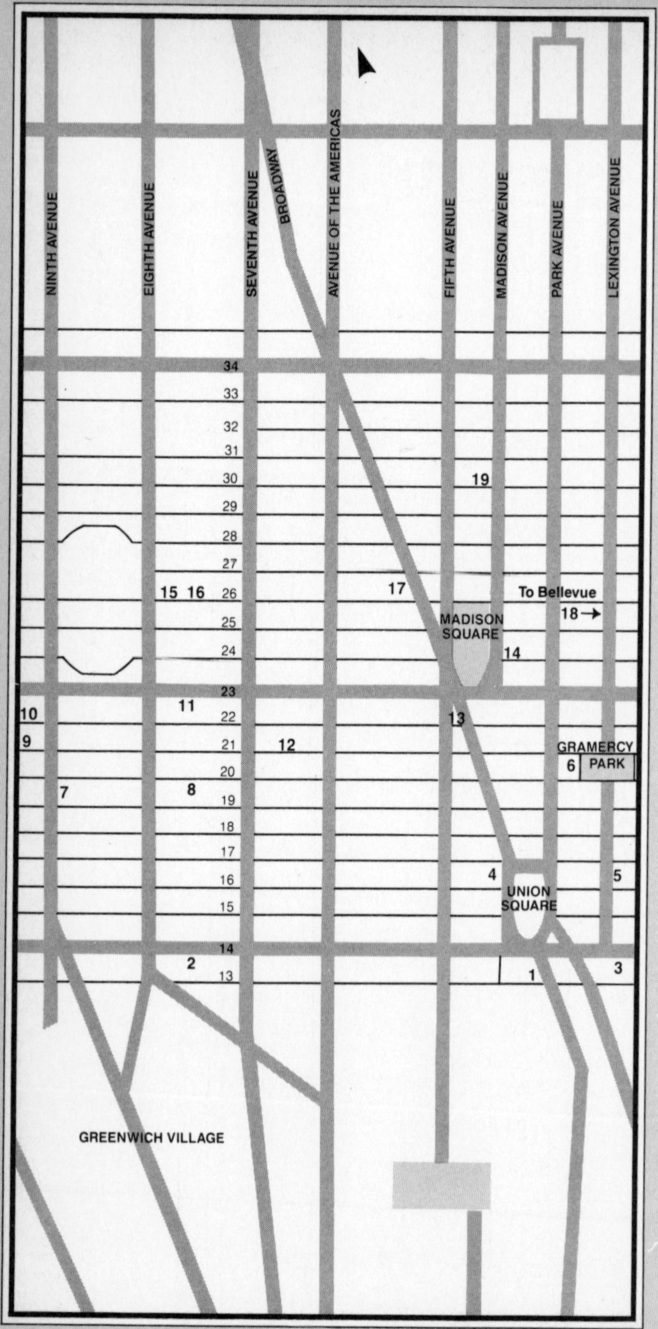

NINTH AVENUE

EIGHTH AVENUE

SEVENTH AVENUE

BROADWAY

AVENUE OF THE AMERICAS

FIFTH AVENUE

MADISON AVENUE

PARK AVENUE

LEXINGTON AVENUE

34
33
32
31
30
29
28
27
26
25
24
23
22
21
20
19
18
17
16
15
14
13

15 16

11

10
9

7

8

2

12

19

17

13

12

4

18 →

To Bellevue

MADISON
SQUARE

14

GRAMERCY
6   PARK

5

1

3

UNION
SQUARE

GREENWICH VILLAGE

UNION SQUARE/ GRAMERCY PARK/ CHELSEA

Fantasy on 14th Street

*Belle of 14th Street: Biograph
starlet Mary Pickford*

I N 1909, when a teenaged Broadway actress named Mary Pickford
decided it was time to think seriously about getting into the
movie business, she hopped a Fifth Avenue bus and headed
downtown toward Union Square. Her destination was the Biograph
Studios, at 11 East 14th Street, where she was instantly cast in a
D. W. Griffith potboiler that marked the beginning of one of the
most spectacular careers in film history. If Mary hadn't been so
lucky at Biograph, however, she could have continued her job search
at any number of other studios—Kalem, Craftsmen, Edison,
Reliance-Majestic, American Kinograph—that were headquartered
in the lofts and office buildings of nearby Gramercy Park and
Chelsea.

Today, while no longer in the film business, these same neighborhoods provide a mixed bag of delights for the movie lover who
ventures here. These include the old studio buildings of Chelsea
(one of which is now used by CBS for producing soap operas), the
storefront that housed the world's first Kinetoscope parlor, the turn-
of-the-century high-rise on whose rooftop James Stewart and Kim
Novak once spent a romantic evening (on film), two of the "factories" where the late Andy Warhol turned out underground films
in the 1960s, one of Manhattan's most exclusive residential enclaves
. . . and possibly the best movie memorabilia store on earth.

1. BIOGRAPH STUDIOS SITE
841 Broadway

The American Mutoscope & Biograph Company was the rather
exotic name of one of the first motion-picture companies to mount
a serious challenge to Thomas Edison's monopolistic hold on the
early film industry. Biograph produced initially a better-quality image (by using larger-sized film) and enjoyed the participation of
W. K. L. Dickson, a former—and the most influential—player on
the team that developed motion pictures at Edison. Biograph's first
studio was on the roof of the Hackett Carhart Building, a great
Victorian fortress with ornate columns, pediments, and turrets that
still stands on the northwest corner of Broadway and East 13th
Street. Similar to the "Black Maria" studio that Dickson had done
for Edison in West Orange, Biograph's rooftop facility was mounted
on tracks and revolved with the sun. The foundations of this primitive studio are still in place atop the restored Hackett Carhart
Building.

Unfortunately, the site of some of Biograph's greatest cinematic
triumphs—a brownstone studio at 11 East 14th Street to which it
moved in 1906—was razed in the 1960s to make way for a big,
uninteresting-looking brick apartment building. It was at the Union
Square studio that D. W. Griffith directed his first film, *The Adventures of Dollie,* in 1908. Griffith went on to become the studio's
top director, and brought such talents as Mary Pickford, Lillian
and Dorothy Gish, Blanche Sweet, Lionel Barrymore, Wallace Reid,
Mabel Normand, Mae Marsh, Harry Carey, and Mack Sennett into

*Left: Hackett Carhart Building today—site of Biograph's first studio;
Right: Biograph's 14th Street base*

the Biograph fold. When Griffith left the studio in 1913 for the
Mutual Film Corporation, Biograph's status fell quickly, and in
1915 the company was dissolved. Many of its films survive, however,
thanks both to Griffith, who saved copies of all his productions,
and to the Museum of Modern Art, which acquired Griffith's collection in the mid-1930s for its new Film Department.

In 1975, a plaque was dedicated by former Biograph beauties
Lillian Gish and Blanche Sweet at the site of the historic townhouse
studio at 11 East 14th Street. The day after the ceremony, however,
the plaque had mysteriously disappeared, and there have been no
further efforts to put up a new one. There should be. And while
we're talking about plaques, there also ought to be one at Biograph's
original studio site at 841 Broadway.

Biograph's revolving rooftop stage atop the Hackett Carhart Building, 1896

2. JERRY OHLINGER'S MOVIE MATERIAL STORE
242 West 14th Street

If you're looking for movie-star glossies, film stills, lobby cards, posters, or screen magazines, Jerry Ohlinger's has them by the thousands. Open seven days a week from 1 to 8 P.M., the store also handles telephone and mail orders.

Phone: (212) 989–0969.

3. PALLADIUM
126 East 14th Street

One of NYC's trendiest night spots, the Palladium is the paradigm of state-of-the-art movie-palace recycling. Originally the Academy of Music, designed by the noted theater architect Thomas Lamb in 1926, this vast showplace has hosted opera, vaudeville, burlesque, movies, and rock concerts in its sixty-odd-year history. A likely target for demolition in the early 1980s, the theater was saved by nightclub entrepreneurs Steve Rubell and Ian Schrager of Studio 54 fame and infamy (the duo spent time in prison for tax evasion). No strangers to the theater-recycling business (Studio 54 had been created from a former theater), Rubell and Schrager called on visionary Japanese architect Arata Isozaki to oversee the Palladium's conversion to a nightclub. What Isozaki did was to incorporate a futuristic club featuring a suspended dance floor, twenty-five-screen video wall, and a glamorous glass-and-steel "stairway to heaven" within the existing theater building in order to retain many of the decorative elements, including the gilded-dome ceiling, the marble columns, and the ornate frescoes and friezes of its original design. The result is a stunning melding of a 1920s movie-palace fantasy with the highest of late-1980s high-tech.

Of special interest to movie lovers at the Palladium may be its Mike Todd Room, a bar/lounge area named in honor of the late film producer/Liz Taylor-husband-number-three who once had his offices in the Palladium building. Of further interest may be the fact that the decor of the Mike Todd Room—all peeling paint, crumbling plaster, broken mirrors, bent candelabra, and bizarre Jean-Michel Basquiat murals—was inspired by Jean Cocteau's surreal 1946 film, *Beauty and the Beast*.

Movie lovers will also find the Palladium to be a showcase for the newest form of moviemaking: video art. Among the top video artists who have designed "pieces" for the club's fantastic multimonitor "screen" are Rebecca Allen, Laurie Anderson, Carter Burwell, George Delmerico, Eric Fischl, John Girono, Keith Haring, Sean Kelly, Komar and Melamid, Mitchell Kriegman, Maureen Nappi, Michael O'Donoghue, David Salle, Grahame Weinbren, and Peter Wollen. No ordinary disco, the Palladium just might be the world's first video palace.

Andy Warhol's 1968–1973
Factory (on right)

4. THE FACTORY SITE
33 Union Square West

It was the best of times, it was the worst of times . . . it was the 1960s. Underground avant-garde films were the rage—especially those created by a platinum-blond NYC artist named Andy Warhol. Andy made his films—which often used stationary cameras and ranged from quickies like *Blow Job* to six-hour epics like *Sleep*— at a series of New York City studios he called "factories." Andy's first factory, which he occupied between 1963 and 1967, was at 231 East 47th Street. With its walls covered in silver mylar, the place hosted a constant stream of drop-ins from the street, many of whom wandered in and out of whatever film Warhol and his associates happened to be shooting at the time. Just like in the old days of Hollywood, this wacky, carefree moviemaking organization also boasted its own superstars. Among them were Viva, Ultra Violet, Baby Jane Holtzer, Paul America, and Edie Sedgwick, whose brief, tragic, fast-lane life and subsequent death of a drug overdose were documented in both the 1982 bestselling book *Edie* and in the 1972 film *Ciao! Manhattan*.

Doing a film at the Factory was a unique experience. "Superstar" Ultra Violet had this to say about her Warhol work to writer John Wilcox in 1971:

Making a film for Andy is very glorious for a person because it gives you a chance to find who you are or who you want to be, and then when you see the rushes you can see yourself without any direction or put on, or any direction given to you, so it's really you, and it gives you a chance to find your own identity, and I think it's just fantastic. He doesn't mess you up. In Hollywood you have to learn lines, you have to say them in a certain manner, it's such a put on. It's just the total opposite, it's wide open to reality, it's a search of a really great reality with no magnification, and no sensation.

In early 1968, Warhol and company moved from their 47th-Street base (which was about to be demolished for the apartment building that now stands on the spot) to the sixth floor of a turn-of-the-century loft building at 33 Union Square West. Although now the walls were painted white and everything was very crisp and minimal, the moviemaking at the new Factory was just as freewheeling as it had been uptown. Things changed radically, however, in June 1968, when a young woman named Valerie Solanis wandered into the Factory, pulled a gun, and fired it at Warhol, supposedly because he had refused to produce a screenplay she had written. Andy survived his wounds, but from then on security at the Factory became much tighter, and the mood became more tense. Another change that took place after the shooting was that Warhol turned over most of the directorial duties to his associate, Paul Morrissey, who went on to do more commercial features such as *Flesh* (1968), *Trash* (1970), and *Heat* (1972) at the Union Square studio.

In 1973, the Factory moved again, to a building a few hundred

Factory worker: Andy Warhol with underground movie star Gerald Malanga

feet across Union Square at 860 Broadway. The space was enormous, but ultimately not much film making took place here, and by 1984 Warhol's enterprises, which now included the very successful *Interview* magazine, had moved into conventional offices at 22 East 33rd Street. With this move and then with Warhol's untimely death owing to complications (and possible negligence) following heart surgery in 1987, the grand days of Andy Warhol movies and of the 1960s were definitely over.

5. WASHINGTON IRVING HIGH SCHOOL
40 Irving Place

A huge bust of the great American writer Washington Irving stands at the northwest corner of this big old Gramercy Park school building that bears his name. But movie lovers will be more interested in the autographed portrait of another American legend that hangs in the high school's library. Presented to her alma mater in 1986 by a small contingent of loyal fans led by actor Andrew Achsen, the portrait commemorates the most famous member of Washington Irving's Class of 1921: Lily Chauchoin, better known as Claudette Colbert. More interested in art and fashion design than in the theater during her Washington Irving days, little Miss Chauchoin nonetheless appeared in several school plays. The experience must have served her well, because two years after leaving Washington Irving she changed her name to Claudette Colbert, made her debut on the stage of the Provincetown Playhouse in Greenwich Village, and has not stopped working since. Well into her eighties, the ageless, glamorous star, who won an Oscar in 1935 for *It Happened One Night,* still performs on Broadway and in road companies. In 1986 she delighted her fans by returning before the motion-picture cameras (her last film role had been as Troy Donahue's mother in *Parrish* in 1961) to star with Ann-Margret in the TV mini-series "The Two Mrs. Grenvilles."

In addition to Claudette Colbert, Washington Irving High also boasts at least two other movie stars as former students: Sylvia Miles (Academy Award-nominated for Best Supporting Actress, both in 1969 for *Midnight Cowboy* and in 1975 for *Farewell My Lovely*); and Whoopi Goldberg, who garnered an Academy Award nomination (for Best Actress) for her 1985 film debut in *The Color Purple.* Miss Miles, who attended Washington Irving sometime in the 1940s, was Sylvia Lee at the time; Miss Goldberg, who dropped out of Washington Irving sometime in the 1960s, did so as plain-old Caryn Johnson (she had yet to meet that "burning bush" in California that, she says, came up with her current name).

P.S. For anyone who wonders why Washington Irving produced only actresses, the answer is that the school has been an all-girls institution for most of its life. In fact, Washington Irving was the only remaining all-girls public high school in New York City up until the fall of 1986, when the Board of Education ruled that it had to admit boys.

6. GRAMERCY PARK
East 20th and 21st Streets between
Park and Third Avenues

One of New York City's most attractive residential enclaves, Gramercy Park dates back to 1831 and, as its main attraction, boasts a locked, fenced-off private park that can be entered only by owners and tenants of the townhouses and apartments that surround it on four sides. In the last century, the legendary American actor Edwin Booth spent the final years of his life in the handsome Stanford White–designed townhouse at number 16 Gramercy Park South, which was also the headquarters for The Players, the famous theatrical club that Booth helped found in 1886. Today The Players—which counts among its current and former members John and Lionel Barrymore, Irving Berlin, John and Keith Carradine, Dick Cavett, Alistair Cooke, Joseph Cotton, Walter Cronkite, Hume Cronyn, Alfred Drake, Maurice Evans, José Ferrer, Richard Gere, George Grizzard, Rex Harrison, Hal Holbrook, Raul Julia, Jack Lemmon, Garson Kanin, Charles Kuralt, Burgess Meredith, Carroll O'Connor, Sir Laurence Olivier, and Frank Sinatra—is still housed at the same landmark Gramercy Park location. Booth's former bedroom, where he died on June 7, 1893, has been kept just as it was back then; and outside in the Park he is remembered with a bronze statue of him in the role of Hamlet.

No statue commemorates another show-business personality who also died here, although newspapers made quite a story of actor John Garfield's fatal heart attack, which he suffered in 1952

John Barrymore building: 36 Gramercy Park East

Number 3 Gramercy Park West—where John Garfield died

during a late-night visit to number 3 Gramercy Park West, townhouse of actress-turned-interior decorator Iris Whitney. Although rumor had it that Mr. Garfield died in Miss Whitney's bedroom, Garfield's biographer, Larry Swindell, in *Body and Soul: The Story of John Garfield* (Morrow, 1975) writes that the forty-year-old star expired in the guest bedroom with nothing more sensational by his side than an unfinished glass of orange juice on the night table.

Over on the east side of the park, two bizarre apartment buildings at numbers 36 and 34 stand out and are of special interest to movie lovers. Number 36 is a Gothic white-marble affair of twelve stories guarded by statues of knights in armor. Between 1910 and 1916, John Barrymore kept an apartment in this building during the period that he appeared in his first films for the Famous Players Company, which conveniently had its main studio on nearby West 26th Street. Movie lovers with eagle eyes may also recognize 36 Gramercy Park East from the 1949 MGM film *East Side West Side* in which its exterior was used as the apartment house where Barbara Stanwyck's parents supposedly lived. Next door to the *East Side West Side* building, a marble-columned entrance leads to the dark foyer—with stained-glass skylight and mosaic-tiled floor and walls—of 34 Gramercy Park East. This mysterious turreted urban castle was the long-time, and wonderfully appropriate, New York home of *The Wizard of Oz*'s Wicked Witch of the West, Margaret Hamilton. Character actress Mildred Dunnock, actor John Carradine, and legendary Warner Bros. tough guy James Cagney are three other former star residents of number 34.

More Gramercy Park names and addresses: silent-screen siren Theda Bara, who between 1916 and 1919 had an apartment in the brick-and-stucco building just off the Park at 132 East 19th Street; and Marion Davies, who claims to have been brought up in a townhouse on the Park, although in her memoir, *The Times We Had*

(Bobbs–Merrill, 1975), she can't seem to remember just which house it was that she lived in. One address Miss Davies does remember, however, is that of a townhouse just up the street from Gramercy Park at 123 Lexington Avenue. It seems that when Marion was a little girl, she and some of her childhood chums pulled a Halloween prank that involved ringing the house's doorbell and throwing vegetables at the butler who answered it. The incident was especially memorable because the kids got caught and were hauled off to the police station. Later, little Marion learned that the house belonged to a great and powerful publisher whose name was William Randolph Hearst. As the world knows, Hearst went on to play a major role in Miss Davies's subsequent personal life and film career. Trick or treat?

7. TWENTIETH CENTURY ANTIQUES & GALLERY
156 Ninth Avenue

Inside this Chelsea boutique, movie lovers will find a treasure trove of kitchy motion-picture memorabilia and souvenirs. In addition to unusual film posters and photos of performers, Twentieth Century Antiques & Gallery tempts with James Dean dolls and cut-outs, Joan Crawford pencil sharpeners, Marilyn Monroe toothpicks, John Wayne wrapping paper, and long-forgotten record albums such as the 1960s Tony Perkins L.P. "On a Rainy Afternoon." We all remember what a hit that was, don't we?

Of special interest to Marilyn Monroe fans: the Gallery's "Monroe-abilia Show," held annually from June 1 (her birthday) to August 5 (the date of her death) and featuring a staggering array of Monroe artifacts.

NOTE: *Twentieth Century Antiques & Gallery is open daily from 12:00 noon to 6:30 P.M.; phone: (212) 691–4587.*

Margaret Hamilton's "castle": 34 Gramercy Park East

Inside the 10th Precinct: Ted de Corsia, Barry Fitzgerald, Don Taylor, and Howard Duff in The Naked City, *1948*

8. TENTH PRECINCT
230 West 20th Street

Cinematographer William Daniels won an Academy Award for his brilliant camerawork in the 1948 film *The Naked City*. Directed by Jules Dassin, the picture was shot entirely in NYC and is considered, along with Louis de Rochemont's *The House on 92nd Street*, to be a landmark in 1940s on-location film making. Among the many spots used in *The Naked City*—from Wall Street to the old Roxy Theater on Seventh Avenue at 50th Street—none was more important than the Tenth Precinct, described by the film's narrator, Mark Hellinger, as "a rather shabby building on a rather shabby street." Used both for exteriors and interiors, the Tenth Precinct was supposedly the base from which the team of detectives and cops headed by Barry Fitzgerald as Inspector Muldoon worked on solving the murder of Howard Duff's girlfriend. The murder, by the way, took place at an apartment building at 52 West 83rd Street. Why Chelsea's Tenth Precinct, some sixty blocks away from the scene of the crime, was in charge of the investigation, we are never told. But then, as we all know, "there are eight million stories in the Naked City," so nothing should surprise us! Today, the Tenth Precinct and the block it occupies look just as they did in the classic 1948 film that immortalized them.

9. ANTHONY PERKINS TOWNHOUSE
467 West 21st Street

In the 1960s and 1970s, Mr. Perkins was the live-in landlord of this Chelsea brownstone. Movie lovers will remember that the actor had his greatest success on screen in a real estate role: as manager of the Bates Motel in *Psycho* (1960).

10. "THE TORN PAGE"
435 West 22nd Street

Married in 1961, actress Geraldine Page and actor Rip Torn lived in the same Chelsea townhouse—which they nicknamed "The Torn Page"—for several decades. In 1986, the often-Oscar-nominated Miss Page (for *Hondo* in 1953, *Summer and Smoke* in 1961, *Sweet Bird of Youth* in 1962, *You're a Big Boy Now* in 1967, *Pete 'n Tillie* in 1972, and *Interiors* in 1978) finally won an Academy Award for her starring role in *The Trip to Bountiful.* A year later, while appearing on Broadway in Noël Coward's *Blithe Spirit,* Miss Page suffered a fatal heart attack at her Chelsea home. The memorial service at the Neil Simon Theater (where *Blithe Spirit* had been playing) turned out to be an SRO event that brought forth a bevy of Miss Page's former colleagues, including Paul Newman, William Hurt, Angela Lansbury, James Earl Jones, Sissy Spacek, and Richard Chamberlain. Remarking on the stellar turn-out, Rip Torn said simply, "Yeah, Gerry would have liked this."

11. CHELSEA HOTEL
222 West 23rd Street

A 23rd Street landmark, the red-brick, iron-balconied, mansard-roofed Chelsea Hotel opened in 1884 as one of the city's first cooperative apartment houses. In 1905 it became a hotel, but throughout its history the Chelsea has catered to long-term tenants. Over the years, too, it has been especially popular with the literati: Mark Twain, Eugene O'Neill, O. Henry, Thomas Wolfe, Tennessee Williams, Vladimir Nabokov, Brendan Behan, Arthur Miller, Dylan Thomas, and William Burroughs have all called the Chelsea home from time to time. Plaques in the lobby commemorate many of these famous former residents. Sci-fi-movie lovers will be intrigued to learn that novelist Arthur C. Clarke penned the script for *2001: A Space Odyssey* while living at the Chelsea.

It was Andy Warhol, however, who put the Chelsea on movie

Chelsea Hotel

lovers' maps back in 1966 when he started shooting artist Brigid Polk in her Chelsea hotel room. This footage formed the basis for *The Chelsea Girls,* the film considered by many critics to be Warhol's best, and also the first of Andy's flicks to score a solid commercial success. Recently the Chelsea was again seen on screen in *The House on Carroll Street* (1988) and in *Sid and Nancy,* the 1986 British film, set in the 1970s, that focuses on the ugly, druggy life and times of Sex Pistols rock star Sid Vicious. Also, in an ironic bit of film making coming full-circle, the 1987 low-budget film *Anna* features the Chelsea as well as former Warhol actress Sally Kirkland.

12. KALEM FILM COMPANY SITE
131 West 21st Street

In 1907 a group of film pioneers set up operations in this little Chelsea loft building. With a director named Sidney Olcott in charge of production, the Kalem Film Company specialized in westerns, which it shot on location across the Hudson River in the "badlands" of New Jersey near Fort Lee. In its heyday, Kalem came out with over two hundred short films a year, and was also noted for productions done in more exotic locations such as Florida, California, Ireland, and the Middle East. In fact, one of its greatest successes was a feature based on the life of Christ, *From the Manger to the Cross,* which was lensed in Palestine in 1911, and which featured Robert Vignola (who later became a top Hollywood director) as Judas. An even earlier Kalem success also had a Biblical theme— a one-reel version of the novel *Ben Hur* in which Manhattan Beach in Brooklyn doubled as the Holy Land. Since Kalem had not acquired the motion-picture rights to General Lew Wallace's book (motion-picture rights didn't even exist at the time), Kalem was sued and eventually paid the Wallace estate $25,000 in a landmark 1911 out-of-court settlement. In 1916, a financially troubled Kalem, which had continued to concentrate on short films at a time when most of the industry had switched over to features, was bought by Vitagraph and never heard from again.

13. FLATIRON BUILDING
175 Fifth Avenue

When it went up in 1902, the three-sided, twenty-two-story Fuller Building was one of New York's most unusual-looking structures, as well as its first full-fledged skyscraper. Instantly nicknamed the "Flatiron Building" on account of its shape, the new architectural wonder became one of Manhattan's best-known landmarks in the early part of the twentieth century. In addition to its height and shape, the Flatiron Building was also believed to occupy one of the windiest corners in Manhattan and was thus popularly considered a prime place to catch a glimpse of a lady's ankle—or, better yet, her knee—should the wind catch her skirt at the right

Flatiron Building

moment. Interestingly enough, it was this aspect of the new building and not its architecture that caught Crescent Films' camera in early 1905 when it made a risqué little docudrama entitled *The Flatiron Building on a Windy Day.* This enthusiastic description of the film from a catalogue of the time gives an idea of what turned early movie audiences on:

> This side-splitting scene was taken January 25, 1905, when the wind was blowing a gale, and gives one a general idea of what women experience on a windy day around this noted corner. The great velocity of the wind can be plainly seen by the manner in which the pedestrians are clutching at their hats and skirts and grasping at anything for support. It is at this corner where one can get a good idea of the prevailing types in hosiery and lingerie. This is the finest picture that has ever been taken at this corner, and we can safely recommend it as something exceptionally fine.

Some fifty years later, the Flatiron Building again furnished the setting for an erotic, although far more sophisticated, cinematic interlude, when James Stewart and Kim Novak find themselves in a passionate clinch atop its roof in *Bell, Book, and Candle.* "Where are we?" asks a love-dazed Stewart of the beautiful witch played by Miss Novak, who has transported them to this ultraromantic spot in the 1958 comedy about magic in modern Manhattan. "On top of the Flatiron Building," she replies. "You liked its shape and you wanted to be on top of a tall building. We had no luck at the Empire State Building."

When star actor/director Warren Beatty came to New York to do location shooting for *Reds* in 1980, he wound up at the bottom of the Flatiron Building. Needing an early twentieth-century backdrop for the sequence where Louise Bryant (Diane Keaton) arrives in Manhattan, Beatty found that the venerable 1902 landmark served his purposes perfectly. To shoot the scene, street and traffic lights around the building were removed, but little else had to be altered. The snow in the scene was not artificial, by the way; it was a lucky happenstance that not only added to the beauty of the shot, but that also meant that the cameraman didn't have to worry about catching the towers of the World Trade Center off in the distance because the snow obligingly blocked them out.

14. METROPOLITAN LIFE INSURANCE COMPANY
11 Madison Square

It was in this monumental Manhattan office building that the Vietnam vet/janitor played by William Hurt supposedly swept up and mopped marble floors in the 1981 thriller *Eyewitness.* It was also here that a Vietnamese businessman was brutally murdered at the beginning of the film, which is the incident that ultimately gets Hurt involved with TV-news reporter Sigourney Weaver. The location where much of *Eyewitness* was shot is the handsome 1932 North Building of the Metropolitan Life Insurance Company. An especially dramatic architectural feature of the building is its set of four massive arcaded, golden-gated entryways—one on each corner of the block-square structure. For *Eyewitness,* director Peter Yates made extensive use of the southwest entrance, which provided an intriguing backdrop for the sequences where Ms. Weaver and her camera crew interview Hurt after the murder. The fact that Madison Square is just across the street was an added attraction of the location, since it offered an interesting space for Hurt to park his motorcycle; and the beautiful Greek-temple-like building of the Appelate Division of the New York State Supreme Court next door was icing on the cake, further adding to *Eyewitness*'s visual appeal. All in all, this location not only worked—it was a director's dream. Other New York directors to cash in on the Metropolitan Life's cinematic assets are Martin Scorsese, who made it Griffin Dunne's office in *After Hours* (1985), and Woody Allen, who used it to represent a broadcasting network office building *Radio Days* (1986).

Sigourney Weaver with Eyewitness *William Hurt outside the Metropolitan Life Building*

Bogie's Restaurant

15. BOGIE'S RESTAURANT
249 West 26th Street

A stained-glass Maltese Falcon hangs in the window of this offbeat Manhattan bistro that claims to be "the only mystery-oriented restaurant and bar in the world." Inside Bogie's, named for we-all-know-who, movie lovers will find many more Maltese Falcons plus posters, lobby cards, and stills that immortalize Humphrey Bogart's film career. On "Sinister Sundays," Bogie's presents old radio mysteries, classic *films noirs,* and occasionally features talks by noted detective story/mystery writers such as Robert B. Parker (of the "Spenser" series), Walter B. Gibson (who wrote "The Shadow" pulp-magazine novels under the name of Maxwell Grant), Whitley Streuber (author of *Wolfen* and *The Hunger,* both of which were made into films shot in New York), and Chris Steinbrunner (author of such works as *Great Monsters from Screenland* and *The Mystery Encyclopedia*). Several times each month at Bogie's, murder—performed by professional actors and actresses—is on the menu, and dinner guests help solve who dunnit.

NOTE: *For reservations, movie/mystery lovers should phone (212) 924-7935 . . . if they dare!*

16. PRODUCTION CENTER STUDIOS
221 West 26th Street

This great brick barn of a building was originally headquarters for the city's Ninth Mounted Cavalry division. When the unit moved to 14th Street in 1914, pioneer film producer Adolph Zukor found the spacious armory—which came complete with a tethering ring for its former equine occupants—a great place for making movies, and he turned it into a studio for his Famous Players Film Company. Featuring "Famous Players in Famous Plays," Zukor's company relied on talent from the New York stage and his was the first movie company to bring Broadway matinee idol John Barrymore to the screen in *An American Citizen* and *That Man from Mexico,* both of which were produced on 26th street in 1914. Other early Famous Players names were Marguerite Clark, Hazel Dawn, May Irving, and H. B. Warner.

Famous Players' biggest star was Mary Pickford, although by the time Zukor scooped her up in 1913, she had already made her mark both on Broadway and in films. A clever businesswoman, "Little Mary" made film-business history in 1916 when Zukor signed her to a then unprecedented two-year, $2-million-plus contract. It was also in 1916 that Zukor's Famous Players merged with Jesse Lasky and Samuel Goldwyn to form the company that eventually became Paramount Pictures. Zukor continued to use the 26th Street studios, along with various other facilities in the city, until the end of the 1910s, at which time, the Famous Players–Lasky Company consolidated their operations into one large new studio complex in Astoria, Queens.

From 1920 on, the old Famous Players studio on West 26th Street had various incarnations, but in the 1950s the place wound up back in the movie business when producer Hyman Brown bought the property, gutted it, and created two soundstages inside. Since then, Production Center Studios has seen constant movie/TV activity. Among the features that have been shot here since the 1950s are MGM's *Butterfield 8* (1960); Sidney Lumet's *Twelve Angry Men* (1957), *Long Day's Journey into Night* (1961), and *The Anderson Tapes* (1971); William Friedkin's *The Night They Raided Minsky's* (1968), *The Boys in the Band* (1970), and *The French Connection* (1971); Mel Brooks's *The Producers* (1967); and Francis Ford Coppola's *You're a Big Boy Now* (1967), which he presented as his thesis for his Master of Fine Arts at U.C.L.A.

Production Center Studios' TV hits have included Phil Silvers's "Sergeant Bilko" series, CBS's "Show of the Week," the "Patty Duke Show," "Inner Sanctum," episodes of Jackie Gleason's "The Honeymooners," and the CBS soap opera "The Guiding Light," which has been based at the historic studio since the early 1970s.

Famous Players Film Company, ca. 1915

1894 Kinetoscope parlor site, now "Broadway Fantasy"

Inside a Kinetoscope parlor, ca. 1895

17. KINETOSCOPE PARLOR SITE
1155 Broadway

On April 6, 1894, the Holland Brothers' Kinetoscope Parlor opened in a storefront in a small brick building that still stands on the southwest corner of 27th Street and Broadway. A great illuminated dragon with green eyes and a red tongue was suspended above the entrance and invited customers inside to see the latest bit of wizardry from Thomas Edison: a peep-show-like contraption, called a Kinetoscope, which provided the public with its first glance at true motion pictures. The films lasted less than a minute and documented such simple scenes as a man sneezing, a woman dancing, or a baby being given a bath, but it wasn't the subject matter that pulled the crowds in to 1155 Broadway, it was the novelty, indeed the magic, of seeing real life captured on celluloid. The Kinetoscope parlors were an overnight sensation, and they quickly proliferated all across the country. Their moment in the sun was brief, however, for just two years later Edison unveiled his first projector, the Vitascope, and this turned movies from private peep shows into public spectacles. But the Kinetoscope parlor paved the way for films as we know them, and thus 1155 Broadway is a very important site in the history of the movies. Today, a novelty shop called Broadway Fantasy occupies the storefront that gave birth to one of the most fantastic industries on earth.

18. BELLEVUE HOSPITAL CENTER
First Avenue from 25th to 30th Streets

To millions of movie and TV lovers, the word "Bellevue" is synonymous with psycho ward. And no wonder: In *Miracle on 34th Street,* Macy's eccentric Kris Kringle is sent to Bellevue for observation; in *The Lost Weekend,* the chronic alcoholic played by Ray Milland has a very bad time of it in Bellevue's detox unit; and more recently, according to a line in the script, the deranged psychiatrist played by Michael Caine in *Dressed to Kill* supposedly "did some work at Bellevue." Although Bellevue is best known for its psychiatric facilities, it is actually a vast and diverse New York City healthcare facility. Tracing its beginnings to 1736, it is also the oldest general hospital on the North American continent.

The motion picture that best captured the scope of Bellevue's operations was undoubtedly the 1950 Universal-International *film noir—The Sleeping City.* Shot totally on location at the historic hospital, the film takes us on a two-hour tour that provides insider glimpses of rarely seen areas such as the residents' dorms, the chapel, cocktail lounge, pool room, trauma ward, basement, and Victorian rooftop (where the film's dramatic climax takes place). Just as interesting as *The Sleeping City* is the disclaimer that precedes it. It seems that when Bellevue officials saw the film—which deals with drugs, blackmail, and murder inside Bellevue—they became quite upset. In order to appease the hospital authorities and get *The Sleeping City* into release, Universal-International had to shoot a special opening sequence in which the film's star, Richard Conte, assured the audience that what they were about to see on screen was totally fictitious. In what then amounted to a "commercial" for the hospital, Conte went on to extol the virtues of the "real" Bellevue and wound up showing architectural renderings of the additions that hospital administrators planned to build around the haunting, original Victorian brick buildings used so effectively in *The Sleeping City.*

19. AMERICAN ACADEMY OF DRAMATIC ARTS
120 Madison Avenue

This landmark 1905 Georgian building was designed by Stanford White for the ultra-exclusive women's club The Colony. Since 1963, however, it has been headquarters for the American Academy of Dramatic Arts, which had been based at the ANTA Theater (now the Virginia) on West 52nd Street and before that had operated out of a basement studio at Carnegie Hall. Actress Helen Hayes was very influential in orchestrating, and helping to raise the funds for, the Academy's move to Madison Avenue; and today the Academy's theater is named in honor of Miss Hayes's actress daughter, Mary MacArthur, who died of bulbar polio in 1949 when she was just nineteen years old.

Founded in 1884, the American Academy of Dramatic Arts claims to be "the oldest school of professional dramatic training in the English-speaking world." Over the years, the number of pros who have studied with the institution is staggering. Among the biggest names: Lauren Bacall, Jim Backus, Conrad Bain, Anne Bancroft, John Cassavetes, Hume Cronyn, Robert Cummings, Brad Davis, Cecil B. De Mille, William Devane, Danny DeVito, Colleen Dewhurst, Kirk Douglas, Vincent Edwards, James Farentino, Ruth Gordon, David Hartman, Florence Henderson, Judd Hirsch, Kate Jackson, John James, Jennifer Jones, Grace Kelly, Dina Merrill, Agnes Moorehead, Don Murray, William Powell, Robert Redford, Don Rickles, Thelma Ritter, Jason Robards, Eric Roberts, Edward G. Robinson, Gena Rowlands, Rosalind Russell, John Savage, John Saxon, Joseph Schildkraut, Renee Taylor, Spencer Tracy, Claire Trevor, and Robert Walker.

Offering two-year programs of study, the Academy often brings back its distinguished graduates—such as Robert Redford, John Cassavetes, and Gena Rowlands—to talk to students on the trials and triumphs of a career in show business. Tuition, by the way, for the Academy's basic course currently comes to over $4,000 a year.

AMERICAN ACADEMY OF DRAMATIC ARTS HALL OF FAME QUIZ
Can you name these famous former students?
(Please turn page.)

1. Kirk Douglas
2. Agnes Moorehead
3. Jim Backus
4. Joseph Schildkraut
5. Cecil B. DeMille
6. Spencer Tracy
7. Rosalind Russell
8. Robert Redford
9. Edward G. Robinson
10. Danny DeVito
11. Grace Kelly
12. Anne Bancroft

Answers:

1 L. 2 H. 3 G. 4 K. 5 D. 6 C. 7 J. 8 I. 9 E. 10 F. 11 B. 12 A.

A

B

E

F

I

J

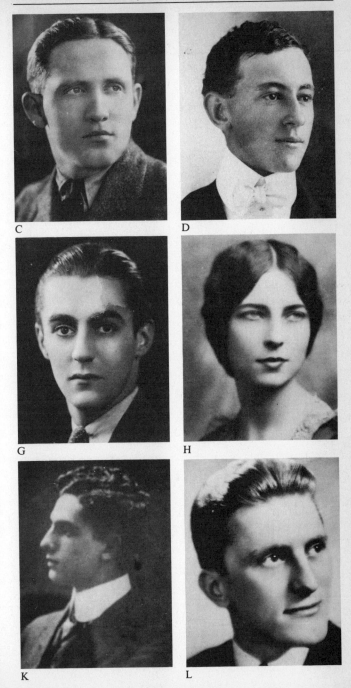

C

D

G

H

K

L

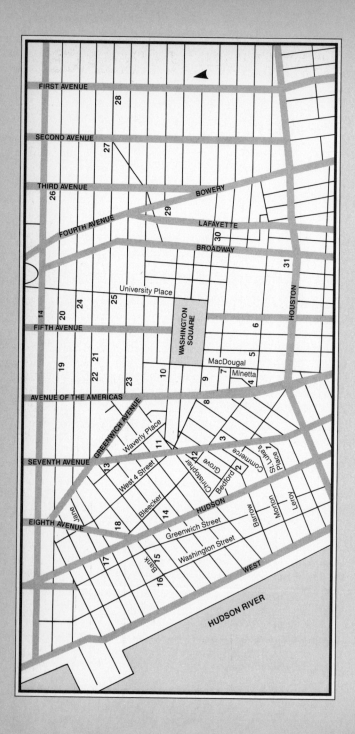

GREENWICH VILLAGE

The Big Backlot

6

Jane of Washington Square:
Fonda in Barefoot in the Park, *1967*

GREENWICH VILLAGE is New York City on a different scale. It is low-rise; there are lots of trees; people live in houses; you can see the sky. Needless to say, with so much going for it visually, the Village has been one of the most photographed areas of the city. This is especially true nowadays, with the resurgence of film making in New York, and on practically any given day you can find a movie, television series, or commercial being shot somewhere in the Village. Quite simply, the Village is New York City's backlot—and in this chapter, movie lovers will discover some of the favorite Greenwich Village addresses found in directors' and location managers' notebooks. These include, by the way, some of the classic Village clubs and cabarets that not only have appeared in films but have also provided employment (both on- and off-stage) to future stars during the dues-paying periods of their careers.

Besides being popular as a place where movies are shot, the Village is also one of New York's most popular neighborhoods for going to the movies. Abounding with small, often avant-garde, theaters that cater to a variety of eclectic Village tastes, the Village has a movie house for practically everyone—including one that boasts Joan Crawford's footprints in the forecourt! And if that's not enough to sell a movie lover on the Village, what is?

1. ST. LUKE'S PLACE

This may well be NYC's most beautiful and most frequently photographed block. Lying between Seventh Avenue South and Hudson Street, St. Luke's Place boasts trees, old-fashioned street lamps, and fifteen elegant brick townhouses all in a row. Built in the 1850s, these Italianate beauties have been home to a number of famous New Yorkers. Mayor Jimmy Walker—whose wild and woolly life was romanticized by Bob Hope in the 1957 Paramount film *Beau James*—once lived at number 6. Playwright Sherwood Anderson occupied number 12, poet Marianne Moore had number 14, and Theodore Dreiser, whose novel *An American Tragedy* became the 1951 Paramount film *A Place in the Sun,* starring Elizabeth Taylor and Montgomery Clift, called number 16 home.

This beautiful block has also lured many film makers. Its most famous screen appearance was in *Wait until Dark* (1967), with the house at number 4 serving as the NYC apartment where the blind woman played by Audrey Hepburn was terrorized by a thug (Alan Arkin) who operated out of a van parked across the street in front of the playground. Part of the playground, by the way, is occupied by a public swimming pool, which movie lovers will recognize as the spot where Cathy Moriarty and Robert De Niro met up in Martin Scorsese's *Raging Bull* (1980).

Back across the street, number 10 St. Luke's Place is the prime-time townhouse where Bill Cosby resides with his Huxtable TV family on "The Cosby Show." *Ragtime* (1980) and *The Survivors*

"Cosby Show" townhouse, St. Luke's Place

(1983) have also used St. Luke's Place as a location. In addition to films, this beauty of a block has been seen in countless TV commercials and print ads.

2. GREENWICH VILLAGE "BACKLOT"
Bedford/Grove/Barrow/Commerce Streets

In the days when Hollywood's Paramount Studios still had its backlot, the New York section was said to have been modeled on this cluster of blocks in Greenwich Village. Indeed, wandering around this enchanting enclave of tiny townhouses, fantasy cottages, ivy-covered apartment buildings, cozy courtyards and mews, you wonder for a second whether you're really in New York or in some Hollywood art director's vision of the city. You may be further confused if you happen to have ventured onto Bedford, Grove, Barrow, or Commerce Streets on one of the many days or nights when a film crew is on the scene with trucks, trailers, lights, cameras, stars, and extras.

Directors love to shoot in this neighborhood—not only for the varied architecture, but because these little streets are easily sealed off from traffic and crowds. Major landmarks for movie lovers to look for—either on screen or on a walking tour of NYC's own "backlot"—are Chumleys, a former speakeasy at 86 Bedford Street that is now a bar/restaurant and that still has no sign. Chumleys has been used as a typical NYC tavern in the features *Reds, Wolfen,* and *Bright Lights, Big City,* on television in "The Equalizer," and in the mid-1970s TV movie based on the life of Walt Whitman, *Song of the Wind.* In addition to its main entrance on Bedford Street, Chumleys also has a "secret" doorway off a flagstone courtyard at 58 Barrow Street.

Close by, at 38 Commerce Street, the tiny Cherry Lane Theater, founded by poet Edna St. Vincent Millay in 1924, is a famous Off-Broadway playhouse. In the movies, it has doubled as the historic Provincetown Playhouse in *Reds,* and has been used as a location for *Bolero* and *The House on Carroll Street.* It has also been used in TV's "The Equalizer," and in the video version of Tina Turner's hit song "What's Love Got to Do with It?" In real life, the Cherry Lane saw James Dean perform on its stage in the 1954 Off-Broadway production of *Women of Trachis,* and thirty years later starred Brad Davis and Maxwell Caulfield in Joe Orton's *Entertaining Mr. Sloane.*

Over on Grove Street, the lovely little red house at number 12 belonged to Angela Lansbury in *The World of Henry Orient.* Next door, another secret courtyard—Grove Court—conceals six small houses and a lovely garden. The space is a bit too confined, however, for film making and thus has appeared in few films. Closer to Bleecker Street, 26 Grove Street was where John Ritter cavorted in *Hero at Large* (1980). Around the corner, the half-timbered place with the twin-peaked roof at 102 Bedford Street was supposed to have been a trendy discothèque in *The April Fools* (1969), which starred Jack Lemmon and Catherine Deneuve. Next door, the historic clapboard cottage at 100 Bedford was the workshop of the sashmaker who once lived in the frame house on the corner at 17 Grove Street. The main house was built in 1822, and in 1970, Sandy Dennis and Jack Lemmon were seen scaling down the side of it in *The Out of Towners.* In 1985, Woody Allen and Mia Farrow passed by this picturesque corner in their pursuit of metropolitan happiness in *Hannah and Her Sisters.* And in late 1987, Mr. Allen again turned up on Grove Street to shoot sequences for his 1988 NYC feature.

For architecture buffs, Greenwich Village's oldest house (which dates back to 1799!) is the brick-and-wood dwelling at 77 Bedford. For movie lovers, however, the skinny house next door at 75½ Bedford may be of more interest, since it was one of John Barrymore's

Commerce Street "backlot"

early New York residences. The city's narrowest house, at just nine-and-one-half feet wide, it was also home to poet Edna St. Vincent Millay.

3.   "HESTER STREET" BLOCK
Morton Street between Seventh Avenue and Bleecker Street

Hester Street was a charming little black-and-white film about Jewish immigrants living on NYC's Lower East Side at the beginning of the century. But the film's director, Joan Micklin Silver, had a hard time finding the Lower East Side of her story in 1970s New York. The real Hester Street, having turned into a thriving commercial district of discount clothing and electronics stores, looked all wrong; whereas other parts of the historic neighborhood were too devastated even to consider. So *Hester Street* and company headed uptown and created their own "Lower East Side" on a wonderfully isolated block of Morton Street that is pretty much unchanged architecturally since the early 1900s. The metamorphosis of Morton Street involved masking streetlamps and adding awnings to some of the buildings to create historically accurate storefronts. Props such as pushcarts and vintage automobiles completed the picture.

NOTE: *Other Village blocks that have been "dressed" for the movies include East 6th Street between Avenues A and B* (The God-father) *and East 11th Street between Avenues A and B* (Ragtime).

Hester Street *on Morton Street*

Serpico *apartment*

4. "SERPICO" HOUSE
5-7 Minetta Street

Based on a true story, *Serpico* (1973) was a hard-hitting Sidney Lumet film that starred Al Pacino as a New York cop who uncovered and tried to rectify major corruption among New York's Finest. In the film, the title character, Frank Serpico, was an offbeat guy from Brooklyn who fancied Greenwich Village life. He took courses at New York University, tried hanging out with the coffee-house crowd, and lived in a basement pad with a tiny rear garden where he could often be found listening to opera records. The quintessential Greenwich Village apartment building used for *Serpico* stands just off the Avenue of the Americas on Minetta Street. Only one block long, Minetta Street is especially attractive to cinematographers because it is easy to block off and because it curves in such a way that there's never any danger of seeing anything else—such as the nearby Avenue of the Americas—even in a long shot.

5. JAMES AGEE RESIDENCE
172 Bleecker Street

James Agee was one of the most important film critics of this century. His reviews in *Time* and *Newsweek* during the 1940s were immortalized in the two volumes that form the classic *Agee on Film,* a frequently used text in many university film courses. Besides critiquing movies, Agee also wrote screenplays for a few of them, notably 1951's *The African Queen* (which he adapted from C. S. Forester's novel) and *The Night of the Hunter* (1955). From 1941 to 1951, Agee had an apartment in this Bleecker Street building on the lively block between the Avenue of the Americas and Mac-Dougal Street.

Caffe Reggio

6. BLEECKER STREET CINEMA
144 Bleecker Street

The best place in town to have seen *Desperately Seeking Susan* (1985) since this is the very movie house where Aidan Quinn supposedly worked as a projectionist in Susan Seidelman's offbeat look at life in Lower Manhattan. Village history buffs will be interested in the fact that the two buildings that house the Bleecker Street Cinema were once the home to a landmark restaurant of the 1880s called Mori's.

Phone: (212) 674–2560.

7. CAFFE REGGIO
119 MacDougal Street

The ultimate Greenwich Village coffee house—dark, smoky, with tiny tables, background classical music punctuated by the constant whoosh of the espresso/cappuccino machine. No wonder Paul Mazursky used it as a location for his tragicomic take on early-1950s Bohemian life in *Next Stop, Greenwich Village* (1975). The same *caffé* also turns up in such other set-in-the-Village epics as *Shaft* (1971) and *Serpico* (1973), and flashes by, too, in *The Godfather, Part II* (1974) and *The Next Man* (1976).

8. WAVERLY THEATER
323 Avenue of the Americas

"I met a boy named Frank Mills/In front of the Waverly/But, unfortunately,/I lost his address." The world heard about this Greenwich Village neighborhood movie house from the song "Frank Mills" in the legendary 1960s Broadway musical *Hair*. But, unfortunately, movie goers didn't get to see the Waverly in Milos Forman's film version of *Hair* in 1979, because the sequence didn't make the final cut. Other than its *Hair* connection, the Waverly has little to offer in the way of architecture or history; it was formerly a church and was converted into a 550-seat movie house in 1937. What the Waverly does have going for it is its location. Situated at the top of the stairs of Greenwich Village's bustling West 4th Street subway station, the Waverly is a place where people from different parts of Manhattan, Brooklyn, Queens, and the Bronx can rendezvous fairly easily for a night at the movies. This central location may have accounted for the success of its midnight shows which have pulled in teens from far and wide for cult classics like *The Rocky Horror Picture Show, Eraserhead,* and *Polyester.* Twinned in 1980, the Waverly is still one of the Village's most popular neighborhood movie theaters, and it still features midnight shows on weekends.

Phone: (212) 929–8037.

9. JOHN BARRYMORE RESIDENCE
132 West 4th Street

John Blythe Barrymore lived on the top floor of this West 4th Street townhouse off Washington Square between 1917 and 1920. Although Barrymore had appeared in films for Adolph Zukor's Famous Players Company since 1913, he was still better known as a Broadway matinee idol than a movie star. Nonetheless, Barrymore's 1920 screen performance in *Dr. Jekyll and Mr. Hyde* brought him great acclaim, and his transformation from mild-mannered M.D. to monster, supposedly done without the aid of trick photography, was much discussed at the time. *Dr. Jekyll and Mr. Hyde* was made in New York at the Famous Players Studio that once stood at 130 West 56th Street.

Meanwhile, back in Greenwich Village, Barrymore's penthouse was lavishly appointed with gilded Chinese wallpaper, expensive European antiques, and a large roof garden. To create the latter,

John Barrymore, right, as Mr. Hyde in Dr. Jekyll and Mr. Hyde, *1920*

Barrymore brought in some thirty-five tons of topsoil and planted wisteria, cherry trees, and grapevines. This was his secret hideaway during an uncharacteristically introspective period of his life. It is reported that Barrymore, who was known for his amorous adventures, even shunned the company of women for the first year or so that he spent in his Greenwich Village aerie. His fling with celibacy and the contemplative life did not last long, however, for he soon met and fell in love with Blanche Thomas, a very married poetess who went by the name of Michael Strange. A tempestuous courtship ensued, and in 1920 Mrs. Thomas became Mrs. Barrymore, and the couple moved to White Plains.

10. "BAREFOOT IN THE PARK" HOUSE
111 Waverly Place

In the play version of Neil Simon's *Barefoot in the Park,* newlyweds Corie and Paul Bratter spend three acts coping with the perils of setting up housekeeping in pre-Yuppie Manhattan on the top floor of a brownstone in the East Forties. For the film version, however, Neil Simon and director Gene Saks decided that Greenwich Village would offer a more picturesque backdrop than the Upper East Side. Thus they transplanted the Bratters, played by Robert Redford and Jane Fonda, to a red-brick "brownstone" with a steep stoop and wrought-iron balustrades on Waverly Place, just off Washington Square Park. Other Village locations used for the

Barefoot in the Park
house

film (interiors were done at Paramount Studios in Hollywood) included a Sixth Avenue deli, West 10th Street, lower Fifth Avenue, and, of course, Washington Square Park, where, toward the end of the film, we find a tipsy Robert Redford dancing . . . barefoot in the Park.

11. THE LION'S HEAD
59 Christopher Street

"Of all the jobs I had for survival, it was by far the most pleasant. Something was happening. It was the pinnacle." Thus spoke Academy Award–winning actress Jessica Lange of the Greenwich Village basement pub where she was a waitress prior to her being "discovered" by producer Dino De Laurentiis for the role of *King Kong*'s love interest in the 1975 mega-remake of the famous 1933 monster movie. Besides Ms. Lange, who still pops into the Lion's Head when she's in NYC, this famous writer's hangout has a number of other celebrities connected with its mystique. Actor Rod Steiger, for example, at one time spent so much time at the Lion's Head that he picked up mail there. On the other hand, Norman Mailer, when he ran for mayor of New York in the 1970s, used the Lion's Head for his unofficial campaign headquarters. And people still talk about the time that Peter O'Toole, after a particularly lively night on the town, had to be carried out of the place feet first! Another regular is "Hill Street Blues" writer/producer Robert Ward. What is it about the Lion's Head? Perhaps author James Baldwin put it best when called it "the last place that feels like the old days."

12. THE DUPLEX
55 Grove Street

A Village cabaret founded in 1950, the Duplex is where unknowns like Joan Rivers, Jo Anne Worley, Rodney Dangerfield, Stiller and Meara, and Woody Allen got some of their first professional gigs. Of Woody's Duplex days it is said that when the comic couldn't get a rise out of his audience, he pencilled in a mustache and started doing Groucho Marx's jokes. If they laughed, then he knew that his material needed work; if they didn't, he could blame it on the audience.

13. VILLAGE VANGUARD
178 Seventh Avenue South

Opened in a cellar on nearby Charles Street in 1934, this classic Greenwich Village night spot moved to its present location a year later and is known mainly for jazz these days. Back in the early 1940s, however, cabaret acts were frequently booked at the Village Vanguard, and one of these, a group called the Revuers, saw several of its members—notably Judy Holliday, Betty Comden, and Adolph Greene—lured to the West Coast by a Hollywood talent scout.

Dover Garage of "Taxi" fame

Ironically, their first Hollywood film was a 1944 Don Ameche/Carmen Miranda musical titled *Greenwich Village.* But their roles in the picture were minuscule, and before long all three performers found themselves back in the real Greenwich Village once more. Several years later, however, the Revuers had considerably better luck: Holliday became a Broadway star—via *Born Yesterday,* and went on to Hollywood film fame in *Adam's Rib* (1949) and in the 1950 screen version of her Broadway success—while Comden and Greene became important screenwriters and lyricists at MGM, where they helped create such classics as *On the Town* (1949), *Singin' in the Rain* (1952), and *The Band Wagon* (1953).

14. DOVER GARAGE
534 Hudson Street

It ran on prime-time TV from 1978 to 1983, and its ninety-three episodes are still big on the syndication circuit. It made a pair of New York actors named Judd Hirsch and Danny DeVito famous and glorified a group of other New York City professionals frequently vilified on their own turf: taxi drivers. Supposedly, "Taxi" took place at this honest-to-goodness taxi garage on the corner of Hudson and Charles Streets in Greenwich Village. In reality, except for some second-unit exteriors, the Sunshine Cab Company was headquartered on a soundstage at Paramount Studios in Hollywood.

15. HB STUDIO
120 Bank Street

Based on Bank Street since 1957, this prestigious acting school was founded in 1943 by Austrian-born actor/director Herbert Berghoff. Among the many former HB students who have found show business fame are Matthew Broderick, Peggy Cass, Jill Clayburgh, James Coco, Robert De Niro, Faye Dunaway, Harvey Korman, Jack Lemmon, Dina Merrill, Bette Midler, Liza Minnelli, Al

Pacino, Christopher Reeve, Eva Marie Saint, Lily Tomlin, and Sam Waterston.

Noted for its star teachers as well as for its famous graduates, HB counts playwright/screenwriter Horton Foote (*The Trip to Bountiful*), actors William Hickey (*Prizzi's Honor*), Charles Nelson Reilly, Jerry Stiller, and Sandy Dennis as recent members of its faculty. The studio's legendary top teacher is Herbert Berghoff's wife of many years, Uta Hagen, who originated the role of Martha in Edward Albee's *Who's Afraid of Virginia Woolf?* on Broadway in 1963. Movie lovers will remember that Elizabeth Taylor won her second Oscar when she played the same role in the 1966 film version of the play. After many years on the stage, Miss Hagen finally made her film debut in 1972 as the Russian grandmother of those strange twin boys in *The Other.*

16. WESTBETH
463 West Street

Since 1970 this huge complex of brick loft buildings has provided low-cost housing for Manhattan artists. Dating back to 1896, the buildings of Westbeth—as the place is known in its present incarnation—were originally the headquarters of the Bell Telephone/Western Electric Laboratories, one of the most important research facilities in communications technology in the country. Among the wonders developed here were the vacuum tube and the condenser microphone, a dynamic duo that made it possible to electronically amplify, as well as to record, sound. These discoveries, in turn, paved the way for something that Edison had wanted to do with motion pictures from the very beginning: make them talk. It was not until 1923, however, that Western Electric scientists came up with a practical system of synchronized sound for the movies. Offering the process—which was dubbed "Vitaphone," and which

Westbeth, formerly Bell Telephone Laboratories

Making movies talk: the Vitaphone system at work

featured a sound disc that was synchronized with the camera—to various movie studios, Western Electric met with little interest from an industry that was content to make fabulous profits from silent films. Only one company had the foresight to realize the potential of sound: Warner Bros., which quickly signed an exclusive agreement to use the Vitaphone sound-on-disc technology for its films.

Interestingly enough, Warners didn't want Vitaphone to make its pictures talk, but rather to add background music. In this way, Warners could provide movie houses all over the country with films that had the same symphonic accompaniment and special sound effects that big-city first-run houses equipped with staff orchestras had previously offered. Thus, in Warners' first Vitaphone film, *Don Juan* (which premiered in 1926), star John Barrymore never uttered a word. The film made history because it featured a prerecorded score played by the New York Philharmonic Orchestra. It was Warner's second Vitaphone production, *The Jazz Singer,* that changed the course of motion-picture history when it opened a year later in 1927. Not only did Al Jolson sing, he *spoke.* He didn't speak very much, mind you, because *The Jazz Singer,* like *Don Juan,* was essentially a silent film that was relying on Jolson's singing to pull in audiences. But when the star insisted on ad libbing here and there, the film's director, Alan Grosland, wound up keeping some of Jolson's patter in the picture. No one at the time had any idea of the powerful effect that Jolson's speaking, especially his now famous "You ain't heard nothing yet," would have on motion-picture audiences. A new, intimate connection was instantly established between audience and screen actor. The sound revolution had begun and there could be no turning back. In addition to Mr. Jolson, the scientists at 463 West Street in Greenwich Village played major roles in starting the revolution.

17. "SHAFT" BAR
621 Hudson Street

He was a tough black private eye who got caught in the middle of a bitter battle between a Harlem gangster and a white mob. The year was 1971, and *Shaft* was one of the first of a slew of successful black-exploitation films that were big on violence, racial tension, jivey dialogue, and heavy sex. Much of the latter took place in John Shaft's pre-Levelor-age apartment—a duplex with exposed-brick walls, louvered wooden shutters, serious shelving, and leather furniture—which would have been on Jane Street across from the No Name Bar at 621 Hudson. The apartment was a set, but the No Name was a real place, which also saw a lot of action in the film. Today, alas, it's a deli.

18. LAUREN BACALL APARTMENT
75 Bank Street

Betty Bacall was still seventeen when she and her mother moved into this large brick apartment building at the corner of Eighth Avenue and Bank Street. With high school behind her, Betty balanced making the rounds of modeling agencies and photographers' offices with ushering for $8.00 a week at various Shubert theaters, as well as being a volunteer hostess at the Stage Door Canteen. All the while she hoped and waited for that big show-business break. The break was not, it turned out, her winning the rather dubious title of Miss Greenwich Village in 1942; nor was it when she landed a small part in the Broadway play *Franklin Street* later that same year (the show closed out of town). Finally, however, dame fortune showed her face when Bacall was introduced to *Harpers Bazaar* editor Nicolas de Gunzburg, who in turn introduced her to the legendary fashion editor Diana Vreeland. Bacall subsequently appeared in seven issues of *Harpers Bazaar,* but it was her cover in March 1943—showing her posing in a chic suit in front of a Red Cross blood donor office—that caught the attention of the country, including such Hollywood heavyweights as Columbia Pictures, Howard Hughes, David O. Selznick, and Howard Hawks. With firm offers from both Columbia and Hawks, it was goodbye Bank Street, hello Hollywood, as Betty Bacall decided to sign with Hawks. It was also goodbye "Betty," as Hawks quickly rechristened his discovery "Lauren." Now all he needed was the right vehicle for his gorgeous new star. By the end of 1943, both the vehicle, *To Have and Have Not,* and the co-star, Humphrey Bogart, had been found.

19. RAMBUSCH
40 West 13th Street

This pie-shaped seven-story loft with the whimsical Gothic archway as its main entrance has housed the offices and studios of

Rambusch studios

the noted Rambusch design firm since 1898. Specializing in stained-glass windows and in decorating the interiors of churches, the Rambusch company found a whole new outlet for its creativity and craftsmanship with the rise of the movie palace in the 1910s and 1920s. Responsible for the gilding of hundreds of theaters all over the country and the world was Harold W. Rambusch (son of the firm's founder), whose grandest achievement was the lavish interior of the now-demolished Roxy Theater at 50th Street and Seventh Avenue. Besides his work on the Roxy, Rambusch also decorated the Paramount and Loew's Kings in Brooklyn, the Beacon on Broadway in Manhattan, and the Loew's Jersey in Jersey City. Feeling that the opulent movie houses he helped create were more than just places for the public to see films, Rambusch wrote in 1929: "In our big modern movie palaces there are collected the most gorgeous rugs, furniture, and fixtures that money can produce. No kings or emperors have wandered through more luxurious surroundings. In a sense, these theaters are social safety valves in that the public can partake of the same luxuries as the rich and use them to the same full extent." Much of that luxury and splendor was conceived at the Rambusch atelier on 13th Street.

20. THE LONE STAR CAFE
61 Fifth Avenue

Country & Western music's main Manhattan outpost has a suprisingly fashionable Fifth Avenue address—as well as a huge, eye-grabbing lizard atop its roof. Over the years, the Lone Star has featured Waylon Jennings, the Judds, and the Eagles on its stage.

In 1978, however, the late Bob Fosse took over the club to film a crucial sequence in his many-layered, semi-autobiographical epic, *All That Jazz*. The scene in point has actor Cliff Gorman delivering a Lenny Bruce-like monologue on death, which the Bob Fosse-like character played by Roy Scheider constantly reruns throughout the film.

21. DUSTIN HOFFMAN RESIDENCE
16 West 11th Street

It was all coming together for Dustin Hoffman in March 1970. The years of struggling to break into the acting business—years that included being everything from a janitor to an orderly in a mental hospital—were all behind him. His overnight success as a confused college student in Mike Nichols's *The Graduate* (1967), coupled with his poignant portrayal of street-person Ratso Rizzo in John Schlesinger's *Midnight Cowboy* (1969), had not only earned him two Academy Award nominations but had assured him of bankable superstardom. Among the fruits of Hoffman's success was an apartment in a handsome Greek Revival townhouse on a very posh block off Fifth Avenue in the Village. Here, Hoffman lived quietly and privately with his first wife, Ann. On March 6, 1970, however, all New York learned of Hoffman's address when the house next door, 18 West 11th Street, exploded and caught fire, killing one person and causing pandemonium on the block with police cars, fire engines, TV crews, newspaper reporters, and streams of gawkers. Hoffman was reportedly seen carrying paintings and at least one Tiffany lampshade out of his own house, which suffered considerable damage in the blast, before police prevented him from reentering the premises.

The blast story stayed in the papers for quite some time. At first, it was thought that the explosion had been an accident caused by a gas leak, but later it turned out that the basement of 18 West 11th Street had been used as a bomb-manufacturing center by the radical 1960s terrorist group, the Weathermen, and that the "accident" had been caused by all the explosives on the premises. Today, a modern, oddly angled brick townhouse now occupies the site of all the commotion back in 1970, and Mr. Hoffman has long since deserted the Village for the Upper East Side.

22. ANNE BANCROFT/MEL BROOKS TOWNHOUSE
52 West 11th Street

One of show business's longest lasting and most famous marriages, actress Anne Bancroft and producer-director-writer-comedian Mel Brooks shared this posh Greenwich Village townhouse in the 1970s. Life was less grand back in the days when she was Anna Maria Louise Italiano of the Bronx and he was Melvyn Kaminsky of Brooklyn.

23. THE LION SITE
62 West 9th Street

Today an expensive Italian eatery called Bondini's, this prime piece of Village real estate was once a gay cabaret called the Lion. In the summer of 1960, the Lion held talent contests on Thursday nights, and awarded the winner with a week-long engagement at the club plus free dinners and drinks. On one of those Thursdays, an eighteen-year-old woman from Brooklyn wowed the audience with her rendition of "A Sleeping Bee" from Cole Porter's *House of Flowers,* and won the contest hands down. Broke at the time, the realistic young songstress was more interested in the week's worth of free meals than in the week's booking. She said later of her Lion gig, "In those days, I could be had for a baked potato." In case you haven't guessed who the winner was, it was Barbra Streisand.

24. CINEMA VILLAGE
22 East 12th Street

At this well-known revival house, the double bill changes every two or three days and the fare is a pleasing mix of old and new, domestic and foreign films.

Phone: (212) 924–3363.

25. THE BEAUCAIRE
26 East 10th Street

A veritable high-rise Venetian palazzo—never mind the French name—this 1927 apartment building near New York University has housed, in separate units, Susan Sarandon and Richard Gere. These days, the reclusive Mr. Gere is said to prefer the privacy of his $1.5 million country house in the Pound Ridge section of Westchester County to the bustle of East 10th Street.

Variety Photoplay Theater

26. VARIETY PHOTOPLAY THEATER
110 Third Avenue

One of the candidates for "Oldest Movie Theater in New York" honors, this little picture palace dates back to 1914 according to theater historians—but to 1909 according to its current house staff. Standing on the site of an amusement palace that showed films as early as 1906, this may well be the oldest *site* in NYC where films have been shown continuously. No matter where the Variety Photoplay stands in the chronological scheme of things, this tattered nickelodeon—with its detached ticket booth and neon marquee (a 1930s modification)—is a charming piece of the past that has survived into the 1980s thanks to such films as *Carnal Olympics, Little French Maid,* and *Expose Me Now.* Also a survivor is the theater's wonderfully anachronistic name, which harkens back to the days when motion pictures were neither films nor movies, but "photoplays."

27. ST.-MARKS-IN-THE-BOWERY CHURCH
10th Street and Second Avenue

One of the city's most historic houses of worship, St. Marks was established in 1799. Movie lovers may recall its Georgian façade as well as its stained-glass-windowed interior from Sidney Lumet's 1966 film, *The Group.* It was at St. Marks that Kay Strong, the ambitious character played by Joanna Pettet, marries Harold Peterson, the "master of unproduced plays" portrayed by Larry Hagman. The film's best St. Marks scene has Blackie (Candice Bergen) arriving at the wedding in a glamorous Morgan sportscar. At the end of the film, St. Marks again figures in the picture as the setting for Kay's funeral, after the stresses of climbing the corporate ladder result in her committing suicide. Both *The Group*'s wedding and funeral sequences were shot by Lumet on the same day.

And speaking of funerals, movie lovers who visit St. Marks will find on the property the grave of New York's first governor, Peter Stuyvesant, who died in 1672 and whose estate once occupied the site on which St. Marks now stands.

28. THEATER 80
80 St. Marks Place

For the movie lover, Theater 80 is pure heaven. Featuring double bills of revivals and nothing but revivals, Theater 80 shows all the classics—*All About Eve, Sunset Boulevard, On the Waterfront, Stage Door, Now Voyager, Casablanca, The Maltese Falcon*—that you can see on your VCR but that come off so much better when viewed on a real movie screen in the company of a live audience. In addition to well-known films, Theater 80 also presents rare and seldom-seen titles like Paramount's NYC-made, Florenz Ziegfeld-directed *Glorifying the American Girl,* with Helen Morgan, Eddie

Crawford at Theater 80, 1971

Cantor, Rudy Vallee, and the legendary nightclub owner Texas Guinan. This early (1929) musical also featured a lavish Technicolor finale in which Johnny Weissmuller made his screen debut playing Adonis!

The fun at Theater 80 goes beyond the delights offered on its screen. Out in front of the theater, for example, if you look down, you may be surprised to see concrete slabs with the handprints, footprints, and autographs of such stars as Myrna Loy, Gloria Swanson, Alexis Smith, Ruby Keeler, Joan Blondell, and Joan Crawford. Theater 80's owner/director Howard Otway didn't raid Grauman's Chinese in Hollywood for these treasures—they were inscribed by the stars themselves in the early 1970s in order to celebrate and publicize Otway's conversion of an Off-Broadway theater into a full-fledged film-revival house.

Mr. Otway remembers with amusement the evening that his long-time friend Joan Crawford came to the theater for her sidewalk ceremony. Playing the star to the hilt, Miss Crawford arrived in a huge limousine; and since she was still a paid spokesperson for her late husband's company, Pepsi-Cola, she had seen that the limo was fitted with cushions that looked like giant Pepsi-Cola bottle caps. Once inside Theater 80, Miss Crawford happened to notice a young assistant drinking a Yoo-Hoo. "*What* are you doing?" she demanded of the frightened young man.

"Oh, I'm sorry," he responded. "I didn't know you were coming, Miss Crawford."

"Don't apologize," Crawford boomed. "Hide it!"

Less in character was Joan's sidewalk signing in which the legendary fussbudget ran out of cement before finishing her last name. "Let them know I don't plan ahead," she quipped.

Today movie lovers can still make out Crawford's signature on the East Village sidewalk in front of Theater 80; and they can see her portrait hanging in a special plant-filled niche inside the lobby. The portrait, which was done for her 1934 film *Forsaking*

All Others and which was used in 1962 in *What Ever Happened to Baby Jane?*, was given by Joan to Howard Otway only two weeks before her death in 1978. Besides the Crawford painting, movie lovers can also delight in Theater 80's lobbyful of stars'—Gloria Swanson, Bette Davis, Myrna Loy, Katharine Hepburn, Tallulah Bankhead, Henry Fonda, James Stewart—blowup photos and vintage movie posters that decorate the adjacent coffee bar.

Phone: (212) 254-7400.

29. PUBLIC THEATER
425 Lafayette Street

Built between 1853 and 1881 to house the Astor Library (the city's first free public library), this exotic Romanesque palazzo now houses producer Joseph Papp's New York Shakespeare Festival/ Public Theater complex. Known for developing such landmark theatrical productions as *Hair* and *A Chorus Line,* the Public Theater also lures movie lovers to its premises with its dynamic "Film at the Public" presentations, featuring first runs of foreign and U.S. films that don't get wide distribution as well as revivals and retrospectives. Recent Film at the Public offerings have ranged from German director Edgar Reitz's *Heimat*—a sixteen-hour chronicle of his country's twentieth-century history—to one of the most complete programs of Charlie Chaplin's work ever put together.

Phone: (212) 598-7171.

30. SILK BUILDING
14 East 4th Street

Taking over the ground floor of this restored nineteenth-century loft building is the downtown-Manhattan branch of Los Angeles's ultimate audio emporium: Tower Records. Meanwhile, living in a $1.25 million triplex penthouse in the same building is another L.A. transplant: Cher! Fellow rockstar Keith Richards and actress Kelly McGillis have been her neighbors at the Silk Building.

31. CINEMABILIA INC.
611 Broadway

On the second floor of this renovated cast-iron loft building, movie lovers will find in Suite 203 the bookstore of their dreams. Cinemabilia claims to be the largest retail and mail order film bookstore and gallery in the country. In addition to their complete stock of contemporary titles, they carry a large number of back titles and extremely rare film books and memorabilia. The shop also has stills, posters, souvenir programs, shooting scripts, sheet music, clipping files, and current movie magazines.

NOTE: *Cinemabilia is open Tuesday to Friday from 11 A.M. to 7 P.M., and on Saturday from 11 A.M. to 6 P.M. Phone: (212) 533-6686.*

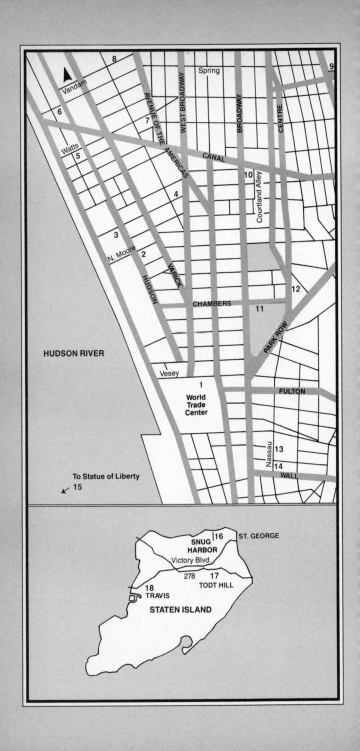

Vandam

8

6

Watts
5

AVENUE OF THE AMERICAS

7

Spring

WEST BROADWAY

BROADWAY

CENTRE

9

CANAL

10

Courtland Alley

4

3

N. Moore 2

HUDSON

VARICK

CHAMBERS

11

12

HUDSON RIVER

Vesey

1
World
Trade
Center

PARK ROW

FULTON

Nassau

13

14

WALL

To Statue of Liberty
15

16

SNUG
HARBOR
Victory Blvd.

ST. GEORGE

278

17

TODT HILL

18
TRAVIS

STATEN ISLAND

LOWER MANHATTAN/ STATEN ISLAND

The "New" New York

On the Town *at Federal Hall: Gene Kelly, Frank Sinatra, Jules Munshin*

THE 1980s may well be remembered in New York film history as the decade the movies went downtown. Classic examples of the "downtown" genre are *Desperately Seeking Susan* and *After Hours,* which show us a Manhattan of New Wave night-clubs, Art Deco diners, and lofty living arrangements—all decidedly *below* Houston Street and with stars rarely over thirty. Lower Manhattan, the oldest part of New York, is today the newest part of the city. Encompassing trendy neighborhoods like SoHo and TriBeCa and the brave new condo colonies of Battery Park City, downtown is a New York that is still evolving both visually and spiritually—which may explain its current appeal to film makers.

At the same time, Lower Manhattan is of interest to both movie lovers and moviemakers because it contains some of the city's oldest and most august landmarks. Ranging from the New York Stock Exchange to Federal Hall to the great lady of New York Harbor, the Statue of Liberty, many of these hallowed monuments are symbolic not just of the City of New York but of the United States of America, and over the years they have played major roles on screen, often providing ironic counterpoint to the mood or message of the scenes in which they appear.

This chapter also heads across New York Harbor to that *terra incognita* (for most Manhattanites) called Staten Island. The borough's relative obscurity, however, has proved to be its major attraction for movie location managers, who have found that Staten Island can be a convenient and surprisingly authentic-looking stand-in for other parts of the country—from the Midwest to New England—in New York–made films. Talk about trick photography!

1. WORLD TRADE CENTER
1 and 2 World Trade Plaza

Completed in 1970 and 1977, respectively, the two identical 110-story towers of the World Trade Center, at 1,350 feet each, are New York City's tallest buildings. Because of their paramount role in the city's late-twentieth-century skyline, they have popped up in countless made-in-NYC motion pictures over the last fifteen years. Often used to represent the ultimate New York City office building, the World Trade Center was where Cliff Robertson appeared to be an ordinary business executive in *Three Days of the Condor* (1973), although he was really a C.I.A. baddie. It was also at the World Trade Center that Jane Fonda headed up her murdered husband's international monetary firm in *Rollover* (1982).

Some of the most interesting uses of the World Trade Center as a location have been in fantasy films. In both *Godspell* (1971) and *The Wiz* (1978), for example, the Center's four-acre plaza provides an open-air sound stage for musical production numbers. In *Escape from New York* (1981), the rooftop of one of the World Trade towers becomes a tarmac where Kurt Russell lands a plane in this bizarre sci-fi film that portrays the island of Manhattan as a maximum-security prison of the 1990s. And then, of course, there's

World Trade Center

King Kong, Dino De Laurentiis's monumental 1976 remake of RKO's 1933 classic ape-loses-girl love story, in which the upstart World Trade Center won out over the tried-and-true Empire State Building for the film's star skyscraper role. Supposedly, however, Paramount's negotiations with the New York and New Jersey Port Authority, who own and manage the World Trade Center, proved difficult, and there were moments when it looked as if the Empire State Building would get the part after all. Meanwhile, the Empire State Building was quite annoyed at being overlooked by the new *King Kong,* and its owners registered their ire by stationing men dressed as apes carrying picket signs atop the observation tower.

Unlike the original *King Kong,* which was done entirely in Hollywood with a little help from some New York process shots, De Laurentiis decided to go on location for his film's New York sequences. In addition to the dramatic production values, filming in New York promised to provide lots of publicity for a picture that was already running way over budget. The publicity began with the Hollywood-to-New York journey of the forty-foot Kong model. This involved dismantling the monster into ten pieces, which were then shipped in special vans painted with "King Kong" in huge letters. Press releases kept the country informed of Kong's progress.

For the actual shoot, the producers wanted five thousand extras. To fill this large order, the production company "invited" the public to the World Trade Center Plaza on the nights of June 21, 22, and 23, 1976, to take part in the excitement of moviemaking. Thousands of New Yorkers showed up and, despite brawls, trouble with the Port Authority over security, and threats of rain, *King Kong* got its crowd scenes—and its headlines. Indeed, for three days the great ape was the city's brightest star. Almost lost in all the excitement was the blonde model who was making her film debut in the project as Kong's gal-pal. How did Jessica Lange enjoy shooting her first film? Best not ask Miss Lange. Since 1981, the Oscar-winning actress, supposedly embarrassed by the picture that launched her career, refuses to discuss *King Kong.* Unfortunately, just when the world had forgotten Lange's *King Kong* connection, Dino De Laurentiis released *Kong Lives* in 1986, which featured footage of Jessica and the great ape once more.

2. FIREHOUSE
14 North Moore Street

When "Saturday Night Live" superstars Bill Murray and Dan Aykroyd took their talents to the big screen, none of their films was ever quite as hysterical—or successful—as 1984's runaway hit *Ghostbusters.* In the film, the boys venture into the ghost-exterminating business and wind up saving Manhattan from some rather frightening ectoplasmic infestations. For their headquarters in the film, the Eight Hook and Ladder Eight firehouse in TriBeCa provided the perfect location. At least for the exterior sequences. The interiors, it turns out, were all done at a firehouse in Los Angeles. Why two firehouses? For one thing *Ghostbusters,* whose principal photography was based at the Burbank Studios in L.A., was on a tight schedule for its location shots in New York. For another, the Moore Street firehouse is still in the business of fighting fires. On the other hand, the firehouse used for the interiors in Los Angeles was one that had been decommissioned.

Ghostbusters *firehouse*

3. SCORSESE AND COMPANY
151 Hudson Street

Director Martin Scorsese and actors Harvey Keitel and Robert De Niro have much in common. They were all born and raised in New York City; they have all worked together professionally (Keitel in Scorsese's 1968 New York University thesis film *Who's That Knocking at My Door?;* Keitel and De Niro in Scorsese's 1973 *Mean Streets* and 1976 *Taxi Driver;* and De Niro in Scorsese's 1977 *New York, New York* and 1980 *Raging Bull*). And, finally, they have all lived at 151 Hudson Street. When Mr. De Niro's in town, he can often be found renting movies from Greenwich Street Video at 368½ Greenwich Street.

4. AMERICAN THREAD BUILDING
260 West Broadway

Built in 1896 as the headquarters for the New York Wool Exchange, this handsome eleven-story structure facing TriBeCa Park is one of Lower Manhattan's most luxurious addresses. Among its glamorous tenants are rock's madcap Cyndi Lauper, and Ingrid Bergman's model/movie-actress daughter, Isabella Rossellini. In the early 1970s, Ms. Rossellini made ends meet in Manhattan by teaching Italian classes at the American Express Language Center and at the New School.

5. BETTE MIDLER APARTMENT
451 Washington Street

Formerly of Barrow Street in the West Village, the Divine Miss M has headed further downtown to this many-gabled 1891 landmark building on the fringes of SoHo. Besides Bette, the building is also home to the trendy, high-ceilinged Capsouto Frères restaurant.

6. "AFTER HOURS" BAR
289 Hudson Street

"Different rules apply when it gets this late. It's like . . . after hours." Thus speaks a SoHo bartender to Griffin Dunne in Martin Scorsese's gritty tale of an Upper East Side Yuppie's harrowing/hilarious all-night odyssey in Lower Manhattan. Club Berlin, the bar where Dunne gets much of his downtown education, was formerly the Blue Note. Today, despite its featured film role, it has become a deli.

Another *After Hours* bar is just a half block away at 308 Spring Street. In the film, it catered to a leather crowd; in real life, it's the Emerald Pub, a standard-issue Irish taproom.

7. FILM FORUM
57 Watts Street

Once a garage, this little brick bunker just north of the entrance to the Holland Tunnel was gutted in the mid-1970s, refitted with two small movie houses, and today reigns as the city's most important showcase for foreign, offbeat, and often-overlooked motion pictures. In her constant quest for the new and the noncommercial, Film Forum's director, Karen Cooper, is credited with turning on New York audiences to the new German directors Herzog, Wenders, and Fassbinder long before they became fashionable with the mainstream. Similarly, Film Forum introduced American audiences to black-sheep Soviet film maker Andrei Tarkovsky and his bizarre sci-fi visions of twentieth-century life in *Solaris* and *The Stalker.* A nonprofit operation, Film Forum is the only full-time facility in the United States devoted exclusively to year-round premieres of foreign art features and American independent films. Film Forum is supported by the New York State Council on the Arts, the National Endowment for the Arts, several foundations and corporations, and, most important, by individual movie lovers who pay from $15 to $1,000 a year to become Friends of Film Forum. In return, these Friends get to see all Film Forum's features for half price.
Phone: (212) 431-1590.

8. THALIA SOHO
15 Vandam Street

Despite the sad demise of the 95th Street Thalia—which reigned for half a century as the city's premier revival house—its spirit, its name, and its double bills are happily being kept alive by this little theater which opened in Lower Manhattan in 1985.
Phone: (212) 675-0498.

Griffin Dunne in an After Hours *bar, 1985*

Williamsburg Bridge as seen in The Naked City, *1948*

9. WILLIAMSBURG BRIDGE

Its neighbor to the south, the Brooklyn Bridge, made history when it opened in 1883. Not only was the Brooklyn Bridge an architectural and engineering marvel, it was a thing of extraordinary beauty. On the other hand, the Williamsburg Bridge, when it came along in 1903, was just another bridge—and not a very pretty one at that, looking more "propped up" than suspended. If it was noted for anything, it had the dubious distinction of opening up the Williamsburg section of Brooklyn to the impoverished masses of the Lower East Side.

Over the years, unlike the glamorous and photogenic Brooklyn Bridge, the lowly Williamsburg span has inspired few film makers. Indeed, when it has been used cinematically, it has usually been as a location for films which emphasize the gritty downside of New York City's mystique. In *The Sleeping City,* the 1950 thriller from Universal–International about drugs and murder at a major metropolitan hospital, for example, Richard Conte plays an undercover cop posing as a doctor at the hospital, and the park at the foot of the Williamsburg Bridge furnishes the gloomy backdrop for a number of secret meetings that Conte has throughout the film.

Perhaps *The Sleeping City*'s director, George Sherman, remembered the Williamsburg Bridge from the landmark New York *film noir* two years earlier that also used it as a location—Jules Dassin's *The Naked City*. This time the Williamsburg Bridge provides a cold, erector-set-like setting for a confrontation between the police and the killer at the end of the film. The killer, needless to say, loses the battle, and winds up falling to his death in the East River. More recently, in Sidney Lumet's depressing look at corruption in the New York Police Department, *Serpico* (1974), the

Williamsburg Bridge again turns up. Here, when street-smart Italian-American cop Frank Serpico (Al Pacino) leaves his Brooklyn home for a new life in a Greenwich Village apartment, he drives into the city in a battered Dodge and takes the Williamsburg Bridge. Clearly the Brooklyn Bridge and even the Manhattan Bridge would have been much too glamorous for this character, this car, this film.

Of the Williamsburg Bridge's film appearances, its most dramatic may well have been in a 1914 silent called *Fighting Death,* in which daredevil movie hero Rodman Law and a young actress both jump from one of its parapets and parachute into the East River. Both performers, it turns out, actually did the stunt, and caused quite a bit of commotion among passers-by and motorists who thought that they were witnessing a double suicide. However, as the *New York Times* reported in its February 6, 1914, edition, "the shouts, shrieks and yells which greeted the double jump stopped for a moment when it was seen that the two had parachuted . . . and as the two struck the water, the breathless crowd on the bridge noticed a tug cruising near them with motion picture cameras aboard." Just another day of Manhattan moviemaking.

10. CORTLANDT ALLEY

In a city that makes movies without the luxury of studio back lots, when an alley is needed for a mugging, gun fight, or fatal confrontation between hero and villain, this Lower Manhattan cul-de-sac is often called on to fill the bill. Movie lovers have seen it in such features as *Highlander, FX,* and *Crocodile Dundee,* and on television in episodes of "Family Honor," "The Equalizer," and "N.Y.P.D."

11. TWEED COURTHOUSE
52 Chambers Street

A monument to the greed of the infamous New York political boss, William Marcy Tweed, this extraordinary Italianate structure was built as a courthouse during the city's corrupt Tammany Hall

Tweed Courthouse

period in the 1870s. Not only did the building take thirteen years to finish, it cost the then unbelievable sum of $14 million, most of which was skimmed off by Boss Tweed and his cronies. Despite its questionable origins, the Tweed Courthouse, now used to house various city offices, is a spectacular space, especially the interior, where a seven-story rotunda is capped with a skylit dome, with cage elevators and two monumental cast-iron staircases adding to the drama.

For film makers, the possibilities offered by the Tweed building as a location are intriguing. In 1974, Joan Micklin Silver used the Tweed's grand staircases to represent the Great Hall of Ellis Island in *Hester Street,* her comedy/drama about turn-of-the-century Jewish immigrants in New York. In 1980, Brian De Palma shot the same staircases from a different angle to create the creepy mental institution where the psychiatrist played by Michael Caine worked in *Dressed to Kill.* Two years later Sidney Lumet turned the Tweed into the Boston courthouse where much of the action of *The Verdict* takes place. Other features that shot at the Tweed include *Kramer vs. Kramer, Turk 182, Alphabet City,* and *Angel Heart.* Declared a landmark in 1984, the building is bound to wind up in many more movies in years to come—especially now that the Mayor's Office of Film, Theater, & Broadcasting has set aside certain areas specifically for film making. Little did Boss Tweed know back in the 1870s that he was building a 1980s movie studio!

12. NEW YORK COUNTY COURTHOUSE
60 Centre Street

When a shot of this great government building, with its massive columns and dramatic stone steps, turns up in a film, it invariably signals that a courtroom scene is about to follow. It was at the New York County Courthouse that Macy's eccentric Santa Claus supposedly stood trial in 1947 in *Miracle on 34th Street.* Ten years

New York County Courthouse

later, Henry Fonda was a star juror in the same building in *Twelve Angry Men*. For this film, which was made entirely on location in New York, director Sidney Lumet used the courthouse's magnificent interior rotunda as well as its striking façade for several sequences. More recently, *Legal Eagles* superstar lawyers Robert Redford and Debra Winger found themselves at 60 Centre Street, and were followed by Barbra Streisand, who had her day in court here (and also stopped traffic!) for the film *Nuts* (1987). Besides appearing in movies, the building has been seen in the mini-series "Little Gloria, Happy at Last" (1985) and "Rage of Angels" (1986), and episodes of "Kojak," "Cagney and Lacey," "Naked City," "N.Y.P.D.," and "The Equalizer." In addition to its status as Manhattan movie star, the 1926 County Courthouse is also a tourist attraction owing to its amazing architecture and its displays of historic New York documents that date back to colonial times.

13. VITAGRAPH SITE
140 Nassau Street

In 1896, a couple of English immigrants named J. Stuart Blackton and Albert E. Smith hit upon a novel way to perk up their lackluster vaudeville act . . . motion pictures! Aware that the Edison Company had just perfected the Vitascope projector, Smith and Blackton were among the first entrepreneurs to purchase one of these miraculous new machines. Quickly seeing that the film business was a lot more lucrative than vaudeville, the pair decided to switch professions. The only problem was that Edison retained exclusive control over the means of producing films: the camera. Smith, however, was a clever mechanic, and he soon figured how to turn Edison's Vitascope projector into a movie camera. And, thus, the American Vitagraph Company was born.

Vitagraph's first office was in the twelve-story, red-brick Morse Building, which still stands at the corner of Nassau and Beekman

Vitagraph's studio on the Morse Building roof, 1897

streets in Lower Manhattan. Vitagraph's first film, *The Burglar on the Roof*, was shot in the fall of 1897 on the roof of this same building. A makeshift affair, the sixty-second melodrama featured Smith as cameraman, Blackton as the burglar, and a supporting cast made up of the building's janitor's wife, an office boy, and a third Vitagraph executive. According to producer/cameraman Smith, the movie cost a whopping $3.50 to make. It was an inauspicious beginning for a company that would become one of the major forces on the silent-screen scene.

Vitagraph continued to operate out of 140 Nassau Street and to shoot films on its roof for another five years. In 1903, the company's continued success—especially with its film coverage of historical events such as Teddy Roosevelt's inauguration—allowed Smith and Blackton to move to larger quarters over in Brooklyn. Today, Vitagraph's Nassau Street birthplace has been renovated and converted into luxury apartments, and few, if any, of the Wall Street brokers and lawyers who live there have any idea of the building's film-making history. Indeed, few people except for film historians have ever heard of Vitagraph, which disappeared from the face of the earth in 1925 when it was swallowed up by an upstart company headed by a couple of brothers named Warner.

14. FEDERAL HALL
28 Wall Street

Built as a U.S. customs house in 1842, this imposing Greek temple–like structure at the corner of Wall and Nassau streets is now called Federal Hall because it occupies the site of our nation's first capitol. In case anyone has forgotten, New York was the capital of the United States between 1779 and 1780, and at the time its City Hall building was converted into the country's first administrative headquarters and renamed Federal Hall. It was here that the Continental Congress met, and here that George Washington was sworn in as the first president of the Republic. Today, this historic event is commemorated by a statue of Washington which stands in front of the present Federal Hall.

Over the years, the building's dramatic façade—with its massive columns, steps, and towering statue of George Washington—has provided one of New York's most popular photo opportunities for speeches, patriotic rallies, and war-bond drives. Needless to say, the site has also been used by film makers and has furnished a dramatic/historic backdrop for sequences in *Kiss of Death* (1947), *Force of Evil* (1948), *On the Town* (1949), *Wolfen* (1982), and the TV mini-series "The Dane Curse." Movie lovers may also remember Federal Hall from Oscar-winning *Kramer vs. Kramer* (1979), in which its exterior and interiors were used for some of the courthouse sequences in which Meryl Streep battled Dustin Hoffman for custody of their child. Today, besides serving as a location for Manhattan-made movies, Federal Hall is open to the public and features exhibits on the history of its site and on early New York.

15. STATUE OF LIBERTY

Edison filmed this great American lady as early as 1896, and she has been showing up on movie screens ever since. Of her undoubtedly thousands of film appearances, we nominate the following five as among the all-time best: (1) *Saboteur* (1942), where Alfred Hitchcock sets the hair-raising climax of this spy thriller on the Statue's crown, arm, and torch. Besides providing one of the world's most exotic locales for a fight between an all-American hero (Bob Cummings) and a Fifth-Column thug (played by Norman Lloyd of "St. Elsewhere"), Miss Liberty becomes a symbolic battlefield for the struggle of Western democracy vs. Axis fascism that was going on in the real world at the time; (2) *On the Town* (1949), the Statue of Liberty According to MGM, with Gene Kelly, Frank Sinatra, and Jules Munshin looking positively patriotic in their sailor suits as they sing, dance, and frolic at the base of what we're sure was Louis B. Mayer's favorite leading lady; (3) *Superman* (1978), featuring the most romantic close encounter with a major monument ever seen on screen, when Superman gives Lois Lane a whole new look at Liberty late one night as part of his "private" tour of New York; (4) *Splash* (1984)—what better place than Liberty Island for a naked mermaid to make a memorable Big Apple entrance?; and (5) *Remo Williams—The Adventure Begins* (1986), a dreadful film that's worth sitting through (or fast-forwarding to the last fifteen minutes of the tape) for the fight scene atop a Miss Liberty caged in scaffolding. The script for *Remo* asked for nothing more than a building wrapped with scaffolding, but when the film's location manager went scouting for sites in Lower Manhattan in mid-1985, he happened to look out at New York Harbor and saw the Statue of Liberty under restoration, being readied for her 1986 birthday bash. Excited by the possibility of shooting on Liberty Island at this unique point in time, he contacted the film's director who was

Inside Miss Liberty: Robert Cummings in Saboteur, *1942*

equally enthusiastic about the idea. To make a long story short, it took quite a bit of dealing with the Department of the Interior, the Parks Department, the American–French Restoration Committee, and the general contractors in charge of the renovation for *Remo*'s producers to get permission to shoot at the Statue of Liberty—but they managed to pull it off. Most of the close-ups, however, were done in Mexico, where the film's principal photography was based.

NOTE: *Today, unscaffolded and spruced up for the next hundred years, the Statue of Liberty is open to sightseers and movie lovers every day from 9 A.M. to 5 P.M., with ferries leaving Battery Park every hour on the hour. The boat trip may remind movie lovers of yet another classic Statue of Liberty film appearance: the "Don't Rain on My Parade" production number from Barbra Streisand's* Funny Girl *(1968).*

16. MABEL NORMAND HOUSE
91 Tysen Street, Staten Island

These days, not too many people know who Mabel Normand was, much less where she was born. One of the greatest comediennes of silent pictures, Mabel Normand was closely linked professionally and personally with the famous producer/director Mack Sennett. In her heyday, she appeared opposite superstars like Charlie Chaplin and Fatty Arbuckle, and at one point she even had her own Hollywood studio. Not bad for a Staten Island gal who started out in the world on November 9, 1892, in this unprepossessing corner house across from the historic Snug Harbor section of the borough. Miss Normand's eventual Hollywood success was short-lived, however. In the early 1920s a series of tragedies rocked both her emotional stability and her film career. Not only had she become addicted to drugs in the film capital, she was one of the suspects in the scandalous William Desmond Taylor murder in 1922. To make

*Mabel Normand house,
Staten Island*

Mabel Normand

matters worse, she was implicated in another Hollywood shooting shortly thereafter, when her chauffeur was accused of killing a man with a gun that belonged to her. When she died of pneumonia and tuberculosis in 1930, she had not made a feature film in seven years. In 1974, her tragic life was the subject of the Broadway musical *Mack and Mabel,* which starred Queens-born Bernadette Peters (née Lazzara) as Staten Island's Mabel Normand.

17. "GODFATHER" ESTATE
110 and 120 Longfellow Road, Staten Island

Benvenuto a Casa Corleone! This cluster of handsome Tudor homes at the end of a tree-lined cul-de-sac in the fashionable Todt Hill section of Staten Island was used by director Francis Ford Coppola in 1971 to represent the Long Island estate of that nice Italian-American family that we all got to know and love in *The Godfather.* Movie lovers will remember especially the spectacular wedding sequence that was shot in the garden of 120 Longfellow.

The Godfather *estate, Staten Island*

Staten Island wedding: The Godfather, *1971*

It is interesting to note that not too far from *The Godfather* movie mansion, the real-life Mafia kingpin, Paul Castellano, lived in a walled estate on Berodid Road. Castellano's name was all over the news in December 1985 when he was rubbed out at Sparks Steak House on 46th Street in Manhattan.

18. "SPLENDOR IN THE GRASS" HOUSE
4144 Victory Boulevard, Staten Island

Splendor in the Grass . . . great Hollywood movie, right? With some fine location scenes shot in the Midwest, right? Wrong—on both counts, for this classic 1960 tale of hot-blooded teenage love in late-1920s Kansas was shot completely in the New York metropolitan area. The reason for this surprising bit of location maneuvering was because the film's director, Elia Kazan, wanted to be as close as possible to New York, where his father was very ill at the time.

Of the many challenges that *Splendor in the Grass* created for its location people, none was more perplexing than finding the small-town Kansas house in which Natalie Wood's character, Deanie Loomis, lived with her family. To the rescue came Staten Island, which had on its underdeveloped western edge a little settlement of wood-frame homes known as Travis. The corner house at number 4144 Victory Boulevard was selected for the Loomis place, and modified slightly through the addition of a temporary staircase on one side, a bit of gingerbread trim in front, and a fresh coat of paint all over. The shooting took place between May 6 and 17, 1960, and, needless to say, it caused quite a stir in Travis—especially when Natalie Wood's handsome husband, Robert Wagner (it was their first time around), showed up one evening and gave autographs to the crowd of locals who had gathered at the location. Another "surprise" guest that same evening was a Twentieth Century–Fox starlet named Joan Collins who, according to a local newspaper report, was visiting her good friend Natalie Wood. Maybe so—but in Miss Collins's tell-all autobiography, *Past Imperfect* (Simon & Schuster, 1984), she indicates that she had been secretly living with Miss Wood's co-star, Warren Beatty, at the time. Miss Collins goes on to tell of Mr. Beatty's lovemaking prowess as well as of the abortion that she had at his insistence in Newark, New Jersey, during the *Splendor* shooting.

Today, 4144 Victory Boulevard and the community of Travis look much as they did in Kazan's 1960 film set in pre-Depression Kansas.

Staten Island sweethearts: Natalie Wood and Warren Beatty in Splendor in the Grass, *1961*

Big night on Victory Boulevard: Joan Collins and Robert Wagner visit Warren Beatty, Elia Kazan, and Natalie Wood at Staten Island location for Splendor in the Grass

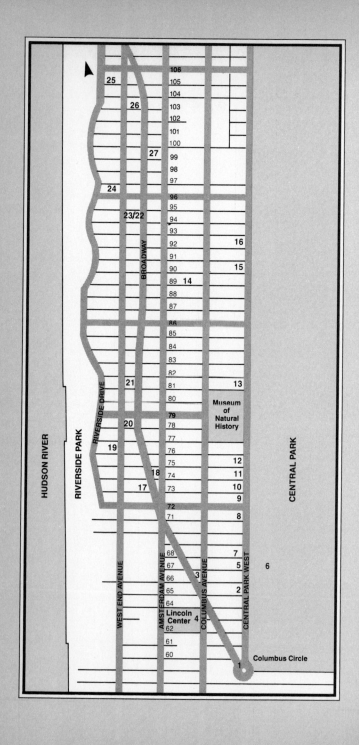

THE
UPPER WEST
SIDE

Rebel Territory

8

Ghostbusters *Harold Ramis, Dan Aykroyd, and Bill Murray on Central Park West*

JUST as there is the East Coast and the West Coast, there is the Upper East Side and the Upper West Side. And despite the fact that there's only Central Park, rather than a whole country, separating these two Manhattan neighborhoods, they are often as different in outlook and spirit as New York is from California. Whereas the East Side has a reputation for being the bastion of establishment Manhattan, the West Side has been noted for its individuality, its liberal politics, its cultural pursuits. Granted, the West Side has lost some of its brashness and originality through recent Yuppie invasions, but old-timers, proud of the way things used to be, are hanging onto their traditions and trying hard to keep their neighborhood from being swallowed up by overpriced pasta places and Euro-trashy boutiques. Classic Upper West Siders from the world of show business include rebels like Lauren Bacall, Barbra Streisand, Mia Farrow, William Hurt, John Lennon and Yoko Ono, Madonna and Sean Penn. It was the West Side, too, that harbored two of the movies' best-known rebels, Rudolph Valentino and James Dean, during their Manhattan days.

Almost as intriguing as the stars who have called the Upper West Side home are the extraordinary buildings that many of them have occupied. Landmarks of Art Deco, Beaux Arts, or Gothic Revival architecture, the great celebrity apartment buildings of Central Park West and Broadway stun by their style and their diversity. Ultimately, diversity is what the Upper West Side is all about—and that includes cultural diversity. Witness the West Side location of Lincoln Center, New York's "acropolis of the performing arts," home to opera, symphony, ballet, theater, and, of special interest to movie lovers, one of the country's most important cinema events—the New York Film Festival, held every September.

1. GULF + WESTERN BUILDING
15 Columbus Circle

The corporate headquarters of the conglomerate known as Gulf + Western is significant to movie lovers because Paramount Pictures—one of G + W's major divisions—has its East Coast offices here. It was in 1970 that Paramount pulled out of the grand old Paramount Building that Adolph Zukor, the studio's founder, had built on Times Square in the 1920s, and headed uptown to Gulf + Western's brand-new forty-four-story Columbus Circle skyscraper. The move signaled the end of the days when movie studios were owned, operated, and cared for by moguls whose names were as well known as those of some of their stars. Despite Paramount's current link to the less-colorful realities of modern-day corporate America, the studio's thirtieth-floor screening room—with cushy swivel seats, individual telephones, and full bar—brings a little Old Hollywood pizazz to Gulf + Western's rather cold, white-marble tower. In the plaza below, the Paramount Theater is a subterranean movie house that shows first-run Paramount pictures to those not lucky enough to catch them on the thirtieth floor. It's a far cry, however, from the spendid Paramount movie palace that was the centerpiece of Zukor's Paramount Building at 43rd and Broadway.

2. "GHOSTBUSTERS" BUILDING
55 Central Park West

New Yorkers often have to put up with a lot for the privilege of living in the Big Apple. Exorbitant rents, ancient plumbing, roaches, noise—but nobody had it quite as bad as Sigourney Weaver when she resided on Central Park West in the 1984 film *Ghostbusters*. Terror dogs! Lecherous arm chairs! Leaping eggs! Evil refrigerators! Who ya gonna call?

For Sigourney's *Ghostbusters* building, a real Central Park West apartment house was used for many exteriors, but the exotic pre-Columbian temple that appeared to be on the roof of 55 Central Park West was created—for long shots—by matte artist Matthew Yuricich. Meanwhile, for medium shots a fifteen-foot model of the temple was used; and for close-ups with actors, a full-scale temple complex was built at the Burbank Studios on the West Coast. For the scene where the street caves in at the end of the film, parts of the sequence were done in New York at 55 Central Park West, while others were lensed at the Columbia Ranch in Burbank, California, where the façade of the New York apartment building was reconstructed, along with a hydraulically controlled collapsing street! Ultimately the whole sequence was put together in the editing room.

This Central Park West address, it turns out, was not the *Ghostbusters* company's first choice for an apartment building. They really wanted to use 1 Fifth Avenue—both for its Art Deco architecture and its proximity to Washington Square. In fact, they planned on using it, and had already started to design a rooftop temple for the building when 1 Fifth's co-op board nixed the plan.

3. ABC "CAMPUS"
West 66th/67th Streets

Although the main office of the American Broadcasting Company is still at 1330 Avenue of the Americas, the corridor formed by 66th and 67th streets, from Central Park West to West End Avenue, is fast becoming what the network likes to call its "campus." TV fans may be interested in checking out the following campus addresses: 47 West 66th Street—where "World News Tonight" originates; 56 West 66th Street—home to the soap opera "One Life to Live"; 101 West 67th Street—for "All My Children"; 7 Lincoln Square—"The Morning Show"; 157 Columbus Avenue—"20/20"; 1965 Broadway—"Good Morning America"; and 320 West 66th Street—the "Loving"/"Ryan's Hope" studios. Eventually ABC's West Side campus may encompass some 2.5 million square feet and employ some five thousand people, which, if coupled with developer Donald Trump's controversial $5-billion "Television City" complex—proposed to rise beside the Hudson River between

59th and 72nd streets—will turn the Upper West Side into Manhattan's major media center.

4. LINCOLN CENTER
Columbus Avenue from 62nd to 66th Streets

Home to opera, ballet, symphonic music, and theater, the Lincoln Center for the Performing Arts is one of the largest and most impressive complexes of its kind in the world. What many people have forgotten is that Manhattan's arts acropolis stands on land that was once a neighborhood of dreary brick tenement buildings. In 1961, before they were torn down to make way for Lincoln Center, these old West Side blocks had a brief fling with show business when they were called on to furnish the realistic locales for some of the scenes in United Artists' *West Side Story.* Later, film making would return to the area in a big way once Lincoln Center made its debut as a dramatic—and camera-ready—New York City landmark.

Especially photogenic is Lincoln Center's main plaza, which clusters the New York State Theater, the Metropolitan Opera House, and Avery Fisher Hall around a black-marble fountain. Movie lovers have seen this beautiful backdrop in everything from *The Turning Point* to *Ghostbusters.* By far its most memorable appearance, however, was in Mel Brooks's outrageous 1967 comedy, *The Producers.* In the Lincoln Center sequence, Zero Mostel is trying to convince Gene Wilder that there's big money to be made in producing a bound-to-flop Broadway musical called *Springtime for Hitler.* When Wilder finally says yes to Mostel's cockamamie scheme, all the lights of the Metropolitan Opera House come up full, the fountain starts going crazy, and fireworks finish off the fantasy.

Serious movie lovers will also be interested in two Lincoln Center buildings beyond the main plaza area. The first is the New

Lincoln Center

York Public Library & Museum of Performing Arts at 111 Amsterdam Avenue. Here, on the third floor, the Billy Rose Theater Collection is one of the country's major research facilities for theater, radio, television, and film. The Collection is open from 10:00 A.M. to 7:45 P.M. on Mondays and Thursdays, and from 10:00 A.M. to 5:45 P.M. on Tuesdays, Wednesdays, Fridays, and Saturdays. Phone: (212) 870–1639.

The other Lincoln Center building that draws movie lovers is Alice Tully Hall, which every September–October hosts most of the presentations of the Film Society of Lincoln Center's prestigious New York Film Festival (Avery Fisher Hall is used for the Festival's opening and closing nights). Credited with staging the U.S. premieres of some of the world's most important films, the New York Film Festival is where New Yorkers first got to see Ján Kadár's *The Shop on Main Street* (1965), Gillo Pontecorvo's *The Battle of Algiers* (1965), Eric Rohmer's *My Night at Maude's* (1969), Bernardo Bertolucci's *The Conformist* (1970), Bob Rafelson's *Five Easy Pieces* (1970), Louis Malle's *Murmur of the Heart* (1971), Peter Bogdanovich's *The Last Picture Show* (1971), Luis Buñuel's *The Discreet Charm of the Bourgeoisie* (1972), Rainer Werner Fassbinder's *The Bitter Tears of Petra von Kant* (1973), Martin Scorsese's *Mean Streets* (1973), François Truffaut's *Day for Night* (1973), Wim Wenders's *The American Friend* (1977), Truffaut's *The Last Metro* (1980), Werner Herzog's *Fitzcarraldo* (1982), Lawrence Kasdan's *The Big Chill* (1983), Akira Kurosawa's *Ran* (1985), Maximilian Schell's *Marlene* (1986), Francis Ford Coppola's *Peggy Sue Got Married* (1986), John Boorman's *Hope and Glory* (1987), and Yurek Bogayerich's *Anna* (1987).

NOTE: *For information on the New York Film Festival, write: Film Society of Lincoln Center, 140 West 65th Street, New York, NY 10023.*

5. HOTEL DES ARTISTES
1 West 67th Street

Originally built to house painters and sculptors, this beautiful 1918 building—with studios that feature double-height windows and wonderful light—quickly began to draw artistic residents from other fields. One of these was America's hottest male movie star, Rudolph Valentino, who rented a bachelor pad at des Artistes in 1922, even though he was married to his second wife, Natasha Rambova, at the time. Actually, he was only sort-of married to Miss Rambova, because his divorce from his first wife, Jean Acker, would not be final in California until the following year. Like many movie people at the time, Valentino had tried to get around California's tough divorce laws by wedding Natasha in Mexico. Upon their return to California, however, there was an uproar that resulted in Valentino's being charged with bigamy and his having to spend a night in jail. Fed up with Hollywood's provincialism and also with his studio (Paramount) for offering him little help with his

Above: Hotel des Artistes

Left: The Valentinos in New York: Rudolph and wife Natasha Rambova

legal difficulties, Valentino and Natasha escaped to New York. Not wanting to risk any more trouble with the authorities or with the press, however, Valentino moved into des Artistes alone. This wasn't too much of a hardship though, because Natasha resided with an aunt who lived on the same West 67th Street block. Also, by the following year Valentino's divorce had gone through, and both Valentinos were able to live together legally at des Artistes. It was during his des Artistes period that Valentino also settled his differences with Paramount and went on to make his two New York pictures, *Monsieur Beaucaire* and *A Sainted Devil,* at the Astoria Studios in Queens. But by 1924, Valentino was working and living in Hollywood once again; and by 1925, his marriage to Natasha was on the rocks. Ironically, when he died while visiting New York the following year, his famous funeral took place at the Frank E. Campbell Funeral Church, which at the time was on Broadway between 66th and 67th Streets, just two blocks away from his old apartment in the Hotel des Artistes.

Besides Valentino, des Artistes also counts among its famous former and current residents artist Norman Rockwell, dancer Isadora Duncan, novelist Fannie Hurst, playwright/performer Noël Coward, Algonquin Round Table wit Alexander Woollcott, former New York City mayor and sometime newscaster John Lindsay, and actors Richard Thomas and Joel Grey.

Taking over much of the ground floor of the Hotel des Artistes is the elegant Café des Artistes—noted for its naughty murals by erstwhile resident Howard Chandler Christy. The restaurant has been featured in Louis Malle's 1981 *My Dinner with André* as well as in the Richard Benjamin–directed 1986 farce *The Money Pit.*

6. TAVERN ON THE GREEN
Central Park West at 67th Street

The Land of Oz is alive and well in Central Park at Tavern on the Green. A sheepfold in the 1870s, the building became a restaurant in the 1930s, but it wasn't until Warner LeRoy got his hands on the place in 1974 that Tavern on the Green became one of the city's most dazzling dining rooms. With strong Hollywood roots—LeRoy's father is director/producer Mervyn LeRoy (*The Wizard of Oz*); his mother was Harry Warner's daughter Doris—Warner LeRoy gave Tavern on the Green the total Tinseltown treatment, redoing it with brass, glass, mirrors, crystal chandeliers, and pastel-

At Tavern on the Green: Joseph Cotton and Ethel Barrymore in Portrait of Jennie, *1948*

James Dean apartment building

painted plaster of Paris. Most opulent of the various dining rooms is the Crystal Room, a great glass pavilion that looks out on gardens—and, at night, trees strung with fairy lights—backed by Central Park. Movie lovers may remember the scene in *Ghostbusters* where Rick Moranis, pursued by a red-eyed, fang-toothed "terror dog," pounds on the glass wall of the Crystal Room desperately trying to get the attention of the diners on the other side. In true New York fashion, everyone in the restaurant keeps right on eating, trying their best not to notice the horror show going on outside. Tavern on the Green has also been used in *Only When I Laugh, It's My Turn, Heartburn,* and the mini-series "Rage of Angels." Meanwhile, to see what the place was like in its pre–Warner LeRoy days, movie lovers should check out David O. Selznick's 1948 *Portrait of Jennie.*

7. JAMES DEAN APARTMENT
19 West 68th Street

"Across the room on the shoulder-high shelf that ran the width and length of the entire room were empty beer cans, an open peanut butter jar, an album cover of *Romeo and Juliet,* a baseball bat, a hot plate, a bunch of dried leaves stuck in a Maxwell House can, several sheets of music and a bust of Jimmy gazing down upon a new chrome music stand." That's how (in David Dalton's *James Dean: The Mutant King,* St. Martin's, 1975) an actress friend of his described the tiny 12-by-12 room—with bathroom down the hall—that was James Dean's Upper West Side home before he went off to Hollywood in 1954 to shoot his first major film, *East of Eden.* Despite the fact that he was heading for the big time, Jimmy Dean held onto his minuscule New York City pad, and stayed there in early 1955 when he returned to the city after having wrapped *Eden*

*West Side rebel:
James Dean*

as well as a couple of television shows on the West Coast. It was to
have been a happy reunion with the city he loved—a time to see
old friends, visit old hangouts, and revel in his newfound success.
It turned out to be anything but. Throughout the visit, Jimmy's
behavior was extremely erratic. He was edgy, ill at ease, often nasty.
Some friends accused him of having "gone Hollywood." Others
felt he was strung out on drugs. There was a particularly unpleasant
episode with his former girlfriend, Barbara Glenn, when she broke
the news to Jimmy that she had gotten engaged during his absence
from the city. At first he took it well, and even had dinner with
Barbara and her fiancé. But the next day, he pleaded with her to
come by his apartment for a talk. There, he opened up a suitcase
full of cash and ordered her to help herself to the stash, since she
had lent him money during his starving-actor days. When she refused the money and insisted that it was all over between them,
Jimmy got hysterical, screamed at her, and threw wads of money
at her as she left the apartment. His last words were: "And when I
die, it'll be your fault!"

Jimmy left New York soon thereafter, never to see the city or
his West 68th Street digs again. The car crash that ended his life
and burgeoning career lay just nine months ahead of him. Today,
over three decades later, the little building with the bow windows
that James Dean called home still stands off Central Park West on
68th Street. Ironically, Dean's last NYC address is just five blocks
away from his first, which was a room at the West Side YMCA at
5 West 63rd Street, where he stayed when he landed in the Big
Apple in the fall of 1951.

8. THE OLIVER CROMWELL
12 West 72nd Street

The *real* West Side home of actress Sigourney Weaver, this ornate 1927 building is just a few blocks from 55 Central Park West, where Ms. Weaver lived and was terrorized in the film *Ghostbusters.*

9. THE DAKOTA
1 West 72nd Street

In 1884, the *New York Daily Graphic* called it "one of the most perfect apartment houses in the world." Besides offering the most lavish apartments that New Yorkers had ever encountered, the Dakota also provided some of the best views in town. "Every prominent landmark in the landscape can be discerned from this location," the *Daily Graphic* gushed on, "and the great buildings of the lower city are as prominently marked as if the sightseer were floating over the island in a balloon."

Today, over a hundred years later, the Dakota still has fabulous apartments and drop-dead views. It also boasts one of the most remarkable tenant rosters of any building in the country. Among the Dakota's most famous former and current residents are Lauren Bacall, Judy Holliday, Zachary Scott, Teresa Wright, Robert Ryan, Marian Mercer, Rex Reed, Kent Smith, William Inge, John Frankenheimer, Jack Palance, Roberta Flack, Fannie Hurst, Gwen Verdon, José Ferrer and Rosemary Clooney, Eric Portman, Warner LeRoy, John Lennon and Yoko Ono, Gilda Radner, Connie Chung, and a mild-mannered gentleman whose real name was William Henry Pratt, but whom movie lovers know as Boris Karloff.

The Dakota

Stories of the Dakota's star tenants abound. Boris Karloff, for example, evidently felt very unloved every Halloween, because the kids in the building were too afraid of his horror-film image to take any of the trick-or-treat candy he left outside his door. Another legend of the Dakota, reported by Stephen Birmingham in *Life at the Dakota* (Random House, 1979), is the saga of Lauren Bacall's air conditioners. Since the building has landmark status, the New York Landmarks Commission must give its blessing to any renovations planned by Dakota tenants. When Bacall wanted to knock out some exterior bricks to install through-the-wall air-conditioning units, she asked a fellow tenant who was familiar with the workings of the Landmarks Commission to plead her case before the commissioner. When the official found out just who wanted permission to install the air conditioners, he hinted that he would prefer to see the legendary actress in person. A meeting was arranged at Miss Bacall's apartment at cocktail time. Bacall, whose standard Dakota drag consisted of slacks and an old sweater, pulled out all the stops and received the city official in full Hollywood-star attire. It was a charming cocktail hour, everyone got along beautifully, and Bacall was permitted to knock down all the bricks she wished. Supposedly, a number of other Dakota tenants, who were stuck with their unsightly window air conditioners—and who didn't happen to be living legends—were not amused.

Then there were the Lennons. Not all Dakota residents were thrilled, it seems, to have John and Yoko as neighbors—especially since their presence meant a constant crew of photographers lurking around the building waiting to get a photo of the famous couple. Nor were the Dakota's telephone operators pleased with the fact that they would have to handle a good thirty calls a day from fans asking to be put through to the famous former Beatle and/or his wife. Needless to say, the whole building was saddened and horrified by Lennon's murder outside the Dakota in November of 1980.

At the time of the murder, many Americans were already familiar with the Dakota because of the famous film, *Rosemary's Baby,* which had been shot there twelve years earlier. Movie lovers may also remember the Dakota from its appearance in Twentieth Century–Fox's 1949 film, *House of Strangers,* which starred Edward G. Robinson, Richard Conte, and Susan Hayward.

10. THE LANGHAM
135 Central Park West

Built in 1905, this Central Park West château has furnished luxurious living space to Cyril Ritchard, Lee Strasberg, Merv Griffin, Carly Simon, Maureen O'Sullivan, and Mia Farrow (Miss O'Sullivan's daughter). When Woody Allen starred both Mia and her mom in his 1986 *Hannah and Her Sisters,* he added a bit of Central Park West *cinéma vérité* by featuring Farrow's Langham apartment in the film as well.

11. SAN REMO APARTMENTS
145–146 Central Park West

A long-time favorite address of celebrities, this massive Central Park West landmark has been home at various times to Dustin Hoffman, Mary Tyler Moore, Raquel Welch, Donald Sutherland, Paul Simon, Barry Manilow, Elaine May, Tony Randall, Robert Stigwood, Harold Arlen, and Diane Keaton. When rock-star Madonna tried to buy a $1.2 million co-op apartment in the San Remo in July 1985, Diane Keaton was the lone member of the prestigious building's co-op board who did not reject the singer's application. The others, it seemed, felt Madonna's flamboyant lifestyle—which had included nude layouts in *Playboy* and *Penthouse* as well as a hot-tempered actor fiancé named Sean Penn—would bring unwanted publicity to the San Remo's elegant classical entryways. Expecting trouble with the board, Madonna showed up for her personal appearance dressed in a basic black dress accessorized with a single strand of pearls and two gold crucifixes around her neck. But neither God nor Diane Keaton were enough to get Madonna into the San Remo. She had better luck down the street at 65 Central Park West, where she and Sean ultimately wound up living.

On a sadder note, the San Remo is where the legendary screen goddess of the 1940s, Rita Hayworth, lived out the last years of her life in the apartment of her daughter by the Aly Khan, Princess Yasmin Aly Khan. A victim of Alzheimer's Disease, Miss Hayworth—installed in a suite that tried to duplicate the furnishings of her Beverly Hills home—had nurses round the clock. The single rose that arrived every day up until her death in 1987 was a gift of her *Gilda* co-star and long-time friend, Glenn Ford.

12. THE KENILWORTH
151 Central Park West

Notable for its massive-columned entryway, the Kenilworth was completed in 1908. For many years, the movies' most famous

The Kenilworth

Sherlock Holmes, Basil Rathbone, resided here. Old-time Central Park Westers recall with amusement seeing Rathbone walking in Central Park with his friend Boris Karloff, who lived three blocks away in the Dakota. Needless to say, it's not every day that you run into Sherlock Holmes on a stroll with Frankenstein! Another Kenilworth tenant of note is actor Keir Dullea.

13. THE BERESFORD
211 Central Park West/1 and 7 West 81st Street

A building so vast it has three different addresses, the magnificent Beresford is where Rock Hudson had his six-room home away from Hollywood. After the star died of AIDS in October 1985, most of the contents of his Beresford apartment were auctioned off at the William Doyle Galleries in New York, bringing prices that far exceeded the auction house's expectations. Among the items that fans fought over were a silverplated box inscribed "Dynasty, 100th episode," which brought $900; a needlepoint rug made by Rock ($2,100); a Steinway piano ($6,875); and the footstool that 5-foot-4-inch Elizabeth Taylor used to reach the 6-foot-5-inch actor's Beresford bathroom sink while staying in the apartment in 1981.

The Beresford

Written on the stool in lavender ink are the lines "E. T. stood here, she had to because she couldn't reach the sink. R. H. is a love, and I thank him always—even tho he is one foot taller. Your always friend, Elizabeth." The footstool was sold to a sixteen-year-old girl, a fan of both Taylor's and Hudson's, who paid $1,400 for it.

Other famous former and current Beresford tenants are John McEnroe and Tatum O'Neal, Mike Nichols, Calvin Klein, Beverly Sills, Diane Sawyer, Isaac Stern, and Meryl Streep.

14. CLAREMONT RIDING ACADEMY
175 West 89th Street

This four-story horse barn on West 89th Street saw a lot of action in the 1981 thriller *Eyewitness,* when William Hurt foiled his would-be murderer by letting loose scores of horses in the middle of the Upper West Side. Dating back to 1889, the Claremont Riding Academy has taught riding to the Kennedy kids, the Lawfords, and the children of Diana Ross; it has also rented mounts for romantic rides through Central Park to such celebrities as Jacqueline Onassis and writer-editor Michael Korda. In addition to *Eyewitness,* movie lovers may also recognize Claremont as the stable from which a band of *Hair* hippies stole their ponies for the "Sodomy" production number in the 1979 Milos Forman film.
Phone: (212) 724–5100.

15. THE ELDORADO
300 Central Park West

Lying between 90th and 91st Streets, this twin-towered 1930s apartment building is about as far north as you can go on Central Park West and still claim a fashionable address. Among the stars who have or who once had such claims are Faye Dunaway, Roddy McDowell, Richard Dreyfuss, Carrie Fisher, Bianca Jagger, Martin Balsam, and Phil Donahue and Marlo Thomas. One celebrity who couldn't wangle an Eldorado apartment, however, was Lena Horne, who reports that she and her late husband Lennie Hayton, who was Jewish, were once denied a spot in the building. In her auto-biography, *Lena* (Doubleday, 1965), she writes of her Eldorado experience: "We were caught in three different kinds of prejudice—against Negroes, against Jews, and against mixed marriages. I don't know which of these the management was responding to, but the Eldorado, on Central Park West, refused us an apartment. At the time it was owned by a Negro, Bishop C. M. ('Daddy') Grace."

16. THE ARDSLEY
320 Central Park West

Designed by Emery Roth, the same architect who did the San Remo down the street, the Art Deco Ardsley is home to Oscar-winning New York actress Dianne Wiest. This, too, is where Barbra

Streisand lived (first with, later without, husband Elliott Gould) throughout the second half of the 1960s. When, in late 1969, Ms. Streisand tried moving across Central Park to posher digs in a co-operative at 1021 Park Avenue, she was turned down by the building's board of directors.

17. THE ANSONIA
2107–2109 Broadway

Loaded with towers, mansard roofs, ornate balconies, balustrades, and bay windows, the Ansonia is easily Broadway's most opulent, if not its most beautiful, structure. When it opened in 1903, this extraordinary sixteen-story Beaux Arts building provided tenants with such luxuries as electric stoves, hot and cold filtered water, freezers, a pneumatic-tube system to deliver messages, and even an early form of central air conditioning. The building also had incredibly thick walls, installed to protect against fire, which meant that Ansonia suites were among the most soundproof in the city. For this reason, it is said, many famous musicians took up residence in the building, including Enrico Caruso, Lauritz Melchior, Igor Stravinsky, Arturo Toscanini, Ezio Pinza, and Lily Pons. Besides their musical careers, Pinza and Pons both appeared in the 1947 film *Carnegie Hall,* as well as in various other Hollywood films. Another legendary film personality who once lived at the Ansonia is Billie Burke of *The Wizard of Oz* and *Topper* fame. During her Ansonia days, she was married to the great theatrical impresario Florenz Ziegfeld, who lived with Miss Burke on one floor of the building and who supposedly kept a mistress in an identical apartment on another!

In addition to its famous residents, the Ansonia has been a star in its own right on various occasions. In the 1975 film *The*

The Ansonia

Continental Baths site— where Bette Midler got her act together

Sunshine Boys, it was Walter Matthau's Manhattan apartment house. That same year the building also served as the location for a dramatic sequence in *Three Days of the Condor* that finds Robert Redford narrowly escaping being gunned down in the Ansonia's alleyway. The Ansonia was also the spot where a now-famous singer and movie star got her big break in show business. The star was Bette Midler, who became the toast of New York when she sang, danced, and clowned at the Continental Baths, a gay spa that once occupied the Ansonia's basement and whose cabaret room enjoyed a brief vogue among both gay and straight New Yorkers in the early 1970s.

Today, the Continental Baths is history, but a substantially renovated Ansonia endures as a vital part of the West Side scene.

18. BEACON THEATER
2124 Broadway

Its architect, Walter W. Ahlschlager, was the same man responsible for designing the legendary Roxy Theater, which stood at Seventh Avenue and 50th Street. This was no coincidence since the Beacon Theater was originally conceived as one of a citywide chain of smaller "Roxy" theaters, all under the direction of Samuel L. ("Roxy") Rothapfel, the entrepreneur who gave New York City some of its most famous movie palaces and who gave the world the name "Roxy." Roxy's chain of theaters never got off the ground, however, because by the late 1920s he had started working for William Fox, who wanted him to concentrate on Fox's own enormous national network of movie houses.

Since Roxy had gone over to Fox while the Beacon was under construction, it never opened with his name on it. Originally to have been called Roxy's Midtown, the half-finished house was bought by Warner Bros. and opened in 1929 as Warner's Beacon. Nonetheless, the theater was still essentially the house that Roxy wanted built and it reflected his grandiose taste and style. Its ornate lobby, for example, had a rotunda that was a scaled-down version of the one that Ahlschlager had designed for the original Roxy's grand foyer. Today, that lobby remains pretty much intact as does its auditorium, which stuns with glorious murals, a huge Art Deco chandelier, colossal gilded statues flanking the proscenium, and a fully playable Wurlitzer organ. Unfortunately, movies haven't been shown in the fabulous old movie palace since 1974, although the space has been a popular venue for contests and rock concerts. In 1986 a developer wanted to turn the Beacon—by then an official city landmark—into a discothèque. Although preservationists managed to prevent this from happening, the theater's future is highly problematical as this book goes to press.

19. WILLIAM HURT RESIDENCE
348 West End Avenue

Upper West Siders have a reputation for being serious, sensitive, intellectual, and politically correct (i.e., liberal). Certainly, of today's young New York–based movie stars, William Hurt fits the image of a proper Upper West Sider to a T—right down to his West End Avenue address.

20. APTHORP APARTMENTS
2207 Broadway/390 West End Avenue

With its iron gates, its monumental tunnellike entrances, and its impressive interior courtyard, the Apthorp is one of the city's most dramatic, and most frequently photographed, apartment buildings. In *Heartburn,* when Meryl Streep escapes from her marital problems in Washington, she finds refuge in her father's Apthorp apartment in New York. (In real life, *Heartburn*'s author, Nora

The Apthorp Apartments

Ephron, is a former Apthorp resident.) The Apthorp also turns up in *Network* (1976) as the love nest shared by TV execs William Holden and Faye Dunaway. On the other hand, in *Eyewitness* (1981) it is a TV newscaster (Sigourney Weaver) who resides in the landmark 1908 building. Other Apthorp feature-film credits include *The Cotton Club* (1984), where mobster "Dutch" Schultz keeps his moll Diane Lane in grand style at the Apthorp; plus *The Changeling* (1978), *The Money Pit* (1986), and episodes of "Rags to Riches" and "The Equalizer."

21. JILL CLAYBURGH APARTMENT
440 West End Avenue

In her Oscar-nominated role as a newly single lady in Paul Mazursky's *An Unmarried Woman* (1978), she lived on the Upper West Side and shopped at Zabar's delicatessen at 2245 Broadway. In real life, Jill Clayburgh's a West Side woman as well.

22. THE THALIA
250 West 95th Street

After living for several years under the threat of plans to "re-develop" the site that it had occupied since 1938, New York's oldest and best-known revival house finally closed down in June 1987. It was a great loss for the Upper West Side, with the only consolation being that the theater will live for a long time in the memories of millions of movie-loving New Yorkers who flocked to the Thalia when practically nowhere else in town provided a steady diet of classic and avant-garde films. The Thalia will also live on in Woody Allen's *Annie Hall,* where it turns up as one of the movie houses where *The Sorrow and the Pity*–obsessed hero Alvy Singer (Woody Allen) catches his favorite film. Meanwhile, a downtown reincarnation—the Thalia Soho at 15 Vandam Street—does its best to emulate its dearly departed role model.

The Thalia, 1986

23. POMANDER WALK
260–266 West 95th Street

One of the Upper West Side's best-kept secrets, this tiny Tudor village tucked between Broadway and West End Avenue was built in 1921 to resemble the set of a hit play of the era called *Pomander Walk.* Among the show-biz people who have lived in Pomander Walk's cottages are Humphrey Bogart, Rosalind Russell, and Lillian and Dorothy Gish. In 1986 Woody Allen let film audiences see this enchanting Manhattan hideaway in *Hannah and Her Sisters.* While Sam Waterston has no trouble escorting Dianne Wiest and Carrie Fisher through this private compound, movie lovers who visit Pomander Walk should be aware that its steel gates are often locked. Even so, a peek through the bars is still quite satisfying.

24. RIVERSIDE PARK PLAYGROUND
96th Street at Riverside Drive

For five nights during the long hot summer of 1978, Riverside Park's 96th Street playground saw more film making than residents of the apartment buildings across the way ever wish to see again. The film was Walter Hill's cult classic *Warriors,* which depicts the freaky odyssey of a Brooklyn street gang fighting its way across Manhattan to its home turf on the other side of the East River. For the opening sequence of *Warriors,* close to a thousand dress extras were recruited to play the delegates to a massive convocation of all the street gangs in New York. Since the Screen Actors Guild permits nonunion actors to be hired to fill in crowd scenes that require over a hundred people, the bulk of the extras were recruited from the

Entrance to Pomander Walk

Trouble in Riverside Park: Warriors, *1978*

streets, lured to the shoot by the promise of $30 plus two box lunches a night. At first it was fun, but as the nights wore on, the glamor of film making soon wore thin for some of the background players (a number of whom, it turned out, were gang members in real life!). There were food fights, fist fights, and cases of disappearing actors, disappearing costumes, and disappearing equipment. When it looked as if *Warriors* might have a real gang war on its hands, the producers tried raffling off color television sets to calm everyone down. To add to the nightmare, the apartment dwellers across the park—angered by the noise and bright lights, which, on some nights, didn't let up until five in the morning—often interrupted the shooting with jeers and protests. Sometimes things go better on a backlot.

25. MARION DAVIES MANSION
331 Riverside Drive

In 1918 fifty-five-year-old William Randolph Hearst got serious about turning his twenty-year-old showgirl mistress, Marion Davies, into a full-fledged movie star. Not only did Hearst establish Cosmopolitan Studios to produce Miss Davies' films, he moved Marion, her mother, her sisters, and various other family members into an opulent French château at the corner of Riverside Drive and 105th Street. Hearst saw to it that Marion's new abode was nothing less than a palace fit for a movie queen—especially since the queen would frequently be receiving the press on the premises. Marion's interviews were usually scheduled for her private sitting room, which was decorated with a marble fountain and statues of cupids. Bejeweled and coiffed, the young star would appear in a shimmery pink or white negligee if the reporter were a woman, or turn up in a chic suit if he were a man. Everything was very carefully controlled and

Marion Davies at home

mapped out and, unlike Orson Welles's fictionalized version of the Hearst–Davies relationship in his 1941 film *Citizen Kane,* Hearst's plot to make his mistress a star ultimately was a stunning success. Her first features, while pulling in mixed reviews from the non-Hearst press, were popular with the public, and Marion Davies had developed into a fine screen comedienne by the early 1920s. It was also at this time that Hearst decided that the future of feature films lay in Hollywood and so, just as quickly as he had moved Marion and family to Riverside Drive, he whisked them off to California, where he found them equally palatial quarters on Lexington Road in Beverly Hills.

Today, Marion's former Manhattan mansion belongs to a Buddhist sect, and movie lovers who visit the site will find a huge statue of Shinran-Shonin, the founder of the sect, looming in front of the building next-door.

26. HUMPHREY BOGART HOUSE
245 West 103rd Street

This unimpressive four-story row house on the Upper West Side is where movie idol Humphrey DeForest Bogart was born in 1899, and where he lived off and on until he was in his early twenties. His father, Dr. Belmont DeForest Bogart, a respected surgeon, had his office on the ground floor; his mother, Maude Humphrey Bogart, was a magazine illustrator, and often worked out of a studio on the third floor, where little Humphrey also had his bedroom. Completing the family portrait were Humphrey's two sisters.

Unlike many of the tough-guy characters he would later play on screen, Humphrey Bogart enjoyed a pleasant childhood on what was then a very upper-middle-class Upper West Side. Sent to fashionable private schools, the young Bogart attended Trinity School at 91st Street and Amsterdam Avenue from 1913 to 1917, where

Bogie's block: West 103rd Street

his best subject was religion. He then went to Andover in Massachusetts, as his father had done before him. Unlike his father, however, young Bogart was expelled for disciplinary problems. After that, he joined the Navy, and upon returning to New York and to 245 West 103rd Street, drifted into the theater. It wasn't until Bogie was in his mid-twenties and starting to get small parts on stage that he finally left home and moved downtown to 43 East 25th Street. There he lived with actress Helen Menken, who became the first of the three wives he had prior to marrying Lauren Bacall in 1945.

By 1933, the elder Bogarts had left the family home as well. Owing to financial problems brought on by the Depression, they were forced to sell the house on 103rd Street and move to a small rental apartment in Tudor City. Soon, however, they would have nothing to worry about financially, because in 1936 their son would play a gangster in a film called *The Petrified Forest,* and he would become one of Hollywood's biggest stars. Today, the home where that star got his start in the world still stands on an Upper West Side block.

27. METRO THEATER
Broadway and 99th Street

This jewel of a neighborhood movie house was called the Midtown when it opened "uptown" on Broadway and 99th Street in 1933. Over the years it has featured everything from second-runs to porn to Japanese films to revivals. Now restored and twinned, the Metro is currently showing first-run films. The theater is also under consideration for landmark status, mainly because of its handsome glazed-terra-cotta Art Deco façade. Its new neon marquee is a beauty, too. No wonder Woody Allen used the Metro as a location in *Hannah and Her Sisters.*
   Phone: (212) 222–1200.

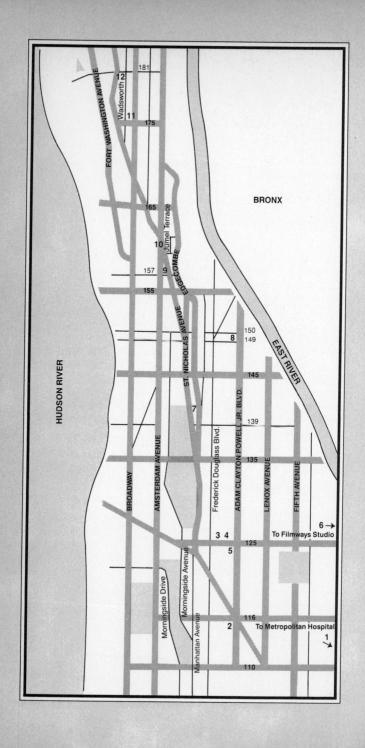

HARLEM/ WASHINGTON HEIGHTS

Surprises Uptown

King of Harlem: Paul Robeson as The Emperor Jones, *1933*

OFTEN written off as a crime-ridden ghetto by many white New Yorkers who've never experienced its grand boulevards, handsome brownstones, hilly streets, and proud spirit, Harlem is one of New York's most surprising and least understood communities. Some old-timers remember Harlem's grandest era— the 1920s and the 1930s—when the town was the undisputed capital of black culture in America. Known as the Harlem Renaissance, this vital period in Harlem's history was marked by music, poetry, theater, and some of New York's liveliest nightclubs and speakeasies. It was a time, too, when most of the country's best-known black entertainers—Paul Robeson, Bill "Bojangles" Robinson, Ethel Waters, Duke Ellington—lived in Harlem, and since they all made significant contributions to America's film history, today their former homes and apartment buildings are high on the list of Harlem must-sees for movie lovers.

Harlem and nearby Washington Heights also preserve some of New York's most historic movie theaters, including one built in 1913 that is considered to be the first movie palace in the City of New York. Although it's still packing people in, it's no longer showing movies; it's a Baptist church these days. Another Harlem theater still going strong is the legendary Apollo, which since the 1930s has hosted the biggest names in the black entertainment world. Closed down in the 1970s and faced with an uncertain future, the theater was brought back to life in the 1980s and is a symbol of a Harlem that's on the upswing. In the words of the Harlem Chamber of Commerce, "You haven't done this town till you've done it Uptown!"

1. METROPOLITAN HOSPITAL CENTER
1901 First Avenue

The Hospital's hospital . . . Metropolitan was the principal location for the 1971 black comedy that fleshed out our worst fears about the medical profession. Paddy Chayefsky won an Academy Award for his screenplay, and George C. Scott received an Oscar nomination for his performance as a hospital honcho in this made-in-Manhattan masterpiece. *The Pope of Greenwich Village* (1984) was another New York film that used Metropolitan Hospital as a location.

2. FIRST CORINTHIAN BAPTIST CHURCH
1212 Adam Clayton Powell, Jr., Boulevard

Now a church, this exuberant tile-faced building with its façade of columns and arches is also a milestone in the history of movie-going in New York: When it made its debut as the Regent Theater in 1913, this was the city's very first *deluxe* theater built expressly for the showing of motion pictures. Before that, movies were presented either in narrow storefront nickelodeons or in vaudeville theaters. The owners of the Regent, however, were banking on the

Regent Theater, 1948

fact that audiences were ready for something new—and better—and so, when the Regent opened, everything in the house was designed to make the experience of going to the movies a truly special event. The Regent featured its own eight-piece orchestra, a separate string trio, the city's first movie-house pipe organ, uniformed ushers, printed programs, and a special screen with black borders that made the picture seem brighter and clearer. Unfortunately, even all of these innovations did not provide enough incentive to fill the new theater, especially since it was all the way up on 116th Street and Seventh Avenue where the locals—who were mostly of German, Irish, and Jewish origin at the time—still felt that their money went further at the neighborhood vaudeville houses where they got a show *and* a movie. Thus, two months after opening, the Regent was in big trouble.

Meanwhile, as the owners of the Regent were trying to figure out how to salvage their investment, a man named Samuel L. Rothapfel, who had had quite a bit of success managing a movie house in Milwaukee, was deciding upon his next career move. Recently arrived in New York with the intention of offering his expertise to Marcus Loew's theater chain, Rothapfel got turned off with the organization after witnessing an ugly argument in the Loew's office on the day of his job interview. Upon leaving Loew's, Rothapfel ran into the owner of the Regent, who had heard of Rothapfel's success in the Midwest and proposed that he try his hand with the floundering theater up in Harlem.

To make a long story a little shorter, Rothapfel took the assignment and quickly set to refining the Regent. First off, he moved the projector from the balcony down to the orchestra floor, which provided a sharper, brighter image on the screen. Next he gave the screen its own special curtain to add drama to the film presentation. Rothapfel's most important innovation, however, had to do with the music. While house orchestras often played during the film portion of a vaudeville show, little attempt was made by the conductor to have the music fit what was going on up on the screen. Rothapfel changed all that by carefully choosing the music and programming it to match the action and mood of the film. In doing this, he added a new dimension to the experience of seeing a film. He also turned around the fortunes of the Regent.

Of the "new" Regent's initial program, *Motion Picture News* wrote: "A remarkable incident in the history of the motion picture took place Monday evening of last week at the Regent Theater, 116th Street and Seventh Avenue, New York City. This sounds serious, and the writer so intends it. . . . The picture was *The Last Days of Pompeii.* This excellent production Mr. Rothapfel centered in an environment so pleasing, so perfect in artistic detail, that it seemed as if the setting were prerequisite to the picture, that to an educated audience the two should, and must hereafter, go together." In short, the age of the movie palace had begun.

After his success with the Regent, Rothapfel moved downtown to the Strand, the Rialto, the Rivoli, and his ultimate triumph, the theater which bore his nickname: the Roxy. Whereas all these theaters have since been demolished, the historic building where Roxy began his New York career in 1913 still stands, reborn as a Baptist church. Hallelujah!

3. APOLLO THEATER
253 West 125th Street

One of America's most important show-business shrines, the Apollo has hosted practically every major black performing artist of the twentieth century on its stage at some point during its over-fifty-year history. Bessie Smith, Billie Holiday, Duke Ellington, Ella Fitzgerald, Louis Armstrong, Pearl Bailey, Aretha Franklin, Ray Charles, James Brown, Dionne Warwick, the Supremes, the Jackson Five have all played the Apollo, and the list could go on and on. It is said that when a teenaged Elvis Presley came to New York for

The Apollo, ca. 1935

the first time, the one place he wanted to see was the Apollo. A decade later, the same story would be told of the Beatles on their first trip to America.

The building that houses the Apollo was built in 1913 as Hurting & Seaman's New Theater, which presented burlesque and vaudeville to a Harlem that was then predominantly white. Twenty years later Harlem was a very different community when entrepreneur Frank Schiffman took over the theater and started showcasing black entertainers on their home ground as well as relying on black audiences to fill the Apollo's seats. This was very different from a number of other fashionable Harlem nightspots (such as the famed Cotton Club), which featured black acts on their stages but refused to allow locals in the audience.

Three years after the Apollo opened, a white reporter for the *New York World Telegram* published the following account of a firsthand visit to what many people at that time considered a very exotic place:

> The Apollo is a sort of uptown Met dedicated to furious jazz, coffee-colored chorus girls and grinning, drawling comedians ... the first stand and last jump-off for the large caravanserai of Harlem entertainers. ... The theater stands behind a gaudy neon sign on West 125th Street, between a haberdashery and a leather-goods store. The sidewalk outside is a favored location for old men lugging sandwich signs and pitchmen unloading razor blades and patent medicines. You buy your ticket at a sidewalk booth (from fifteen cents mornings to a fifty-cent top Wednesday and Saturday nights) and enter through a narrow lobby lined with bathroom tiles, glistening mirrors and photographs of such Harlem idols as Ethel Waters and Louis Armstrong, all affectionately inscribed to the Apollo. At the candy counter you can buy chocolate bars and peanuts, but no gum. That is to protect the seats. In the lobby, three or four colored boys generally are waiting for their dates to show up.

Whereas Harlem's whites-only clubs eventually moved downtown (the Cotton Club relocated to Broadway and 48th Street in the late 1930s) or closed down, the Apollo continued to flourish through the 1960s. By the 1970s, however, when America's color barriers and complexes had been somewhat broken down through the civil rights movement, and when many black entertainers found that they could make better money in the mainstream, the Apollo fell upon hard times. By 1976 the theater, no longer able to book top talent and no longer able to fill seats, closed down. Since then, several attempts have been made to reopen the legendary establishment. The most recent, which took place in the mid-1980s and saw the Apollo totally refurbished and equipped with the latest in video technology, seems promising. Now under black ownership and management, the Apollo celebrated its rebirth with a network television special, "Motown Returns to the Apollo." Taped on the premises in May 1985, it featured Bill Cosby as host. Since then, major stars have returned to the Apollo's stage and/or have used its media facilities to produce music videos. More good news is that the theater has opened an Apollo Theater Hall of Fame, with a photo gallery of legendary Apollo performers as well as a display of memorabilia connected with the theater and its stars. Hooray for Harlem!

For Apollo information, phone: (212) 749–5838.

4. MOVIECENTER 5
235 West 125th Street

A symbol of Harlem on the upswing, this new cinema is housed in the restored shell of the former Loew's Victoria Theater, which had been shuttered since 1970. The theater—distinguished by an exotic ancient-Egyptian-style façade designed by Thomas W. Lamb—opened in 1917 as a 2,225-seat house. The new multiplex, with four theaters in the original Loew's Victoria building and a fifth next door, is significant not only because it has managed to preserve the exterior of architect Lamb's historic structure, but also because it brings first-run movies back to Harlem. In fact, before Moviecenter 5 opened in early 1987, not one movie theater was operating within the Harlem community.

Phone: (212) 222-8900.

5. OSCAR MICHEAUX FILM CORPORATION SITE
200 West 125th Street

A fried chicken joint now marks the spot where one of the country's most prolific and ingenious independent film makers of the 1920s and 1930s once had his headquarters. Unknown to most

A scene from Oscar Micheaux's Underworld, *1936*

white and many black Americans, Oscar Micheaux was a black from the Midwest who came to Harlem in the early 1920s and specialized in producing "race films." These featured all-black casts playing the roles—handsome heroes, glamorous heroines, villainous gangsters—that they were denied in mainstream movies at the time. Literally a one-man film industry, Micheaux wrote, directed, produced, and promoted the majority of his pictures and was successful in getting them distributed not only in Europe but also in the U.S. South, where he convinced many white theater owners of the profits to be made from setting up special matinee showings of his features for black audiences.

With a few exceptions, Micheaux's movies rarely dealt with the important social and economic issues that confronted his race. Instead, he produced highly commercial black versions of the same formula stories that spelled success for Hollywood. Typical Micheaux titles were *Daughter of the Congo,* a 1930 swashbuckler that had a dashing black cavalry officer rescuing a wealthy Negro girl lost in the wilds of Africa, and *Underworld* (1936), a standard 1930s gangster yarn in which both the good guys *and* the bad guys were black. Even Micheaux's stars were marketed with Hollywood counterparts in mind: suave Lorenzo Tucker, for example, was the "Black Valentino," sultry Ethel Moses was the "Negro Harlow," sexy Bee Freeman was the "Sepia Mae West," and Slick Chester, who often played gangsters, was the "Colored Cagney." These stars, by the way, were usually light-skinned, and Micheaux is sometimes criticized today for the unreal black world that his films created. But this criticism is offset by films like *The Exile* (1931), which dealt with the sensitive issue of a black man who falls in love with a woman he thinks is white, and *God's Stepchildren* (1937), which focused on the perils of trying to "pass" for white in a racist society. Ultimately, Micheaux was not a philosopher but a film maker, and his films provided black audiences of the 1920s and 1930s with positive self-images at a time when the major studios systematically kept people of color in their place on screen as maids, mammies, butlers, and shoeshine boys.

6. FOODWAYS
246 East 127th Street

Now an East Harlem supermarket, this barn of a building on the southwest corner of 127th Street and Second Avenue reigned for two decades as one of New York City's most active movie studios. Among the many features that were done at Filmways (which had been a city transit garage before it was made a studio) during the 1960s and 1970s were *Murder Incorporated* (1960), *Splendor in the Grass* (1961), *The Brotherhood* (1968), *Klute* (1971), *The Godfather* (1971), *The Taking of Pelham 1 2 3* (1973), *Annie Hall* (1977), and *Manhattan* (1979). Filmways also saw a number of TV series lensed on its soundstages, the most famous of these being "The Defenders," "The Nurses," and "The Blue Men." When the

Foodways, formerly Filmways studios

studio closed in the early 1980s, one of the reasons was supposedly because the neighborhood had become too dangerous. Fortunately, by then the city had a number of new production facilities such as the reborn Astoria Studios to fill the void caused by Filmways' demise.

Across the street from the Filmways building, another famous movie studio once stood. Also a "conversion," Cosmopolitan Studios was created in 1918 out of a former nightclub on the east side of Second Avenue at 127th Street. The man behind the make-over was William Randolph Hearst, who at the time was obsessed with turning his showgirl protégée Marion Davies into a movie star. In typical Hearstian fashion, the famous newspaper man/movie mogul spared no expense in order to make Cosmopolitan one of the top studios in town. His ultimate extravagance was the special five-piece string orchestra that he hired to play popular melodies in order to keep Miss Davies in a pleasant frame of mind between takes. The group was nicknamed "The Marion Davies Orchestra," and Marion is said to have used them throughout her career.

William Randolph Hearst's Cosmopolitan Studios

7. ETHEL WATERS RESIDENCE
580 St. Nicholas Avenue

Throughout most of the 1920s and on into the 1930s, Harlem not only presented a place for black Americans to find decent housing in a country that usually denied it to them, it also promised intellectual stimulation and creative fulfillment. Popularly known as the Harlem Renaissance, the flourishing of black culture that took place in Harlem in the 1920s and 1930s was marked by large numbers of talented writers, poets, artists, and performers flocking to Upper Manhattan. One of the major centers of the Harlem Renaissance was a posh apartment house at 580 St. Nicholas Avenue in the fashionable Sugar Hill district. Known simply as "Five eighty" to the in-crowd, the building boasted many celebrity tenants during its heyday, but none more famous than Ethel Waters, considered the first black woman to win star billing both on the stage and in the movies. Of her films, *Cabin in the Sky* (1943), *Stage Door Canteen* (1943), *Pinky* (1949), and *The Member of the Wedding* (1952) are the most memorable. Miss Waters was also a star of early television, playing the title role in the "Beulah" series during its first season in 1950–51.

8. DUNBAR APARTMENTS
2588 Adam Clayton Powell, Jr., Boulevard

This cluster of six six-story walk-up apartment buildings between West 149th and 150th streets was built in the late 1920s by John D. Rockefeller as the country's first large cooperative-apartment complex for blacks. Named for the black American poet Paul Laurence Dunbar (1872–1906), the Dunbar offered courtyards

Dunbar resident Leigh Whipper in Of Mice and Men, *1939*

Harlem star Bill "Bojangles" Robinson with Shirley Temple in The Little Colonel, *1935*

and gardens, published its own gossipy newsletter, and housed some of Harlem's toniest citizens. Among those who enjoyed Dunbar luxuries were the dynamic NAACP leader W. E. B. Du Bois, poet Countee Cullen, newspaperman Asa Philip Randolph, and explorer Matt Henson, who was part of Admiral Perry's North Pole expedition and the first Westerner to set foot on the Pole.

The world of show business was represented at the Dunbar by the famed leading man and operatic basso Paul Robeson, stage and movie character actor Leigh Whipper, violinist-composer Clarence Cameron White, and the illustrious musical performer Bill "Bojangles" Robinson, who sang and tap-danced in many major films throughout the 1930s and is especially remembered for his screen appearances with Shirley Temple. In addition to performing with the child star in *The Little Colonel* (1935), *The Littlest Rebel* (1935), *Rebecca of Sunnybrook Farm* (1938), and *Just Around the Corner* (1939), Robinson also choreographed Temple's 1936 film *Dimples*. In 1943, Twentieth Century–Fox's all-black film, *Stormy Weather,* not only starred Robinson but was based loosely on his career in show business.

Today the Dunbar Apartments, after having fallen into disrepair during the 1960s and 1970s, have been renovated and are poised to play a role in what many civic leaders hope will be a second Harlem Renaissance.

*Duke Ellington
residence*

9. DUKE ELLINGTON RESIDENCE
935 St. Nicholas Avenue

A plaque at the entrance of this Harlem Gothic apartment building indicates that it has been declared a National Historic Landmark because Edward Kennedy "Duke" Ellington once lived here. Ellington resided in apartment 4A of the building from 1939 to 1961, and for much of the time his lady friend Beatrice Ellis lived there too. More often known as Evie Ellington, even though Ms. Ellis was never officially married to the Duke, she was still with him when they moved downtown to West End Avenue in the early 1960s. By that time, however, they saw little of one another since Duke was constantly on the road and Evie had become reclusive in her later years.

Although known principally as a musician, composer, and band leader, Ellington was connected with motion pictures throughout his career. As a performer, Duke and his band appeared in a number of films in the 1930s and 1940s, including *Murder at the Vanities* (1934), *Belle of the Nineties* (1934), and *Cabin in the Sky* (1943). In addition, Ellington wrote music for the Marx Brothers' *A Day at the Races* (1936), and did complete scores for *Anatomy of a Murder* (1959), *Paris Blues* (1960), *Assault on a Queen* (1964), and *Change of Mind* (1968). His *Paris Blues* score received an Academy Award nomination. Of Ellington, Orson Welles is reported to have said that, next to himself, Duke was the only genius he had ever known.

Ellington died of lung cancer in 1974 and was buried at Woodlawn Cemetery in the Bronx, beside his parents. When his life partner Evie died (also of lung cancer) two years later, she was laid to rest in the same plot. The site of Duke and Evie's Harlem apartment—where they shared their happiest years together—was given landmark status that same year.

10. PAUL ROBESON HOUSE
16 Jumel Terrace

One of Harlem's many lovely surprises, Jumel Terrace preserves a clutch of handsome townhouses on a small cobbled street. Tourists come here mainly to visit the historic Morris-Jumel Mansion, a columned Georgian residence dating back to 1765, which sits on a grassy hill on the east side of Jumel Terrace. Movie lovers will be more interested in the townhouse at number 16, however, because it was the last Harlem home of the great black actor Paul Robeson. In addition to his stage triumphs—notably in Shakespeare's *Othello* and in Eugene O'Neill's *All God's Chillun Got Wings* and *The Emperor Jones*—Robeson will always be remembered for his screen performances in *The Emperor Jones* and as Joe in Universal's 1936 film version of *Show Boat,* in which he sings "Old Man River."

Robeson is also remembered for his leftist political views, which got him into no end of trouble with the McCarthy committee and the U.S. State Department in the late 1940s and well into the 1950s. Through it all, Robeson remained true to his country—even when the State Department revoked his passport in 1950 and refused to allow him to travel out of the country. When he finally got his

Paul Robeson residence (second from left) on Jumel Terrace

passport back eight years later, he went on to spend several years in Europe and the U.S.S.R. He returned to the U.S. in the early 1960s and moved into 16 Jumel Terrace, where he lived as a virtual recluse until failing health forced him to take up residence with a sister in Philadelphia. He died there in 1976.

P.S. From 1939 to 1941, Robeson lived not far from Jumel Terrace at 555 Edgecombe Avenue. One of Harlem's grandest apartment buildings, 555 Edgecombe Avenue has been declared the Robeson Home National Historic Landmark.

11. UNITED CHURCH
Broadway and 175th Street

This spectacular neo-Assyrian fortress at the northeast corner of Broadway and 175th Street was called "the apogee of the movie palace" when it debuted on February 22, 1930, as Loew's 175th Street Theater. Designed by Thomas W. Lamb, the 175th Street featured an interior that looked like a great gaudy Hindu temple. One of Loew's five "Wonder" theaters (so called because each had a huge Robert Morton Wonder organ), the 175th Street joined the Paradise in the Bronx, the Kings in Brooklyn, the Valencia in Queens, and the Jersey across the Hudson in Jersey City as the final jewel in the crown formed by Loew's most sumptuous New York metropolitan-area movie palaces. Today the Wonder organ is still going strong on 175th Street—not as part of any film presentation, but to back up the religious services now staged here by a charismatic preacher and radio personality known as Reverend Ike.

Reverend Ike's United Church, formerly Loew's 175th Street Theater

Inside Loew's 175th Street

12. THE HEIGHTS
150 Wadsworth Avenue

In October of 1913, a little movie theater called the Heights opened on Wadsworth Avenue just south of 183rd Street in Washington Heights. Today, three-quarters of a century later, the theater, still called the Heights, is still showing movies and can claim to be the oldest movie house in the city to operate continuously under the same name.

Small wonder: the Heights, opened in 1913

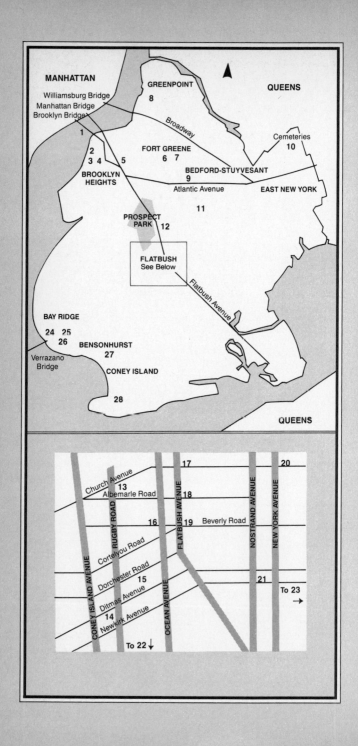

BROOKLYN

Hometown of the Stars

Alice Mann, Fatty Arbuckle, and Buster Keaton in
Fatty at Coney Island, *1917*

MAE WEST, Mickey Rooney, Rita Hayworth, Barbra Streisand, Mary Tyler Moore, Danny Kaye, Susan Hayward, Lena Horne, Woody Allen, George Gershwin, Irving Thalberg, Veronica Lake, Clara Bow, Mel Brooks—the list of megastars who hail from Brooklyn would make a sizable who's who of the entertainment industry. This chapter's itinerary takes in the actual sites where many of Brooklyn's illustrious natives were born and raised and also visits such star Brooklyn neighborhoods as Flatbush, with its pastoral streets and landmark mansions, one of which starred in the film *Sophie's Choice* . . . Bensonhurst, land of *Saturday Night Fever* . . . Coney Island, an inspiration to film makers from the 1890s through the 1980s . . . and Brooklyn Heights, whose ivy-covered townhouses, landmark churches, and knockout views of the Lower Manhattan skyline across the harbor have made it a favorite location for New York movies. Other discoveries awaiting movie lovers in Brooklyn are the site of the legendary Vitagraph Studios, a major force in the film industry at the turn of the century and still being used for NBC television productions . . . Erasmus Hall High, boasting an impressive pedigree (it was founded in 1887), dazzling architecture, and stellar alumni . . . and Cypress Hills Cemetery, where fans can pay their respects to Miss Mae West, who, despite her fifty years in Hollywood, never forgot her Brooklyn roots. Which is true of the best of Brooklynites and is perhaps the secret of their success: They always remember where they came from—and therefore always know who they are.

1. BROOKLYN BRIDGE

Fredric March and Carole Lombard sailed under it in *Nothing Sacred* (1937); F. Scott Fitzgerald wrote about it in *Brooklyn Bridge* (1940)—a script he did for a Columbia film that was never produced; Johnny Weissmuller dove off it in *Tarzan's New York Adventure* (1944); Gene Kelly, Frank Sinatra, and Jules Munshin danced over it in *On the Town* (1949); Superman flew Lois Lane alongside it in

Brooklyn Bridge, 1880s

Superman (1978); Sidney Lumet covered it with yellow linoleum so that Diana Ross, Michael Jackson, and a cast of hundreds could "Ease On Down the Road" across it in *The Wiz* (1978); Meryl Streep, Kevin Kline, and Peter MacNicol drank champagne atop it in *Sophie's Choice* (1982); and there have been hundreds more films that have taken advantage of this century-old architectural wonder of Gothic arches and spider-web steel cables linking downtown Manhattan with Brooklyn. Surprisingly, one of the most memorable film sequences featuring the Brooklyn Bridge is in the 1978 disco-docudrama *Saturday Night Fever,* when, toward the end of the movie, the youth played by John Travolta has finally gotten up the nerve to leave his provincial Brooklyn neighborhood to try his luck in near-but-oh-so-far Manhattan. Travolta's crossing the Brooklyn Bridge is a poignant, pivotal moment in the film—a rite of passage. Whereas the Verrazano-Narrows Bridge was the scene of the immature, dangerous games of Travolta and his friends earlier in the story, the Brooklyn Bridge—older, more substantial, and leading to Manhattan rather than Staten Island—comes to represent the challenge of moving on, growing up. Quite clearly, at least in the movies, this is not just another pretty bridge.

2. BROOKLYN HEIGHTS PROMENADE

The dramatic view of the Brooklyn Bridge, Lower Manhattan, New York Harbor, and the Statue of Liberty that can be seen from the Brooklyn Heights Promenade may well by NYC's ultimate photo opportunity. Built in 1951 to protect Brooklyn Heights residents from the sight and some of the sounds of the Brooklyn-Queens Expressway, which runs beneath it, this paved esplanade—with its trees, shrubs, and park benches—quickly became one of the most popular spots in the neighborhood for strollers, joggers, romantic couples—and film makers. Indeed, sometimes it seems as though directors deliberately "house" a major character in Brooklyn Heights just so they can feature a scene set on the Promenade. A case in point: *Three Days of the Condor,* where, because Faye Dunaway happens to live in Brooklyn Heights, Robert Redford (whom she happens to be hiding in her apartment) is able to have a dramatic Promenade confrontation with bad-guy Cliff Robertson. Other features in recent years that have also used the Promenade to add to the drama—and often the romance—of a scene or two are: *Moonstruck* (1987), *Prizzi's Honor* (1985), *Luna* (1979), *Saturday Night Fever* (1978), *The Sentinel* (1977), and *Sweet November* (1968). And let's not forget the "Patty Duke Show," which was filmed in Manhattan, set in Brooklyn Heights, and showed off the Promenade during its opening credits for several prime-time television seasons in the 1960s. In addition to its TV and film appearances, the Promenade is constantly used for print ads and fashion photography. For movie lovers planning to visit the Promenade, don't leave home without your cameras!

Prizzi's Honor *mansion*

3. "PRIZZI'S HONOR" MANSION
3 Pierrepont Place

New York actor and acting teacher William Hickey was nominated for an Academy Award in 1986 for his portrayal of the dying Mafia chieftain, Don Corrado, in John Huston's *Prizzi's Honor*. In the film, the fabulous brick palazzo with magnificent gardens that was Don Corrado's home and headquarters was actually a landmark Brooklyn Heights mansion built in 1857 for a wealthy local named Abiel Abbot Low. Low's son, Seth, went on to be mayor of Brooklyn, president of Columbia College, and eventually mayor of New York, after Brooklyn and the other boroughs were consolidated into the City of New York in the 1890s. Little did Mr. Low know that his handsome family home would one day be in the hands of the underworld.

P.S. Another *Prizzi's Honor* location—standing just across the street from the Pierrepont Place palazzo—is the Brooklyn apartments at 57 Montague Street. It was here that Jack Nicholson had that pad with the great view of the Brooklyn Bridge.

4. "THE SENTINEL" BUILDING
10 Montague Terrace

It looks like an idyllic place to live, this beautiful Brooklyn Heights brick building with its wrought-iron gate, lush front garden, and elegant stained-glass entryway. But in the 1977 supernatural thriller *The Sentinel,* Cristina Raines found anything but peace and quiet when she rented an apartment here. For, unbeknownst to her, she had entered "the gates of hell," and for the rest of the film she battled all manner of ghosts and ghouls as neighbors. The real

Brooklyn Paramount, ca. 1930

estate agent who got Miss Raines into this otherworldy mess was none other than Ava Gardner, playing one of the many cameo roles that have kept her more or less in show business for the last two decades.

5. PARAMOUNT THEATER SITE
385 Flatbush Avenue Extension

The sweeping marquee that once wrapped around Flatbush and DeKalb Avenues is gone, as are the two nine-story-high neon signs that told all of Brooklyn that this was the fabled Paramount Theater. With 4,126 seats, the Brooklyn Paramount reigned as the borough's biggest movie palace from 1928—when it opened with Nancy Carroll starring in *Manhattan Cocktail*—to 1962, when its last picture show was *Hatari* with John Wayne. Designed by Rapp and Rapp, the architectural firm responsible for the Paramount Theater on Times Square, the Brooklyn Paramount was just as famous for its Paramount–Publix stage shows as for its films. Early in the theater's history, a chorus girl named Ginger Rogers leapt successfully from the Paramount stage-show circuit to Broadway and eventually to the Paramount Studios in Astoria.

By the time the 1950s rolled around, the once-lavish stage shows at the Paramount had given way to rock-and-roll extravaganzas, many hosted by New York D.J.s Alan Freed and Murray the K. By that time, too, Long Island University had acquired the office building that towered over the Paramount, and in 1962, when the theater shut down permanently, L.I.U. turned the massive auditorium—with its mighty Wurlitzer organ and its star-studded "atmospheric" ceiling—into a gymnasium. It's still that today.

6. MICKEY ROONEY BIRTHPLACE
57 Willoughby Avenue

Although Mickey Rooney's mythological "Andy Hardy" hometown of Carvel was bulldozed into oblivion in 1970 after MGM had sold off its backlot to real estate developers, his real-life hometown, Fort Greene in Brooklyn, endures. In fact, the residential block where Mickey's family was living when he came into the world as Joe Yule, Jr., on September 23, 1920, looks as if it hasn't changed that much in the last seventy years—with the unfortunate exception that Micky's house is no longer on the street. He probably wouldn't remember it anyway, because he didn't spend much time on Willoughby Avenue. Two weeks after his Brooklyn birth, little Joe went "on the road" with his vaudevillian parents. He was fifteen months old when he made his stage debut, seven when he became famous on film through the *Mickey McGuire* shorts, and seventeen when he did his first (of fifteen) *Andy Hardys* for MGM.

7. BARBARA STANWYCK BIRTHPLACE
246 Classon Avenue

A vacant lot in a run-down neighborhood near Brooklyn's Pratt Institute is all that marks the spot where Ruby Stevens was born on July 16, 1907. The youngest of five children, Ruby had a tough childhood. Not only did her mother die when she was two years old but her father deserted the family soon thereafter, leaving Ruby to be cared for by an elder sister, who often farmed her out to board with other families. But Ruby was tough, too, and at age fifteen she started working as a chorus girl in a nightclub atop the Strand Theater on Broadway. Since then, the woman who became Barbara Stanwyck has never stopped working. Witness, some sixty-five years after her show-biz debut, Stanwyck's recent starring role in the prime-time TV soap opera, "The Colbys."

Early Stanwyck,
ca. 1929

Brooklyn bombshell:
Mae West

The Astral, where Mae
West may have been
born

8.   MAE WEST BIRTHPLACE?
184 Franklin Street

One thing is certain, she was definitely from Brooklyn. Just
where in Brooklyn is another story. Indeed, Ridgewood, Bushwick,
Flatbush, and Greenpoint have all claimed Mae West as their own.
Perhaps not wanting to disappoint any of her fellow Brooklynites,
Mae offers no help in her autobiography, *Goodness Had Nothing
to Do with It* (Prentice Hall, 1959), where all she has to say on the
subject of her birthplace is: "I was born on a respectable street in
Brooklyn." In addition to the question of where, there is also the
question of *when*. Mae claimed that she came into the world in
1893—but there are those who have calculated the year to be more
like 1887. And just who was her father? Mae's stories had John
Patrick West being everything from a prize fighter to a detective to
a medical doctor. In reality, it seems, Mr. West ran a livery stable
in Brooklyn. Which brings us back to where. This exotic Gothic
"fortress" on Franklin Street between Java and India streets in
Greenpoint is frequently said to be Mae's birthplace. Ironically,
Mae's Hollywood home of some fifty years was an exotic Art Deco
fortress apartment building called Ravenswood.

9. LENA HORNE HOUSE
189 Chauncey Street

She made history in 1941 when she became the first black woman to be signed to a long-term contract by a major Hollywood studio. Before that, black performers freelanced in Hollywood, picking up jobs as they came along at whatever studio happened to be casting maids, butlers, bootblacks, etc. in the less-enlightened times and movies of the 1920s and 1930s. But Lena Horne changed all that with her MGM contract—or so she had hoped. As it turned out, Lena was usually featured on screen as an exotic lead singer in a production number that could easily be cut from the film when it played in the South.

Lena Horne was born in Brooklyn, and spent the first seven years of her life in her paternal grandparents' three-story brownstone on Chauncey Street in the Bedford–Stuyvesant district. Because her parents separated not long after her birth, Lena spent her formative years growing up under the strong influence of her grandmother Cora Calhoun Horne. A vigorous civil rights activist and a stalwart member of the black bourgeoisie, Cora Horne taught her grand-daughter to be polite to the less-advantaged white families that lived in the neighborhood, but refused to allow her to play with any children—white or black—whose behavior and language did not meet her high standards.

Lena's life on Chauncey Street was filled with cultural opportunities. While Cora often took the child along to her many club meetings, Lena's grandfather exposed her to museums, theater, and movies. Indeed, all that Lena missed were her parents. Occasionally she would be visited by her father, who had shunned middle-class respectability for the freewheeling life of a Harlem gambling man.

Lena Horne house
(on left)

Lena in Hollywood: Stormy Weather, *1943*

Less often, her mother, who was a sometime actress and who didn't get along with Grandmother Horne, would arrange to see Lena away from Chauncey Street.

Lena's life took an abrupt turn when she was seven years old and her mother decided that it was time to have her daughter live with her. Thus began a long period of instability that had Lena moving all over the South and the Midwest. Sometimes she would live with her mother; other times, when her mother was pursuing her theatrical career, Lena would be put up with relatives or family friends. Eventually, when her mother realized that she couldn't provide a proper home for her daughter, Lena, now in her early teens, returned to the house on Chauncey Street.

Unfortunately, Lena's grandparents died within three months of one another a year or so after her return, and she was uprooted once again. Lena's next home was with a woman-friend of her grandmother's. As it turned out, the woman was a very kind lady who encouraged Lena in dance and theater. But then Lena's mother, who had recently remarried, again entered the picture and moved Lena in with her and her new husband. There followed a series of dreary apartments in Brooklyn, the Bronx, and finally Harlem. By this time, Lena was old enough to help support the family, and she wound up auditioning for the chorus of the famous Harlem night spot, the Cotton Club. She got the job, and suddenly a whole new life began.

Like her old life, however, show business would also involve frequent uprootings, and the same loneliness. In her autobiography, *Lena* (Doubleday, 1965), Miss Horne speaks movingly of her life-long affection for her grandparents' Brooklyn brownstone: "The Brooklyn house was coming, I suppose, to symbolize normalcy and stability to me. I felt I belonged there and all through my life— until my father finally sold it a few years ago—the existence of that house, the knowledge that it was there, unchanged, was a comfort to me."

Dear Lena Horne, it's still there.

10. CYPRESS HILLS CEMETERY
833 Jamaica Avenue

One of the many cemeteries that are clustered along the border between northern Brooklyn and southern Queens, Cypress Hills is a vast hilly enclave of trees, flowering shrubs, and graves that range from traditional headstones to architecturally exotic mausoleums to small stone slabs embossed with Chinese characters. Toward the back of the property, near the Queens border, stands a huge white-granite building with stained-glass windows and a dramatic col-umned entryway. This is the Cypress Hills Abbey mausoleum, and inside, off to the right, along aisle EE, movie lovers will discover a whole wall of crypts that bear the name "West." At the bottom of the stack is John E. West, 1900–1964; above him are John West, 1862–1935; Beverly West, 1898–1982; Matilda West, 1875–1930; and, at the very top, one of Brooklyn's most illustrious native daughters, the legendary Mae West, 1893–1980. Reportedly, when Mae was first interred in the Abbey, she had been put in the number-three slot. Once her will was read, however, it became quite clear that Mae would not settle for anything less than top billing, and Cypress Hills saw that her wishes were carried out.

Besides Mae, Cypress Hills Abbey also houses the crypt of comic character-actor Victor Moore as well as that of prizefighter James J. ("Gentleman Jim") Corbett (1866–1933). While best known for his boxing exploits, Corbett occupies a unique position in motion-picture history because in 1894 he signed an exclusive deal with the Kinetoscope Exchange Company (the company that marketed Edison's Kinetoscope motion-picture viewing device) to appear in filmed fight sequences *only* for that company. In so doing, Corbett was the first performer to sign a motion-picture-star contract.

Mae West crypt,
Cypress Hills Abbey

11. BARBRA STREISAND BIRTHPLACE
457 Schenectady Avenue

In the early 1940s, the Brooklyn phone directory listed Emmanuel Streisand as living in this six-story brick apartment building not far from Kings County Hospital. Streisand was an English teacher married to Diana Rosen, the daughter of a Brooklyn cantor who also worked in the garment district. The couple had a son, Sheldon, born in 1935, and a daughter, Barbara, who came into the world in 1942. Less than a year later, Mr. Streisand died and Mrs. Streisand left Schenectady Avenue and moved herself and her two kids into her parents' home in nearby Williamsburg.

12. PROSPECT PARK

One of Brooklyn's greatest treasures, Prospect Park provides the borough with 345 acres of streams and ponds, green lawns and gardens. Designed by Frederick Law Olmsted and Calvert Vaux—the same team responsible for Manhattan's Central Park—Prospect Park was completed in 1874, some twenty-four years before the independent City of Brooklyn would become part of the City of New York.

Movie lovers, especially, will be interested in one of the park's 1986 additions—the Celebrity Path—which wraps around an enchanting lake over by the Japanese Garden. Brooklyn's answer to Hollywood's star-studded Walk of Fame sidewalk, the Celebrity Path honors the talents of artists, performers, and athletes who were born or who flourished in Brooklyn. Among the stars who are remembered here with their names inscribed on stepping-stones around the lake are Woody Allen, Clara Bow, Mel Brooks, Dom DeLuise, Vincent Gardenia, George Gershwin, Jack Gilford, Harry Houdini, Moss Hart, Susan Hayward, Lena Horne, Edward Everett Horton, Danny Kaye, Arthur Miller, Zero Mostel, Phil Silvers, Neil Simon, Barbara Stanwyck, Gene Tierney, and Mae West.

Harder to find, but also a must for movie lovers visiting the park, is the tiny, fenced-off Quaker cemetery at the center of the property (best reached from the 16th Street and Prospect Park Southwest entrance). A private burial ground that dates back to 1849 (some twenty-five years before Prospect Park was built), this is a peaceful preserve of green hills, big trees, and ancient gravestones. One of the newer memorials, on the slope to the right of the main gate (which is always locked), marks the grave of Montgomery Clift, who was buried here in 1966. Although Clift's funeral was held at the Episcopal Church of St. James in Manhattan, he rests in Prospect Park because his mother, Sunny Clift, had become enamored of the Quaker religion in her later years. Clift's simple headstone, by the way, was designed by John Benson, the same artist responsible for John F. Kennedy's at Arlington National Cemetery in Virginia. The crocuses that once bloomed in front of Clift's grave were planted by his good friend and colleague, actress Nancy Walker.

Sophie's Choice *house,*
Flatbush

13. "SOPHIE'S CHOICE" HOUSE
101 Rugby Road

They painted this wonderful Queen Anne–style Victorian mansion shocking pink for the 1980s film based on William Styron's 1970s novel about 1940s Brooklyn, *Sophie's Choice.* As Yetta Zimmerman's Brooklyn boarding house, this "Pink Palace" was where a young writer from the South named Stingo (Peter MacNicol) first lived in New York, and where he slowly discovered the dark secrets of his fellow tenants Sophie (Meryl Streep) and Nathan (Kevin Kline). The Pink Palace, actually a private house on a magnificent residential block of Flatbush, was painted back to gray once the film crew had gotten all their shots.

14. MARY PICKFORD HOUSE
1320 Ditmas Avenue

According to local legend, this handsome half-timbered Tudor house was built for Mary Pickford by the executives of the Flatbush-based Vitagraph Company so that their new star would have a luxurious Brooklyn bungalow near the studios. The same story goes on to say that Miss Pickford never moved into this Brooklyn house because Vitagraph moved to Hollywood before the place was finished.

To set the record somewhat straight, Vitagraph never *moved* to Hollywood; it did set up studios there, but these were always in addition to its Brooklyn operations. Also, Miss Pickford was *never* a Vitagraph artist, although in the spring of 1916 it looked as if she might become one. Shopping around for a new studio at the time, Miss Pickford was in serious negotiations with Vitagraph's head, Albert E. Smith, when a very minor incident—detailed in Terry Ramsaye's *A Million and One Nights* (Simon & Schuster, 1926)—occurred to nix the whole proposition. It seems that during a final

Mary Pickford house, Flatbush

meeting between Mary and Smith, there had been much small talk about the new baby that had just been born to Smith and his wife. When at the end of the meeting, Pickford and Vitagraph had still not come to terms, Mary, fully expecting another meeting, kept everything cordial by asking when she might see Smith's new baby. To this, Smith, more interested in contracts than in babies, answered: "Just as soon as we get this business signed up and out of the way." Not appreciating Smith's crass sense of priorities, the ever-so-proper Miss Pickford came back with, "If that's it, I'll never see the baby," and kissed Vitagraph goodbye.

It wasn't a bad move on Mary's part, as it turned out, because six weeks later she signed a new contract with the studio she had just left, Adolph Zukor's Paramount. It was quite a contract for 1916: Mary would get more than a million dollars over a two-year period—plus an extra $300,000 when her pictures earned out. In addition, her name was to be the only one featured in any advertisements for her films, and the type-size of her name had to be larger than the title of the movie. She would also receive her own exclusive studio plus script, cast, and directorial approval. Needless to say, Mary never moved to Ditmas Avenue in Flatbush.

15. HELEN MORGAN HOUSE
466 East 18th Street

Ann Blyth starred in this singer's tragic life story in the 1957 Warner Bros. film, *The Helen Morgan Story.* Born on a farm in Illinois in 1900, Helen Morgan became the 1920s' most famous torch singer, appearing both on the stage—often in the Ziegfeld Follies—and in early talking pictures. Her greatest triumph on screen was in Rouben Mamoulian's 1929, made-in-Astoria musical,

Helen Morgan house, Flatbush

Applause, in which she sang "What I Wouldn't Do for That Man."
Miss Morgan also appeared as Julie in two screen versions of Jerome
Kern's *Show Boat,* a 1929 part-talking production that now is lost,
as well as the much more famous 1936 Universal extravaganza that
also starred Irene Dunne, Allan Jones, Paul Robeson, and Hattie
McDaniel. In 1941, Helen Morgan died of cirrhosis of the liver
brought on by years of alcoholism. In the 1920s and 1930s, she
called this barny 1899 Flatbush Victorian house home.

Helen Morgan in
Applause, *1929*

*Star apartment house:
the Buckingham Court*

16. BUCKINGHAM COURT
726 Ocean Avenue

It's all very Hollywood—the tapestry-brick façade, the bay windows and ornate iron grills, the gabled and tiled roofs. Add a few palm trees and it could almost be the set for a Raymond Chandler murder mystery. Actually, back in 1913, when the exotic Buckingham Court apartments were built at 726 Ocean Avenue, fantasy played a rather major role in Flatbush life—what with the Vitagraph studios churning out "eighty-seven miles of film a year" down on Elm Street. In those days, many of Vitagraph's actors, technicians, and executives lived in Flatbush, and it seems that Buckingham Court was an extremely popular address with the Vitagraph crowd. Indeed, the building's exotic architecture may well have been an attempt by developers to cater to the theatrical tastes of the Flatbush film colony. Locals say that Douglas Fairbanks, Mary Pickford, Fatty Arbuckle, and Norma and Constance Talmadge once lived at Buckingham Court. In the cases of Pickford, Fairbanks, and Arbuckle, this would seem highly unlikely, since none of them ever worked for Vitagraph. On the other hand, it is quite possible that the Talmadge sisters did reside at Buckingham Court—along with their forceful stage-mother, Peg, and their other sister, Natalie, who made some films in the 1910s but never became a star. Today the building is popular with the many West Indian immigrants who live in this section of Brooklyn.

17. ERASMUS HALL HIGH SCHOOL
911 Flatbush Avenue

Founded in 1787, Erasmus Hall High School is the oldest secondary school in New York State, and the second oldest in the U.S. Among the many famous Brooklynites educated within its hallowed halls are lyricist Betty Comden, record-company executive Clive Davis, chess star Bobby Fischer, Broadway producer Morton Gottlieb, *Vogue* features editor Amy Gross, radio personality Larry King, comedian Gabe Kaplan, diva Beverly Sills, pop star Stephanie Mills, novelist Mickey Spillane, and songwriter/performer Neil Diamond. And then there are the motion picture folk: Jeff Chandler (Ira Grossel during his Erasmus days), Susan Hayward (Edythe Marrener), Barbara Stanwyck (Ruby Stevens), Barbra Streisand, Jane Cowl, Aline MacMahon, Eli Wallach, Norma and Constance Talmadge. Movie lovers may remember, too, a famous fictional Erasmus student. Her name was Phoebe, and in her brief appearance at the end of *All About Eve,* we find her coveting Broadway star Eve Harrington's Sarah Siddons Prize, as the Eve Harrington–Margo Channing cycle is about to go round once again.

Today's Erasmus Hall is a very different place from the time when most of the people listed above were students there. Reflecting the changes in the ethnic make-up of Flatbush, Erasmus is now 90 percent black and 9 percent Asian. The native language of 25 percent of the students is Haitian Creole and that of another 10 percent is Spanish. In addition to the more traditional disciplines, today's Erasmus offers a strong computer-science program as well as courses in tourism and restaurant management. For future show folk, the school also has a variety of speech, drama, and music classes. Barbra Streisand, by the way, got her start in the Erasmus chorus.

STREISAND, BARBARA
Freshman Chorus, 1, 2; Choral
Club, 2-4.

Class of '59 star graduate

Erasmus Hall High School

18. ALBEMARLE THEATER
973 Flatbush Avenue

Just like the old Stanley Theater in Jersey City, Brooklyn's 2,700-seat Albemarle movie palace later served as a Kingdom Hall for the Jehovah's Witnesses. Among the renovations made to this historic 1920 theater, with its French Empire façade and enormous lobby, has been the installation of a baptismal font in the basement.

19. LOEW'S KINGS THEATER
1049 Flatbush Avenue

With two enormous lobbies, a 3,609-seat auditorium lavished with sculpted columns, magnificent murals, velvet draperies, and gilded ceilings, Loew's Kings brought the splendors of the French Renaissance to Flatbush Avenue. Designed by the Chicago firm of Rapp and Rapp and decorated by Harold W. Rambusch of New York, the Kings opened on September 7, 1929, with a "part-talkie" called *Evangeline,* starring Dolores del Rio, who showed up in person for the glamorous event. Also on the bill was a stage show that featured the revue "Frills and Fancies," Wesley Eddy and his Kings of Syncopation, plus the Chester Hale Girls "direct from the Capitol Theater" (Loew's famous first-run house on Times Square). In addition to the luxuries the theater provided its patrons, it treated its staff pretty well, too, offering them such pleasant perks as a gym and basketball court in the basement.

Like many movie palaces, Loew's Kings started losing its luster—and its customers—during the 1960s. Nonetheless, the place somehow managed to hang on until 1977, when it finally went out of business. Since then, the theater has been frequently in the local news. One group wants to turn it into a community center, another

Splendor on Flatbush Avenue: Loew's Kings

Brooklyn-born Susan Hayward arriving at La Guardia, 1952

thinks it would make a great shopping mall, and, of course, there are those who feel that the best thing to do with it would be to tear it down. As the book goes to press, the controversy continues, and the massive old palazzo just sits on Flatbush Avenue, quietly awaiting its fate.

20. SUSAN HAYWARD BIRTHPLACE
3507 Church Avenue

The daughter of a transit worker, the woman whom the world knew as Susan Hayward was born Edythe Marrener on June 13, 1917 (or June 30, 1918). This three-story brick apartment on a commercial block in Flatbush was her first home.

21. BARBRA STREISAND PROJECTS
3102 Newkirk Avenue

A great brick jungle of aging post–World War II apartment houses rises between Newkirk and Foster, Nostrand and New York avenues, in the center of Flatbush. Today these projects offer housing to low-income, mostly black, families, many of them originally from the Caribbean. Thirty years ago these same buildings housed many of Flatbush's once large Jewish middle class. One family that resided here in the early 1950s was that of Louis Kind, his wife Diana, and their child Rosalind. Also sharing the Kind apartment were Diana's son and daughter from her first marriage, Sheldon and Barbara Streisand. By all accounts, it was not an idyllic situation—especially for little Barbara, who had to contend with a stepfather who is said to have referred to his baby daughter and his ten-year-old stepdaughter as "Beauty and the Beast." At the same time, it seems that Barbara referred to Mr. Kind as "a used car salesman or something," when in reality he was a real estate agent. In any event, Kind didn't last too long on Newkirk Avenue. He moved out in 1953 and never came back.

Meanwhile, Barbara appears to have had a fairly uneventful adolescence. She spent a lot of time watching television on a neighbor's seven-inch set; she also babysat, worked as a cashier at a nearby Chinese restaurant, ushered at the Loew's Kings movie house on Flatbush Avenue, and attended Erasmus High School where she won a medal in Spanish, sang in the chorus, and graduated in 1959 with a 93 percent average. After that, she went to Manhattan because she wanted to become an actress. To pay for acting lessons, she started singing in clubs . . . and, well, we all know the rest.

22. NBC STUDIOS
1268 East 14th Street

On the edge of Flatbush, this little-known branch of NBC's broadcast operations is where the network's hottest property, "The Cosby Show," was taped from 1984 to 1987, and where the soap opera "Another World" is currently based. The history of this NBC facility goes way beyond television, however. In 1903, a young and prosperous film company called Vitagraph established its main studio here and on the adjacent property now occupied by the Orthodox Jewish high school at 1277 East 14th Street. Today, with the exception of NBC's modern front-office structure, the rest of the compound—including all the buildings of the Yeshiva next-door—dates back to the Vitagraph era.

Vitagraph was a studio of famous firsts. In 1907, for example, Vitagraph was the first motion-picture company to put an actress under contract. Her name was Florence Turner, but to movie audiences of the day she was simply "The Vitagraph Girl." Turner was extremely successful and was also one of the first actresses to

Vitagraph's Brooklyn studios

go on a promotional tour to publicize her films, which included *The Merchant of Venice, The New Stenographer, A Tale of Two Cities, Jealousy,* and *The Discarded Favourite.* In many of her films, Miss Turner co-starred with the screen's first matinee idol, Maurice Costello, who set an important precedent for the film industry by refusing to help build sets or paint scenery, activities actors in early films were often called upon by their producers to do.

The greatest star in Vitagraph's firmament was Brooklyn's own Norma Talmadge. Norma was a teenager when she made her first appearance before the Vitagraph cameras rather unexpectedly in 1910. On a visit to the studio with her mother, Norma saw her idol, the aforementioned Florence Turner, and rushed up to meet her. As it turned out, Miss Turner was shooting a scene—which Norma ruined. By 1913, Florence Turner had left Vitagraph, and Norma Talmadge had taken over as queen of the lot. When Norma herself left Vitagraph in 1915 to form her own company with her future husband, Joe Schenck, she had appeared in over 250 Vitagraph pictures. One of her last was *The Battle Cry of Peace,* a World War I epic, heavy on propaganda, that one of the studio's founders, J. S. Blackton, is said to have made both to capitalize on the popularity of D. W. Griffith's Civil War saga, *The Birth of a Nation,* as well as to get Americans geared up to enter World War I.

Other famous Vitagraph players of the 1910s were the heavyweight (three hundred pounds!) comic John Bunny, whose career came to a sudden end when he suffered a fatal heart attack in 1915, and Anita Stewart, who made headlines in 1917 when she signed on with an upstart producer named Louis B. Mayer before her Vitagraph contract had run out. Vitagraph sued, and won, in a landmark case that established for many years the power of producers over their stars. Less well known during their Vitagraph days were Leon Trotsky, the Russian revolutionary, and Rudolph Valentino, the superstar, both of whom worked as $5-a-day extras at the Brooklyn studio long before they became famous.

By the mid-1920s, Vitagraph, which now had studios in Hollywood as well as Brooklyn, was having serious financial difficulties. Unlike many of its competitors, the Vitagraph Company had not developed its own chain of theaters, and ultimately it had trouble booking its features into first-run houses. Thus, when Warner Bros. offered to buy the studio from its cofounder, Albert E. Smith, in 1925, Smith had no choice but to sell. After the sale, Warners held onto the Flatbush facility, and modified it for their new Vitaphone sound system. In addition to carrying out a number of important Vitaphone experiments, Warners also produced short subjects with New York talent at its Brooklyn plant. By 1939, however, there was little actual filming going on at the old Vitagraph lot, and Warners sold off much of the property (the part that's now the Yeshiva) to Technicolor. Then, in 1952, NBC acquired the rest of the studio and equipped it for color-television broadcasting. Among the famous early color "Spectaculars" that came live from Brooklyn was the 1955 production of "Peter Pan" that starred Mary Martin.

*Vitagraph superstar:
Norma Talmadge*

Today, NBC is still here. Granted, things are a lot quieter than in the old days when Vitagraph had twenty-nine directors and hundreds of actors working simultaneously, but the fact that this historic show-business site is still in show business is good news. Viva Vitagraph!

23. VITAGRAPH VAULTS
791 East 43rd Street

This abandoned brick warehouse with row upon row of chimneys of various heights is another vestige of the film making that once went on in Brooklyn. Built by Vitagraph, this bizarre-looking building was a film-storage facility. The fact that the nitrate stock used for early silent pictures needed ventilation to avoid decomposition explains the chimneys. Movie lovers who venture here can still make out a fading "Vitagraph/Warner Brothers" sign on the side of the place.

Vitagraph vaults

Saturday Night Fever
house, Bay Ridge

24. "SATURDAY NIGHT FEVER" HOUSE
221 79th Street

John Travolta took the country by storm in 1978 with his dead-on portrayal of a callow/callous Brooklyn teenager named Tony Manero in Robert Stigwood's *Saturday Night Fever.* Based on a 1976 piece in *New York* magazine by writer Nick Cohn called "The Tribal Rites of the New Saturday Night," the film shot a lot of scenes on location in Brooklyn. For the Manero family abode, this Bay Ridge bungalow got the nod. In the film, as we all remember, John Travolta/Tony Manero worked in a paint store by day and was king of the disco floor at night. In between, he spent a lot of time at home on 79th Street blow-drying his hair, posing in front of his bedroom mirror, and at the dinner table (which was in the kitchen) coming out with some of the foulest four-letter language ever to burst forth from the Dolbys.

25. 2001 ODYSSEY
Eighth Avenue and 64th Street

A decade after *Saturday Night Fever,* the Bay Ridge *boîte* that was used for many of the film's disco sequences is still in business. These days, in addition to its flashy dance floor, light shows, and pulsing music, 2001 Odyssey keeps up with the times by featuring "Male Revues" for ladies on Thursdays and Fridays. Outside the club, if you look up Eighth Avenue, you'll see the towering Verrazano-Narrows Bridge off in the distance. Connecting Brooklyn with Staten Island, this dramatic span also played an important role in *Saturday Night Fever* as the bridge where Travolta and his drunken buddies climbed, clowned, and tempted fate.

*Bay Ridge beauty:
Clara Bow*

26. CLARA BOW HOUSE
857 73rd Street

She was the ultimate flapper and clinched her film fame in the 1927 Hollywood feature *It,* through which she became known forever after as "the It Girl." Whatever "it" was that Clara Bow had, it didn't last long. A combination of nervous breakdowns and sex scandals—including a story of how she had "entertained" the entire starting line-up of the University of Southern California football team—quickly shook the flimsy foundations of her film career. Then talking pictures came along and finished her off entirely.

Born in Brooklyn in 1905, Miss Bow spent most of her adolescence on the second floor of this modest wood-frame house which still stands across from McKinley Park in the Bay Ridge section of the borough. Her father was a waiter and her mother, plagued with the same emotional problems that would later afflict her daughter, died while Clara was in her early teens. At the age of sixteen, Clara managed to escape her dreary Bay Ridge existence when she won a movie-magazine beauty contest. The prize: a small role in a Hollywood film. On the West Coast, Paramount biggie B. P. Schulberg took a liking to the Brooklyn teenager, and Clara's brief fling with fame is often thought to have been the result of her fling with Schulberg.

27. NEW UTRECHT HIGH SCHOOL
Sixteenth Avenue and 79th Street

TV viewers may recognize this Bensonhurst high school from the credit roll of the 1970s hit series "Welcome Back Kotter," the show that Brooklyn-born comic Gabe Kaplan both created and starred in. Kaplan never attended New Utrecht High, however; he was an Erasmus grad and is said to have based "Kotter" on his

Erasmus days. To further complicate matters, the name of the school in the series was neither New Utrecht nor Erasmus, but the created-for-television James Buchanan. Things were different in the old days: New Utrecht got to use its own name when it played a featured role in MGM's 1947 *It Happened in Brooklyn.* In case anyone has forgotten, in the film, New Utrecht High is where returning World War II vet Frank Sinatra solves his postwar housing problem by moving into the basement of the school. Sharing his pad is the school's janitor, Jimmy Durante. Welcome back, Frankie.

28. CONEY ISLAND

In the days when newsreels informed America's movie-going public of what was happening in the country and the world, summers would always bring the standard newsreel puff-piece telling of record-breaking weekend crowds jockeying for a place in the Coney Island sunshine. Accessible by public transportation, this three-mile-long strip of Brooklyn beach was for many New Yorkers the easiest and least expensive way to escape the horrors of summer in the city. And in the days before air conditioning, New York summers were pretty horrendous.

Besides its beaches, Coney Island offered vast bath houses with sports facilities, a boardwalk, penny arcades, side shows, all sorts of food stalls and cafes, and several totally self-contained amusement parks. In its heyday, there was nowhere on earth quite like Coney Island; it was the world's biggest carnival.

When the movies came along in the 1890s, Coney Island was already well established as America's capital of fun and fantasy. Therefore it is not surprising that early film makers were attracted to this magical and infinitely photographable island. Indeed, in 1896, the year that movies were first projected onto screens in front of an audience, one of the titles that the Edison Manufacturing Company offered to its exhibitors was called *Sea Waves at Coney Island.* That same year Edison also produced a twenty-nine-second film called *Shooting the Chutes,* which documented a particularly thrilling Coney Island ride of the day. And in the years immediately following, the list of films with Coney Island in their title would grow and grow. Coney Island was not just one of the movies' first locations, it was easily the single most-photographed spot in New York.

On November 3, 1899, Coney Island was the site of an important event in the history of the American cinema—when the American Mutoscope and Biograph Company filmed a prizefight between two boxers named Jim Jeffries and Tom Sharkey. To capture the event, which took place at night in the Coney Island Athletic Club, Biograph suspended some four hundred lights above the ring. This turned out to be the first time that a film had been successfully made with artificial light. The fighters were not too thrilled about their history-making bout, however, because the heat from all the

Harold Lloyd at Coney Island in Speedy, *1928*

lamps was intolerable. Between rounds, they had to be shielded by umbrellas and fanned by their seconds in order to complete the match.

The famous Edison director Edwin S. Porter also helped make film history at Coney Island. In 1903, his *Rube and Mandy at Coney Island* starred two leading vaudeville comics in an amusing ten-minute-long romp around Coney. Not as significant as some of his story films, *Rube and Mandy* is nonetheless a valuable, and wonderfully photographed, documentary on turn-of-the-century life. More of a landmark is Porter's 1904 *Fighting the Flames at Coney Island,* which captured a mock fire at a resort hotel and took an important step in bringing staged spectacles to the screen. Also important is the director's 1905 *Coney Island at Night.* Just three-minutes long, this beautiful little film was a brilliant experiment in night photography.

More made-at-Coney Island film history: In 1908, the Kalem film company used Manhattan Beach (adjacent to Coney Island) to stage the chariot race for a very low-budget, highly condensed version of *Ben Hur.* Since Kalem had not secured the screen rights for the popular novel on which it had based its little film, the company was sued by the estate of author General Lew Wallace, and wound up settling out of court for $25,000. From then on, screen rights became a force to be reckoned with in the movie business.

Dissolve to 1912, and a film called *Cohen at Coney Island,* produced by a newly formed company called Keystone, which planned to specialize in comedies. Directing as well as acting in the film was one of the new company's founders, Mack Sennett. *Cohen at Coney Island,* as it turns out, was the first in a long line of Keystone Comedies, some of which featured Sennett's legendary Bathing Beauties frolicking in the Coney Island surf long before they got their feet wet in the Pacific. Ironically, four years after Sennett had used Coney Island for his first independent picture, one of his company's greatest stars, Roscoe "Fatty" Arbuckle, left Keystone to set up his own production company. Among the first films Arbuckle directed and starred in for his new company was *Fatty at Coney Island!*

The Coney Island movies went on and on. In 1925, Adolphe Menjou took a hair-raising roller-coaster ride at Coney Island in *The King on Main Street.* The innovative camera work for the sequence was that of James Wong Howe, who would become one of the industry's leading cinematographers, earning Academy Awards for *The Rose Tattoo* (1955) and *Hud* (1963). In 1928, when Harold Lloyd, the bespectacled comic who made most of his films in Hollywood, came to New York to shoot *Speedy,* he couldn't pass up Coney Island as a location. In *Speedy*'s Coney Island interlude, we see Lloyd and his girlfriend riding the airplanes of Luna Park and the famous mechanical racehorses of Steeplechase Park. Today, both of these amusement parks are gone, but film historians recently found a very good print of Lloyd's film—with Czech subtitles!—providing another rare glimpse of a lost world.

In the 1930s the movies started to talk. This meant that increasingly they were made on soundstages or on backlots where noise could be carefully controlled. It also meant that almost all feature-film production moved to Hollywood. Thus, when we get Betty Grable, George Montgomery, Cesar Romero, and Phil Silvers starring in *Coney Island* in 1943, we also get a lot of the backlot at Twentieth Century–Fox in Los Angeles.

By the end of the 1940s, however, things had started to change again. Lighter, more sophisticated cameras and sound equipment that had been developed during the war meant that movies could come back outdoors again. Once this started happening, movies also started coming back to New York, and occasionally to Coney Island. In 1953, Morris Engel did *The Little Fugitive,* a low-budget independent film about a little boy who mistakenly thinks he has killed his brother and who spends a day at Coney Island trying to run away from his fear. The film was shot entirely on location, and was one of the features that helped to reestablish New York as a moviemaking town.

And then, of course, there's Woody Allen, whose career is very much in the tradition of pioneer New York directors like Morris Engel—and who came to Coney Island in 1977 to shoot part of *Annie Hall.* In the film, Alvy Singer's childhood home is under Coney Island's famous Cyclone roller-coaster. Despite the fact that precious little of vintage Coney Island survives today, Allen found his Cyclone as well as some antique bumper cars and successfully managed to evoke the feeling of the place in the 1940s. And speaking of success, *Annie Hall,* shot entirely in New York, won the Academy Award for the best film of 1977, as well as two additional Oscars for Woody's script and direction. Once again, Coney Island had played a role in the saga of film making in New York.

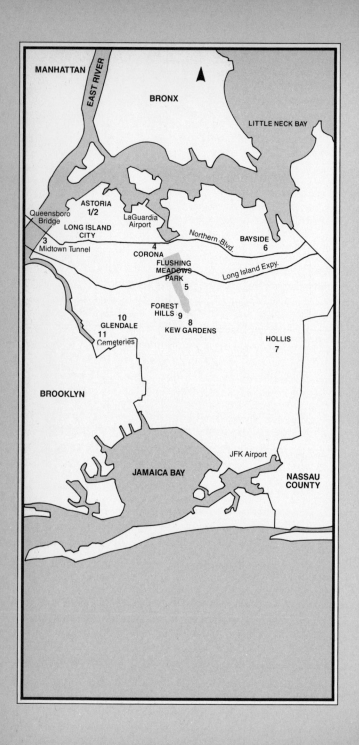

QUEENS

The Return of the Movies

Last Tango in Astoria: Rudolph Valentino in A Sainted Devil, *1924*

A decade ago, the borough of Queens was the site of one of the most important recent developments in New York film history: the renovation and reopening of the Astoria Studios. Representing the renaissance of feature-film making in New York, the comeback of this landmark studio facility is now being upstaged by an equally historic development: the opening, across the street, of the American Museum of the Moving Image. The country's first museum devoted exclusively to the art and industry of film making, AMMI will provide visitors with an insider's look at how films are made, stage special exhibitions, and present screenings of new and classic films and videos. For those who can tear themselves away from this major new tourist attraction in Queens, the borough has other areas that movie lovers may wish to explore. Of these, one of the most interesting is the community of Bayside, which in the early part of the century was a movie colony where New York moguls and film stars like Joe Schenck, Norma Talmadge, Gloria Swanson, Nancy Carroll, and Fatty Arbuckle spent their summers. These days, Bayside is a quiet little suburban community—but who knows, with the comeback of Astoria, perhaps Bayside will regain its former cachet as well? And it's a lot closer than the Hamptons.

1. KAUFMAN-ASTORIA STUDIOS
34–12 36th Street

Of all the links that modern New York has with its proud moviemaking past, this great studio today stands as one of the most visible and most vital. The Astoria Studios were founded in 1920 by Jesse Lasky and Adolph Zukor in order to centralize the production facilities of their Famous Players–Lasky Corporation (known as Paramount Pictures by 1927), which at the time had studios scattered all over New York. Throughout the 1920s and well into the 1930s, Astoria would reign as the most important film studio on the East Coast.

Known as "the Big House" to the old-timers who worked there, the original studio encompassed thirteen acres of an industrial area of Queens that had been "opened up" by the building of the 59th Street Bridge in 1909 and the elevated subway in 1917. As befitted a proper movie factory, Astoria had a dramatic columned entrance, a huge main stage as well as numerous smaller ones, a backlot, scene shop, and commissary, not to mention lavish suites and dressing rooms for its stars.

Among those stars were such legends as Gloria Swanson, who disliked Hollywood's provincialism and who in 1923 decreed to her Paramount bosses that she would work only at Astoria. Since Swanson was the biggest thing in pictures at the time, she got her way—as well as the most glamorous star quarters on the lot, where her enormous closetsful of shoes were the talk of New York.

Another legendary Astoria star of the 1920s was the screen's ultimate male sex symbol, Rudolph Valentino, who made *Monsieur Beaucaire* and *A Sainted Devil* at Astoria in 1924 so that he could

Astoria's backlot, 1929

have more artistic control over his films than the Hollywood studio system permitted. When the news broke that Rudy was coming East, it is said that Astoria real estate agents were deluged with women seeking apartments near where their idol would be working.

Besides Valentino and Swanson, other notable names from Astoria's silent era were Billie Burke, May McAvoy, Richard Barthelmess, Elsie Ferguson, Wallace Reid, Nita Naldi, Louise Brooks, Bessie Love, Adolphe Menjou, Bebe Daniels, Richard Dix, Thomas Meighan, Rod La Rocque, W. C. Fields, Gilda Gray, and William Powell. Among the studio's top directors were Allan Dwan, Robert Vignola, Sidney Olcott, as well as D. W. Griffith, who in 1924 had run into financial difficulties as an independent producer and had made a deal with Adolph Zukor to work at Astoria. Griffith's first Astoria production, *Sally of the Sawdust,* introduced W. C. Fields to movie audiences.

The year 1927 marked the end of Astoria's silent era, and indeed looked like the end of Astoria as well, since Paramount's production head, B. P. Schulberg, had managed to convince the studio's top brass to close their Queens operation and center all feature production in California. Schulberg hadn't counted on the impact of the talkies, however, and when it looked as though they were around to stay, Paramount reopened Astoria in 1928 to capitalize on Broadway plays and Broadway actors. The great names of Astoria's talkie days include: the Marx Brothers, who did *The Cocoanuts* and *Animal Crackers* at Astoria in 1929 and 1930, respectively; Tallulah Bankhead, noted more for her milk baths than for the quality of her films; Ginger Rogers, who made her screen debut with brown hair and the line "Cigarette me, big boy!"; Claudette Colbert, who filmed many of her pictures both in English and in French; Nancy Carroll, considered to be the first star created by the talkies; and Clive Brook, the first Sherlock Holmes of the sound era.

Despite Astoria's sound revival, by 1932 Paramount was having financial difficulties on both coasts. Facing bankruptcy, it therefore again decided to shoot all of its features in Hollywood. It was at this time, too, that one of the company's creditors, the Western Electric Company, took charge of Astoria and changed its name to Eastern Services Studios. With its new management and new name, Astoria remained a major film-making facility on the East Coast and still kept strong ties with Paramount, as is evidenced by the fact that Paramount's newsreel division—"the Eyes and Ears of the World"—continued to be based here. During the 1930s, Astoria/Eastern Services Studios specialized in short subjects, and many of these brought to the screen such New York–based talents as George Burns and Gracie Allen, Jack Benny, Milton Berle, Bob Hope, and Danny Kaye. In the 1930s Astoria was often used for projects that Hollywood wouldn't touch, such as *The Emperor Jones* (1933), which starred the great black actor Paul Robeson. Finally, Astoria in the 1930s was where many promising New York performers made their screen tests. Among this group of Hollywood hopefuls was Fred Astaire. Of his Astoria test, the West Coast casting people noted: "Can't act. Slightly bald. Can dance a little."

By the late 1930s, activity at Astoria had slowed down considerably, and Hollywood was definitely the motion-picture capital of the nation and of the world. With World War II, however, Astoria suddenly found itself back in action in a big way, when it was taken over by the U.S. Army and turned into the U.S. Signal Corps Pho-

Rudolph Valentino in Astoria commissary while shooting Monsieur Beaucaire, *1924*

Maurice Chevalier and Claudette Colbert in The Big Pond, *which they made in English and French at Astoria Studios in 1930*

tographic Center for the production of training and propaganda films. After the war, the Army stayed on at Astoria and shot, among many projects, its television series "The Big Picture."

In 1971, the Army got out of the motion-picture business, and for the next few years the future of Astoria was dicey. Although the government gave the studio to the City University of New York in 1973, plans to turn it into a college campus and/or a film school were never realized. Indeed, by the mid-1970s it looked as if the property would have to be turned back over to the federal government, which might then have auctioned it off as surplus real estate, thus spelling the end of Astoria as a film studio. Seeing its historic significance and its potential role in the resurgence of film making that was taking place in the city at the time, a group of New York film people formed a foundation in 1976 that not only managed to get the Astoria Studios declared a National Historic Landmark, but that also got the facility restored and back in operation.

Today's Astoria Studios—further expanded and modernized in 1983 by real estate developer George S. Kaufman—boasts the country's largest soundstage outside Hollywood, plus seven smaller stages, and a recording studio big enough for a symphony orchestra; in addition, there are scenery rooms, equipment-rental operations, production offices, health club, tennis court, bank, and commissary. Today's Astoria also boasts *The Wiz, All That Jazz, Fort Apache, the Bronx, Wolfen, The World According to Garp, The Verdict, Daniel, Arthur, Going in Style, Ishtar, Radio Days, The Money Pit, The Secret of My Success, Brighton Beach Memoirs, The Glass Menagerie, Orphans,* and *September* as some of the films produced wholly or partially here over the last decade. Indeed, with the rebirth of "the Big House," feature films are alive and well and back in New York City—to stay.

2. AMERICAN MUSEUM OF THE MOVING IMAGE
35th Avenue at 36th Street

Movie lovers who visit the historic Astoria Studios in Queens will find an impressive complex of grey concrete buildings that spreads across several blocks of an otherwise undistinguished neighborhood. Visually, the most memorable landmark here is the columned entrance to the original 1920 soundstages, which will soon be joined by a new ornamental iron gate not unlike the famous Spanish Colonial entrance to Paramount in Hollywood—the one that Gloria Swanson was chauffeured through by Erich von Stroheim in *Sunset Boulevard.* Otherwise, Astoria, in true movie-studio style, looks like a big factory—which, ultimately, is exactly what it is.

For the moment, there are no tours of Astoria for the general public. However movie lovers who venture out to Queens to see the studios can now get an insider's view of the history and technology of moviemaking at the exciting new American Museum of the Moving Image. Housed in a former studio building on the Astoria lot, the nation's first museum dedicated solely to the art and artifice of film making exhibits historic and contemporary props, set models and sketches, posters, lobby cards, annotated scripts, production photos, and equipment. AMMI is a place where movie lovers can marvel at everything from the earliest Edison camera to Valentino's French court costumes for *Monsieur Beaucaire* to the living room set used in the Paul Newman–directed remake of *The Glass Menagerie.* AMMI does more than just display movie memorabilia, however; it has and will continue to develop a number of demonstrations and hands-on exhibits that focus on the process of film making. These currently include a working soundstage where visitors can shoot their own scenes.

Detail of "Tut's Fever," forty-seat fantasy movie house created by artists Red Grooms and Lysiane Luong for the American Museum of the Moving Image, Astoria

A 200-seat movie theater and a 60-seat "screening room" are also part of the AMMI operation, presenting lively and varied programs of silents, classic and contemporary sound films, plus avant-garde film and video art. By 1990, AMMI will have added a penthouse level to include an amphitheater and additional exhibition space. The new museum is a nonprofit project funded in part by the City of New York, the New York State Council on the Arts, and with grants from the National Endowment for the Arts, and by private donations.

It seems Hollywood is planning a similar museum. Theirs, however, won't open until the 1990s. Once again, New York was there first!

NOTE: *For information on hours and screenings at the American Museum of the Moving Image, call: (718) 784–4520.*

3. SILVERCUP STUDIOS
42–25 21st Street

Further evidence of the dramatic rise of film production in New York, the former Silvercup Bakery in Long Island City was turned into a movie studio in 1983. Specializing in commercials—which still account for the bulk of filming that goes on in New York—Silvercup Studios currently has fourteen soundstages within its enormous three-block-long building, and its plans call for an eventual total of forty. If these plans are realized, Silvercup will have the largest number of stages of any studio in the country with the exception of Universal in Los Angeles.

Besides commercials, Silvercup also provides studio space for music videos starring the likes of Billy Joel, Cyndi Lauper, and Billy Idol. In addition, it's hosted various made-in-New York features. Among these have been *Highlander, Compromising Positions, The Purple Rose of Cairo, Broadway Danny Rose, Garbo Talks, Street Smart, Three Men and a Baby,* and *Crocodile Dundee II.*

The birth of the news: television covers RCA founder David Sarnoff dedicating RCA pavilion at 1939 New York World's Fair

Louis Armstrong house,
Corona

4. LOUIS ARMSTRONG HOUSE
34–56 107th Street

From 1942 until his death in 1971, Louis Daniel Armstrong lived in this attractive red-brick home in Corona, Queens. Known primarily for his superstar trumpeting, "Satchmo" also appeared in some two dozen motion pictures, beginning with *Pennies from Heaven* in 1936 and ending with *Hello, Dolly!* in 1969. Today, Armstrong's former Queens home is a National Historic Landmark and bears a plaque from the U.S. Department of the Interior.

5. FLUSHING MEADOW PARK

Much of it was a garbage dump before it was filled in, graded, and built upon for the 1939 New York World's Fair. While some Fair visitors enjoyed riding in shiny new Lincolns along the Ford Motor Company's half-mile elevated highway of the future, and while others marveled at the artificial thunder and lightning generated inside the General Electric pavilion, everyone agreed that the most impressive wonder at Flushing Meadow was on view at the Radio Corporation of America Building: television!

It was in RCA's pavilion—designed to resemble an Art Deco radio tube—that television made its official commercial debut. The five- and nine-inch TV sets on display were not just for looking; they were authentic production models that RCA hoped soon to market all over the country. At the same time, NBC (RCA's network) would be providing several hours of scheduled television programming every day and soon CBS, not to be outdone, would follow suit.

But while TV was a big hit with the masses at Flushing Meadow, it was not a hit with the buying public. Not only did the price tags on those first models—between $199.50 and $600—amount to big bucks for a small screen at the tail end of the Depression, there was also the increasingly disturbing world situation, which meant that Americans had other things on their minds besides television. In fact, by 1941 there were only ten thousand TV sets in the entire country, and once the U.S. entered the war at the end of that same year, all television production as well as commercial broadcasts had been discontinued. When the war ended, however, the story of television would be a very different one. What happened at Flushing Meadow in 1939 was just a sneak preview.

NOTE: *For TV lovers who visit Flushing Meadow Park, little remains of the 1939 World's Fair except the old New York City Building, which is now the Queens Museum. Its main attraction is a wonderful scale model of New York's five boroughs, which was built for the 1964 World's Fair and is continually updated to reflect the architectural changes in the city. Other vestiges of the 1964 Fair at Flushing Meadow are the 140-foot Unisphere globe—the Fair's symbol, which can be seen from both the Long Island Expressway and the Grand Central Parkway. Also hard to miss from the highways skirting Flushing Meadow Park are the futuristic towers of the New York State Pavilion. Adding a surreal dimension to the skyline, they wound up, appropriately, as part of "Munchkinland" in Sidney Lumet's 1978 fantasy musical,* The Wiz.

6. BAYSIDE

Enjoying a prized position on Little Neck Bay, the community of Bayside in northeastern Queens was a fashionable spot for wealthy New Yorkers to have summer estates in the last decades of the nineteenth century. Close to the nerve center of Manhattan, yet delightfully peaceful and rural, Bayside was an especially convenient location for people whose businesses didn't allow them the luxury of being too far from the city. When the twentieth century rolled

Bayside wedding: Norma and Constance Talmadge flank newlyweds Buster Keaton and Natalie Talmadge, 1921

around, it wasn't long before a whole new group of wealthy, hard-working New Yorkers—the stars and executives of the burgeoning motion-picture industry—discovered the many charms of the Bayside summer; and during the 1910s and 1920s they turned the little Queens community into what may have been the world's first movie colony. Long before Malibu . . . there was Bayside!

One of the grandest of the Bayside film colony's summer places was that which producer Joseph Schenck and his movie-star wife, Norma Talmadge, rented from publisher John Ridenour. Ensconced in their hideaway on Little Neck Bay, the Schencks frequently hosted weekend parties that had some of the brightest stars of the era sunning, sailing, and playing croquet. The Schenck compound, it seems, was also a popular spot for celebrity weddings. In 1920, screenwriters Anita Loos and John Emerson tied the knot in Joe and Norma's Bayside garden, and a year later Norma's sister, Natalie, married the famous comedian Buster Keaton there as well. Today the historic property has been seriously subdivided, but the main house with its enormous driveway can still be seen off 222nd Street between Corbett Road and Second Place. The guest house—number 35–45 222nd Street—was used by Gloria Swanson in the summer of 1923 when she was making her transition from Hollywood movie queen to Astoria film star.

Around the corner from the Schencks, W. C. Fields supposedly spent several summers in the split-level frame house at 35–25 223rd Street. Only the back of the place can be seen from the street; the front, which had direct access to the beach and the bay in W. C. Fields's day, is now separated from the shoreline by the Cross Island Parkway.

Movie lovers can get a good look, however, at the handsome turreted mansion that was the longtime Bayside home of boxer James "Gentleman Jim" Corbett at 221–04 Corbett Road. Remembered for inventing the left hook and for defeating John L.

The Joseph Schenck/Norma Talmadge Bayside "cottage"

"Gentleman Jim" Corbett and wife outside their Bayside home

Sullivan in a famous match in 1892, Corbett was also the first celebrity to sign an exclusive contract to appear in motion pictures. The year was 1894—and the company was the Kinetoscope Exhibition Company, one of the firms involved in marketing Edison's Kinetoscope motion-picture viewing devices.

Not far from the Corbett property, at 215th Place and 32nd Avenue, one of the most famous stars of the silent screen had Bayside's most spectacular estate. The owner of the property was Pearl White, queen of the cliff-hanger serials in the 1910s, who is still remembered as the star of the legendary *The Perils of Pauline*. According to one Bayside old-timer, however, in person Pearl cut quite a different figure from the embattled heroine she portrayed on screen. He remembers often seeing the star passing by in a great

Bayside's biggest star:
Pearl White

Pearl White's Bayside mansion

chauffeur-driven motorcar. If the railroad gates happened to be down at the Bell Avenue crossing, Miss White would simply have her chauffeur drive through them, knowing full well the railroad would bill her for the repairs!

Pearl eventually gave up Bayside and the U.S. for a château and a continued life of luxury in France. Meanwhile, theater critic John Golden, for whom Broadway's Golden Theater is named, bought Miss White's estate and eventually bequeathed the property to the city to be turned into a public park upon his death. Today, Golden's wishes have been followed and the former Pearl White/ John Golden estate is now John Golden Park. The main house is gone, but the grounds—with gardens, walkways, park benches, playing fields, and old-fashioned street lamps—make this one of the prettiest spots in Bayside.

Further afield, movie lovers may want to check out a few more Bayside addresses. A house where the great character actress Marie Dressler once lived can be seen at what is now 217–09 39th Avenue, although when she had the place, the address was 221st Street, overlooking the Bay and close to the rest of the movie colony. Dressler, whose greatest film success came with the talkies, lived in Bayside during her "silent" period, which began in 1914 when she played opposite Charlie Chaplin in *Tillie's Punctured Romance.* Four blocks from where the former Dressler home now stands, the brick apartment building at 209–01 43rd Avenue was built on the site of a house once occupied by the exotic silent screen siren Theda Bara.

Character actress Mae Robson—noted for playing society matrons in many movies, but who was nominated for an Academy Award in 1933 for her performance as the baglady-like Apple Annie in Frank Capra's *Lady for a Day*—lived at 42–34 209th Street. Across the way, at 43–25 209th Street, Duncan "The Cisco Kid" Renaldo was in residence until his death in 1980. Further along

Baysider Nancy Carroll
with Richard Arlen in
Wayward, *1932*

209th Street, the Dutch Colonial mansion at number 42–46 was, in the late 1920s, briefly home to a beautiful, frequently forgotten star of the early talkies, Nancy Carroll. In her second film, *Abie's Irish Rose* (1928), originally made as a silent and then turned into a "part-talkie," Carroll was the first woman to sing in a commercial feature film. While many careers were ruined by the talkies, Miss Carroll was considered the first actress to have been made a star thanks to the new medium.

Nancy Carroll shot her first films at Paramount Studios in nearby Astoria but, by 1932, she and most of Paramount's other East Coast stars had packed their suitcases and steamer trunks and had taken off for Hollywood, where feature films would be based for the next couple of decades. The 1930s also saw the end of Bayside as a film colony, and soon the exclusive community on Little Neck Bay was swallowed up by Greater New York and became just another suburb. Meanwhile, out on the West Coast, Malibu was starting to become very popular.

NOTE: *The Bayside Historical Society periodically gives walking tours that take in some of the town's more interesting properties. For information, call: (718) 224–5707.*

7. TABERNACLE OF PRAYER
165–11 Jamaica Avenue

Today the discarded crutches of those who have been healed here hang beneath the two-story vaulted ceiling in the lobby of what is now Apostle Johnnie Washington's Tabernacle of Prayer. Before being born again as a house of worship, this Hollis, Queens, landmark was, from 1929 to 1977, the Loew's Valencia movie house. A dazzling mix of Spanish Colonial and pre-Columbian architecture and decor, the Valencia had an auditorium that gave moviegoers the illusion that they were in a lushly planted patio under a moonlit sky. Today, many of the nude statues that adorned this fantasy patio have been given wings to make them more in keeping with the Valencia's present incarnation.

8. CHARLIE CHAPLIN HOUSE
105 Mowbray Place

Although Chaplin made most of his feature films on the West Coast, at his own studio on La Brea Avenue in Hollywood, the great silent-picture star is said to have acquired this modest Kew Gardens brick bungalow in 1919 to use when his business as producer, writer, and star brought him to the East.

9. WILL ROGERS HOUSE
124 81st Avenue

In the early 1920s, actor/humorist Will Rogers lived with his family in this stately Tudor mansion in Kew Gardens. At the time Rogers was often a headliner in the Ziegfeld Follies on Broadway. By the end of the decade, however, he would have great success in talking pictures and would move permanently to the West Coast, where he wound up living on a vast ranch near the Pacific Ocean. Today, his L.A. estate has become the Will Rogers State Park and is a popular attraction for locals and tourists. Meanwhile, the world has forgotten that Rogers once lived in Queens.

10. "ALL IN THE FAMILY" BLOCK
89-66 to 89-88 Cooper Avenue

ABC had backed two separate pilots of "All in the Family," but in each case had dropped the project. Ultimately, a television series in which the main character was a raving bigot was just too controversial for American TV audiences in 1969—despite the fact that the British series on which "All in the Family" was based ("Till Death Do Us Part") had been extremely successful in the United Kingdom. Indeed, when Norman Lear finally got CBS to take a chance on the project, it was with little enthusiasm that the network put the show on the air. Much to everyone's surprise, "All in the Family" was an instant hit, and it spawned a rash of sitcoms that

Loew's Valencia, Hollis

"All in the Family" block, Glendale

dealt with formerly taboo-on-TV subjects like race, abortion, pre-marital sex, homosexuality, and impotence. "All in the Family" also gave birth to the phenomenon of the spin-off, which started when Edith Bunker's cousin Maude segued into her own series, and was followed by the Bunkers' black neighbors becoming the prime-time "Jeffersons"—not to mention Maude's maid, who went off to have her own "Good Times."

Although the series was taped in California, "All in the Family" supposedly took place in a conservative neighborhood in Queens. For the show's credit roll, however, a real block of middle-class wood-frame houses on Cooper Avenue between Woodhaven Boulevard and 88th Street in Glendale, Queens, was used. The home that was supposedly Archie and Edith's is thought to have been number 89–70 Cooper Avenue. Besides the notoriety that the block gained from its weekly appearances on network TV, it also found itself in some grizzly newspaper headlines in October 1972, when a woman living at number 89–88 Cooper Avenue shot her three children and then turned the gun on herself.

11. MACPELAH CEMETERY
82–30 Cypress Hills Street

The great star of this cemetery is the "Incredible Houdini" (born Erich Weiss), whose grave just beyond Macpelah's main gate is distinguished by a large marble monument topped by a bust of the famous showman. While the world remembers Harry Houdini for his escape artistry and his feats of magic, it has forgotten that, in the late 1910s and early 1920s, Houdini also appeared in a series of swashbuckling, daredevil adventure films that exploited his acrobatic skills and his special-effects expertise. The first of these film projects was a fifteen-part serial called *The Master Mystery,* which Houdini made in 1918 for Octagon Films at their studio in Yonkers, New York. From there, Houdini went to Hollywood, and starred in two features for Paramount–Artcraft Pictures, *The Grim Game* (1919) and *Terror Island* (1920), and he soon became more interested in making movies than in doing live performances. So interested that, in 1921, he formed the New York-based Houdini Picture Corporation which, for its first film, came out with *The Man from Beyond* (1922), featuring Houdini as producer, writer, editor, and star. It also featured a hair-raising sequence, filmed on location at Niagara Falls, and the movie met with critical and box-office success. A year later, however, Houdini didn't fare quite as well with *Haldane of the Secret Service,* in which the fiftyish escape-artist-turned-movie-actor couldn't cut the mustard as a romantic lead. The film failed and Houdini returned to the stage.

Houdini died of a ruptured appendix suffered in October 1926 while he was performing at the Garrick Theater in Detroit. The theatrics surrounding his funeral and burial in New York were reminiscent of those that had attended Valentino's death just two months earlier. And like Valentino's grave at the Hollywood Memorial Cemetery on the West Coast (which continues to draw fans and cultists to this day), Houdini's tomb at the Macpelah Cemetery in Queens has also seen its share of bizarre visitors over the years. Many of these are spiritualists who come to the Houdini crypt annually on Halloween to commemorate the many séances held by Houdini's widow to try to contact her husband after his death. Unfortunately, vandals have also visited the Houdini grave from time to time, and on two occasions they have made off with the great magician/movie star's bust.

Harry Houdini grave,
Macpelah Cemetery

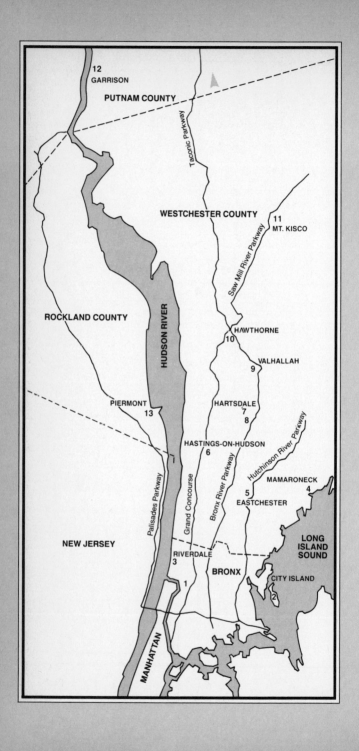

THE
BRONX AND
BEYOND

Final Stops

Rainbow girl: Judy Garland, 1922–1969;
Ferncliff Cemetery, Hartsdale, New York

LIKE Brooklyn, the Bronx is noted for the many stars who were born here. Among them: James Caan, Tony Curtis, Carl Reiner, June Allyson, Anne Bancroft, Carroll O'Connor, Sal Mineo, and director Stanley Kubrick. Besides stars, the borough was also once noted for its movie studios. Perhaps the most important of these was the uptown branch of Biograph, whose large facility at 175th Street and Prospect Avenue dated back to 1905, and which, in its later years as Gold Medal Studios, was used both for feature films (*On the Waterfront, A Streetcar Named Desire, The Fugitive Kind*) and television productions ("Car 54, Where Are You?"). Edison's Bronx facility, which went up in 1908 at Decatur Avenue and Oliver Place as the most advanced movie studio in the world, also hosted during the 1950s and 1960s a number of important TV series ("Man Against Crime," "You Are There," and "I Spy") and film projects (*The Wrong Man, The Last Angry Man,* and *The Hustler*). Both studios are gone now, and preservationists fear for the future of another famous Bronx movie landmark, Loew's Paradise Theater.

The sightseeing picture for movie lovers is brighter north of the Bronx, in Westchester, Putnam, and Rockland counties, areas that traditionally have provided "instant" small town and/or rural locations for New York film crews. But perhaps the greatest attractions awaiting movie lovers north of New York City are the superstar cemeteries of Westchester County, where a surprising number of film legends are buried. Neither depressing nor morbid, these beautiful, peaceful, dignified enclaves are a pleasure to visit and seem fitting finales to the careers of some of the movie world's brightest stars.

1. LOEW'S PARADISE
2417 Grand Concourse

For the first half of this century, the Bronx's Grand Concourse was one of the most glamorous boulevards in the five boroughs. Often compared to the Champs Elysées in Paris, this fabulous thoroughfare was divided by elegant islands and edged with stately apartment buildings. Mention the Grand Concourse today to anyone who grew up in the Bronx in the 1930s, 1940s, or 1950s, and they'll undoubtedly wax rhapsodic about this grand old main street, and they'll invariably go on to talk about its crown jewel—Loew's Paradise Theater. They won't have too much to say about the theater's exterior, because the Paradise had a rather conservative Italianate façade and a simple flat marquee, since Grand Concourse zoning laws forbade projecting marquees as well as big vertical signs. But just wait until they get to the inside!

The interior of this famous 1929 movie house was an extravaganza of baroque balconies and balustrades, columns and cornices, intricately sculpted niches that showcased exact copies of classical statues. To finish off the fantasy, the Paradise had a deep-blue ceiling where white puffy clouds drifted by and stars twinkled. A night at

*Loew's Paradise, Grand
Concourse, ca. 1948*

the Paradise was just about the closest anybody could get to heaven—certainly in the Bronx.

The Paradise's "atmospheric" special effects as well as its overall design were the work of John Eberson, known among movie palace historians as the Father of the Atmospheric Theater. Besides being spectacular, Eberson's designs were amazingly cost-efficient, since the smooth-plaster ceilings of his houses were much less expensive to build than the ornate, chandelier-hung affairs that were customary in nonatmospheric theaters.

Alas, the clouds no longer roll by and the stars no longer shine at Loew's Paradise. It was a sad day both for the Bronx and for movie lovers when this great theater was twinned in 1974 and its lobby statuary painted blue. But that was just the beginning of the bad news. Two years later, the Paradise was triplexed, and in 1981

Inside Loew's Paradise

it was quadded. Today, about all that remains of what was once the jewel of the Grand Concourse are the theater's façade and its lobby, now painted a garish green. What next? Unfortunately, many people who have followed the movie palace's history fear the worst, and expect the whole place to be demolished within the decade. Welcome to Paradise Lost.

2. "LONG DAY'S JOURNEY INTO NIGHT" HOUSE
21 Tiel Street, City Island

Hepburn didn't want to play the part, and producer Ely Landau had to make two trips to Hollywood to convince her that she was both right for it and up to the rigors of doing Mary Tyrone in the 1962 film version of Eugene O'Neill's play, *Long Day's Journey into Night*. And if Landau and director Sidney Lumet had had their way, Hepburn's co-star in the film would not have been Sir Ralph Richardson, who wound up being cast, but rather Hepburn's long-time very close friend Spencer Tracy. But Tracy would have nothing of the $25,000 that Landau was offering to pay him to perform in the very low-budget movie.

"Look, Kate's the lunatic," Tracy is reported to have said to Landau and Lumet in Charles Higham's *Kate* (Norton, 1975). "She's the one who goes off and appears at Stratford in Shakespeare. I don't believe in that nonsense—I'm a movie actor. She's always doing these things for no money! Here you are with twenty-five thousand each for *Long Day's Journey*—crazy! I read it last night, and it's the best play I ever read. If you offered me this part for five hundred thousand and somebody else offered me another part for five hundred thousand, I'd take this!" But five hundred thousand was out of the question and the budget, and Hepburn wound up doing the film without Tracy.

Long Day's Journey into Night, which literally documents a

Long Day's Journey into Night *house, City Island*

long day in the life of the Tyrone family, whose problems range from alcoholism to drug addiction, takes place entirely at their Connecticut waterfront estate. Instead of going on location all the way up to Connecticut, Lumet and Landau found an ideal *Long Day's Journey* house on City Island, that delightfully remote, New England-like community in the Bronx that's linked via causeway to the rest of the borough. Needless to say, City Island was a lot closer than Connecticut to the Production Center Studios on West 26th Street in Manhattan, where the film's interiors were lensed. It was also a lot less expensive. Today, the *Long Day's Journey* property, with its turreted mansion, distinctive gazebo, and low stone fences appears to have changed little since the early 1960s when the film was done. The pristine view across Eastchester Bay is another story, however, now that condo colonies have sprouted up on the other side. To do *Long Day's Journey* today, a producer just might have to go to Connecticut after all—or even further.

3.   JOSEPH P. KENNEDY ESTATE
5040 Independence Avenue, Riverdale

From 1926 to 1929, a very important film producer lived in this big white house at the corner of Independence Avenue and 252nd Street in the exclusive Bronx residential enclave of Riverdale. Although he is better known as the financier father of a U.S. president, two senators, and a number of other celebrity children among his brood of eight, Joseph P. Kennedy was in the film business in a big way in the 1920s. In fact, one of the reasons he moved his family from Boston to the Bronx in 1926 was so that he could head up Film Booking Offices of America (FBO), the production company he had just purchased.

Kennedy's FBO was definitely not a major studio and produced schlock titles like *The Dude Cowboy* and *Hot Hooves.* The company made money, however, and for Kennedy it was a foot in the door

Joseph P. Kennedy fiasco: Queen Kelly *with Gloria Swanson and Walter Byron, 1929*

of a business that he found both seductive and lucrative. By 1929 Kennedy had acquired the Keith-Albee-Orpheum theater chain, and eventually he used his equity in this company to mastermind the merger deal that created RKO.

It was also during the late 1920s that Kennedy became professionally as well as emotionally involved with a great star of the era, Gloria Swanson. Taking a page from William Randolph Hearst's book, Kennedy served as executive producer on Swanson's films, just as Hearst did on the films of his mistress, Marion Davies. At the height of their affair, Kennedy is said to have made so many long-distance phone calls to Swanson that he had the largest private long-distance phone bill in America in 1929. Despite his attentiveness to his movie-star mistress, Kennedy was responsible for Swanson's greatest failure, a picture called *Queen Kelly*. Directed by Erich von Stroheim, the film ran so over budget and was so long that the project was shelved. (A reconstructed version has since been exhibited at film festivals and in art houses.) Then, not long after the *Queen Kelly* disaster, Swanson, who lost around $1 million of her own money on *Queen Kelly,* was also shelved by her producer/lover. By that time, Kennedy, who had somehow managed to make $5 million in the film business, had moved from Riverdale to an even grander estate in Bronxville, New York. Throughout his Hollywood/Swanson phase, Kennedy continued to be married to Rose Fitzgerald Kennedy.

4. D. W. GRIFFITH STUDIO SITE
Orienta Point, Mamaroneck, N.Y.

In 1919, D. W. Griffith was at the height of his wealth, his fame, his power—and his hubris. It was the year that Griffith had joined with Mary Pickford, Charles Chaplin, and Douglas Fairbanks to form the revolutionary United Artists Corporation, which gave its star founders control over both the production and distribution

D. W. Griffith's Mamaroneck studio, ca. 1920

D. W. Griffith (in boater) directs Orphans of the Storm, *1921*

of their films. It was also the year that Griffith had made a separate
deal to do three pictures with First National. Finally, it was the year
that Griffith decided to leave Hollywood and set up his own studio
back East. The place Griffith chose for his operation was the former
estate of Standard Oil/Florida real estate millionaire Henry Flagler,
which occupied a secluded spit of land jutting out into the Long
Island Sound near Mamaroneck, New York. Besides making films
here, Griffith planned to live on the estate, too—a situation which
many felt fulfilled the Southern-born director's fantasies of being
master of the plantation. Others who knew Griffith well also pointed
out that the seclusion of Orienta Point would enable him to carry
on his various romantic liaisons with young actresses far away from
the prying New York press.

The trouble with Griffith's grand Mamaroneck plan was that
he had overextended himself with all of his production deals, as
well as with the enormous costs of converting and maintaining the
Flagler place. But while Mamaroneck would ruin Griffith financially,
his first major film there, *Way Down East* (1920), was a huge success.
Other ventures, such as *Dream Street* (1921) in which Griffith pi-
oneered synchronized sound some six years before Warners released
its first Vitaphone picture, were less successful. As for *Dream Street*'s
sound system, Griffith became its biggest critic and discontinued
its use immediately after the picture opened. In fact, Griffith eventually became one of the industry's most vocal anti-talkie spokesmen:
"It puts us back to Babel," he once told Lillian Gish. "Do you
realize how few people in the world speak English? If we make
pictures that talk, we can't send them around the world. That's
suicide."

Next to *Way Down East,* Griffith's most important film from
his Mamaroneck period was *Orphans of the Storm* (1922). An artistic
success, it also did well at the box office, but wound up losing money

for Griffith due to accounting and copyright problems. For this epic story of the French Revolution, enormous sets depicting eighteenth-century Paris were constructed at Mamaroneck—and Griffith deliberately scheduled the filming of major crowd scenes for weekends in order to use as many of the locals as extras as possible. After *Orphans of the Storm,* however, it was all downhill for the great director, and by 1924 he was forced to abandon independent producing, signing on with Paramount to do pictures at Astoria. That same year, Griffith put his Mamaroneck estate up for sale, and in early 1925 a developer bought most of the property for the purpose of subdividing it.

Today all of the Griffith and Flagler buildings on Orienta Point are gone, and the property is now part of an exclusive, gated community. One wonders how many, if any, of the people who live in the luxurious homes on the other side of the gates have a clue that the French Revolution was once fought in their neighborhood or that Lillian Gish battled the fiercest blizzard in filmdom out on Orienta Point? The least they could have done was to name the place D. W. Griffith Estates.

5. "GARP" RESIDENCE
2 Brassie Road, Eastchester

Of all the crazy things that went on at this big white colonial house where Robin Williams faced the absurdities of life as T. S. Garp in the 1982 screen adaptation of John Irving's bestselling novel *The World According to Garp,* the craziest was when a small plane crashed into its side. While many of the exteriors of *The World According to Garp* were shot at this real house in Eastchester, New York, for that airplane sequence a mock-up of the side of the house was built at a private airport in Lincoln Park, New Jersey, where the "crash" was carefully controlled. Meanwhile, the interiors of the house were done on a soundstage at Astoria Studios in Queens. Sometimes it takes a lot of houses to make a place a home—especially in the movies.

6. WESTCHESTER HILLS CEMETERY
400 Saw Mill River Road, Hastings-on-Hudson

One of Westchester County's star cemeteries, Westchester Hills is a small Jewish burial ground that will intrigue movie lovers from the moment they drive inside. Just beyond the entrance, two large, columned mausoleums stand across from one another on either side of the roadway. The one on the left belongs to the great showman, Billy Rose, whose famous Manhattan nightclub, the Diamond Horseshoe, was immortalized in the 1945 Betty Grable–Dick Haymes musical, *Billy Rose's Diamond Horseshoe.* The mausoleum on the right is that of the Gershwin family, and contains the crypts of the immortal composer-lyricist brothers, George and Ira Gershwin, whose music graced such movies as *Delicious* (1931), *Girl*

*George Gershwin
mausoleum, Westchester
Hills Cemetery*

Crazy (1932), *Shall We Dance?* (1937), and *A Damsel in Distress* (1937). Although George Gershwin died in 1937 at the age of 38, his melodies have continued to inspire film makers and films right up to Woody Allen, who relied exclusively on Gershwin for the score of *Manhattan.*

Up the road from the Gershwins, a large headstone bears the family name of Tuvim. While this name probably doesn't mean much to many movie lovers, a glance down at one of the smaller individual markers, will reveal that Judy Holliday (born Judith Tuvim) is buried here. Judy's first screen appearance was in a small role in Twentieth Century–Fox's musical *Greenwich Village,* in 1944, but it was her Broadway performance in 1946 as Billie Dawn, the loveable blonde of *Born Yesterday,* that made her a star and that ultimately wound up bringing her an Academy Award for her performance in the film version in 1950. (Judy had stiff competition that year, by the way: she was up against Bette Davis in *All About Eve* and Gloria Swanson in *Sunset Boulevard.*) Judy Holliday, "Beloved Mother, Dear Daughter," died in 1965 of cancer at the age of forty-three.

Another star whose light faded prematurely was John Garfield, who was not quite forty when he died in 1952 of an apparent heart attack at the Gramercy Park apartment of a lady friend. Born Julius Garfinkle on the Lower East Side, Garfield lies toward the back of the Westchester Hills property, across the road from a large mausoleum that bears the name Silver. Garfield, "Beloved Husband and Father," became a big film star in the 1940s, but ran into trouble in the early 1950s when he was black-listed for refusing to tell the House Committee on Un-American Activities the names of his Hollywood friends who were suspected of being Communists.

Ironically, the grave of director/producer Robert Rossen lies not too far from Garfield's (up the hill and off to the right where the road ends in a small traffic circle). It was Rossen who directed Garfield in his 1947 hit *Body and Soul.* Like Garfield, Rossen also refused to name names to HUAC in 1951, and his career ground to a halt. Two years later, however, Rossen went back before the Committee and ratted on fifty of his colleagues. Although he made films afterwards—including *The Hustler* in 1964—Rossen is said to have gone to his grave a haunted man. He died in 1966.

Finally, off to the left of Rossen's stone, movie lovers will find Lee and Paula Strasberg, the couple who founded the Actors Studio and who influenced the craft and careers of acting greats from James Dean to Marlon Brando to Marilyn Monroe. Paula Strasberg (1909–1966) was Marilyn Monroe's personal acting coach for many years, and is said to have driven many of Marilyn's directors crazy with the "private" directions she gave on the set to the insecure star. On the other hand, Lee Strasberg (1901–1982), in his later years, managed to practice in front of the cameras what he had been teaching from behind the scenes for so long, when he appeared in—and won an Academy Award nomination for—*The Godfather, Part II* in 1974. Strasberg then went on to act in other films, including 1979's *Boardwalk* and *Going in Style.* His tombstone is easy to miss, since it is in the shape of a rock and blends right in with the terrain of Westchester Hills.

NOTE: *The cemetery is open from 9 A.M. to 4 P.M. from Sunday to Friday; closed on Saturdays.*

7. FERNCLIFF CEMETERY
Secor Road, Hartsdale

It's about as far from Hollywood as anyone can get, this pastoral, very East Coast enclave of rolling hills, green lawns, and big shady trees that lies a few miles north of the town of Hartsdale, New York. The surprise is that two of Hollywood's all-time biggest stars are buried here—Judy Garland and Joan Crawford—both of whom got their start at the same studio: MGM. Who would have thought that they would wind up together in Westchester?

Judy Garland's crypt, Ferncliff Cemetery

Actually, if Sid Luft, Garland's third husband and the father of two of her three children, had had his way, Judy would not have been buried at Ferncliff. Feeling that Hollywood—the town that had made her a star—was her real home, Luft had wanted Judy to be interred there. But Mickey Deans, Judy's fifth and final husband, as well as Liza Minnelli, her eldest daughter, felt that Judy would have preferred an East Coast cemetery because, according to them, she had never been fond of California. Since Deans had custody of Judy's body, and since Liza was handling the funeral arrangements, Sid couldn't argue.

At the time of Judy's death in 1969, Mickey Deans had plans for an elaborate tomb to be dedicated to the memory of his legendary wife of six months. Since the wing at Ferncliff that would house this memorial was still being built (and Deans didn't have the $37,500 to cover the cost of the crypt at the time), Judy was first put in a temporary vault. Deans had hoped to raise the needed money from Judy's friends and fans, but by November 1970, almost a year and a half after his wife's death, he still hadn't managed to pull it off. It was then that Liza stepped in and had her mother placed in a permanent and very simple wall crypt, which says only, "Judy Garland, 1922–1969." Movie lovers who visit Judy will find her on the second floor in the new wing of Ferncliff's main mausoleum (Unit 9, Alcove HH, Crypt 31). There is usually some kind of floral tribute in front of her beige marble slab, which is at floor level. Above Judy is Angelo R. Careccia; on her right are Mae and Leo Mintzer. Were they fans, one wonders? Did they have any idea that they would share billing with Judy Garland?

Downstairs in the old wing of the same building, movie lovers will find Joan Crawford in Unit 8, Alcove E, where her ashes rest in a vault next to that of her fourth and last husband, Pepsi-Cola executive Alfred N. Steele. The inscription is again very simple, just, "Joan Crawford, 1908–1977." Joan's fans may chuckle at these dates, however, because their idol was always notorious when it came to lying about her age, and it seems that at Ferncliff she managed to pull off one final fib. At the latest, Joan was born in 1904, and according to one Hollywood contemporary who knew Joan when, it was really closer to 1901!

Besides Crawford and Garland, Hollywood is further represented at Ferncliff by Basil Rathbone (buried in the cemetery's smaller Shrine of Memories mausoleum), Ona Munson (who played Belle Watling in *Gone with the Wind*), and Harold Arlen (who wrote Judy's "Over the Rainbow"). More Ferncliff names of note include Ed Sullivan, Jerome Kern, Paul Robeson, Moss Hart, Elsa Maxwell, Connie Boswell, Diana Sands, Malcolm X, Sherman Billingsley, "Toots" Shore, "Moms" Mabley, Thelonius Monk, Adolph Caesar, and Sigmund Romberg. Welcome to Forest Lawn East!

NOTE: *Ferncliff is two miles north of Hartsdale on Route 9W. At Secor Road, turn left and continue for 1½ miles until you reach the driveway for the main mausoleum, which is off to the right. Ferncliff is open from 9 A.M. to 5 P.M., daily.*

Hartsdale Canine Cemetery entrance

8. HARTSDALE CANINE CEMETERY
75 North Central Avenue, Hartsdale

The oldest pet cemetery in the U.S., Hartsdale Canine has buried some fifty thousand dogs and cats—as well as several hundred birds, fish, and at least one lion cub—since it opened in 1896. Among its dearly departed doggies are celebrity pets like Diana Ross's German shepherd, which joined Kate Smith's "Freckles," George Raft's "Ruggles," and Gene Krupa's "Jerk" and "Susie." Dancer Irene Castle, actress Gloria (*Summer Stock*) De Haven, 1950s TV queen Dagmar, radio host Barry Gray, band leader Xavier Cugat, and cosmetics empress Elizabeth Arden have also used Hartsdale's "complete interment services" over the years. Those services include transporting the animal to the cemetery, annual flower care, endowment plans for perpetual care—plus a wide assortment of burial vaults, headstones, and satin-lined caskets. Recently, cremation became another option available at Hartsdale. The most bizarre option of all, however, which around 150 people have chosen, is to be buried on the property next to one's pet.

In addition to the pets of the famous that populate Hartsdale Canine, the cemetery also has buried several animals who were celebrities in their own right. Movie and TV viewers may remember a winsome basset hound named Morgan, who appeared on the tube with Perry Como, Jackie Gleason, Arthur Godfrey, and Steve Allen in the 1950s, as well as on screen opposite Dean Martin and Jerry Lewis in *Living It Up* (1954). Morgan is at Hartsdale, along with Boots, a 1940s canine film star credited with helping to raise $9-million-dollars'-worth of war bonds during World War II. When Boots died, his Hartsdale graveside service received national media attention.

NOTE: *The cemetery and office are open Monday to Saturday from 8 A.M. to 4:30 P.M., and on Sunday from 9:30 A.M. to 4 P.M. The staff is very helpful in pointing out who's where.*

9. KENSICO CEMETERY
Lakeview Avenue, Valhalla

Gloriously landscaped, studded with splendid monuments and mausoleums, Kensico is one of the most beautiful cemeteries in the country. For movie lovers the main reason to visit here is to pay one's respects to the enchanting screen actress, Billie Burke, who will always be remembered as *The Wizard of Oz*'s Glinda, Good Witch of the North. Miss Burke also played Cosmo Topper's scatterbrained wife in the *Topper* series as well as a host of leading and character roles in films from the 1930s to the 1950s. Prior to her career in the talkies, Miss Burke was a popular Broadway performer, and in 1914 she married the legendary producer Florenz Ziegfeld (1868–1932), who managed her career until his death in 1932. At Kensico, Miss Burke, who died in 1970 at the age of 85, is buried next to Ziegfeld under a huge weeping willow tree at the end of Powhatan Avenue. The bronze statue of the dancing woman nearby is not Billie Burke, but her circus-performer mother, Blanche Betty Burke, who is interred here as well.

Three other notables at Kensico will please movie lovers. Not far from the Burke–Ziegfeld graves (at the intersection of Powhatan and Ossipee Avenues) lies the tomb of Thomas F. Dorsey, Jr. (1915–1956). Dorsey's headstone is embossed with a trombone, musical notes, and the inscription: "The Sentimental Gentleman." A few steps away, novelist Ayn Rand (*The Fountainhead* . . . Gary Cooper . . . Patricia Neal—remember?) is buried. Further afield, a large Russian Orthodox cross marks the plot where Russian-born composer Sergei Rachmaninoff (1873–1943) and his wife Natalie lie. Movie lovers who pass by may hear the notes of Rachmaninoff's *Variations on a Theme of Paganini,* which figured prominently in MGM's 1953 film, *The Story of Three Loves.*

10. GATE OF HEAVEN CEMETERY
Stevens Avenue, Hawthorne

Yet another of Westchester's superstar cemeteries, Gate of Heaven is the final resting place for some of New York's most famous Roman Catholics. Among those buried here are former New York City mayor Jimmy Walker, "What's My Line" alums Fred Allen and Dorothy Kilgallen, baseball great Babe Ruth, and movie stars James Cagney and Sal Mineo. The Gate of Heaven office staff will provide visitors with a map showing who's where.

NOTE: *Gate of Heaven is open daily from 8 A.M. to 5 P.M.*

11. "RAGTIME" HOUSE
81 Main Street, Mt. Kisco

Although it was set in turn-of-the-century New York, *Ragtime* was shot largely in and around London. One American location that director Milos Forman did use (for both exteriors and interiors)

Ragtime *house,*
Mt. Kisco

in his 1980 film was this handsome hilltopping Victorian mansion in Mt. Kisco. According to *Ragtime*'s art director, Patrizia von Brandenstein, she scouted hundreds of locations before coming up with this one.

NOTE: *The house lies along Route 133 just east of Sand Street.*

12. "HELLO, DOLLY!" VILLAGE
Garrison's Landing

In June 1968, the cast and crew of *Hello, Dolly!* descended upon the tiny village of Garrison's Landing, which lies on the east bank of the Hudson River, just across from West Point. To turn 1960s Garrison's Landing into 1890s Yonkers, Twentieth Century–Fox had spent weeks and used some thousand gallons of paint, six thousand pieces of lumber, three hundred truckloads of earth, and a hundred thousand square feet of lawn. The cost of the operation, which also involved transporting the *Dolly* company to New York from Los Angeles where the principal photography was being done at Fox Studios on Pico Boulevard, was no object because this was a *big* picture, with a *big* director (Gene Kelly), based on a *big* Broadway hit, and featuring the decade's *biggest* star: Barbra Streisand.

There was also *big* trouble on the set between Miss Streisand and her leading man, Walter Matthau, and on one hot, humid, mosquito-swarming afternoon in Garrison's Landing, there erupted a battle that Mr. Matthau describes in Shaun Considine's *Barbra Streisand: The Woman, the Myth, the Music* (Delacorte Press, 1985) as follows:

If the elements were not enough, Barbra kept asking Gene [Kelly] whether he didn't think it would be better if I did this on this line, and that on the other, et cetera, et cetera—and I

Hello, Dolly! *at Garrison train station, 1968*

told her to stop directing the fucking picture, which she took exception to, and there was a blowup in which I also told her she was a pipsqueak who didn't have the talent of a butterfly's fart. To which she replied I was jealous because I wasn't as good as she was. I'm not the most diplomatic man in the world, and we began a slanging match like a couple of kids from the ghetto. I think Gene thought one of us was going to die of apoplexy or something, or that I'd belt her, or maybe she'd scratch my eyes out—or worse, that we'd walk off, leaving twenty million dollars' worth of movie to go down the drain.

Today, anyone visiting Garrison's Landing will find it hard to imagine the above scene having taken place in this green, peaceful spot with its glorious views of the Hudson River. Besides the charm of the setting, movie lovers who visit Garrison's Landing will also find various vestiges of the *Hello, Dolly!* shoot. Most notable is the pretty white gazebo with the weathervane on top that is the centerpiece of the village's waterfront park, both of which were built for the film. (Actually, the gazebo is a replica of the Fox original, which had rotted so badly in the 1970s that it had to be replaced.) Not far from the gazebo, a barber shop advertises ten-cent haircuts and five-cent shaves. On closer inspection, the place turns out to be a façade. The Golden Eagle Inn around the corner is for real, however—a solid three-story bed-and-breakfast establishment with a big verandah. If it looks familiar, that's because it served as Horace Vandergelder's grocery store in *Dolly*. Today its glass doors are still embossed with a large "V" and the name "Vandergelder." Meanwhile, the little train station that Dolly used to go from Yonkers down to Manhattan is—and was then—a working station. Supposedly, when its sign was changed from Garrison to Yonkers for the film, it confused quite a few commuters.

13. "PURPLE ROSE OF CAIRO" TOWN
Piermont

When Woody Allen passed through the tiny Hudson River village of Piermont, New York, in the fall of 1983, the local paper called it a "miracle." Not because Allen had chosen the place as the principal location for his film, *The Purple Rose of Cairo,* but because the film company had magically turned Piermont's clock back over half a century. The man behind the miracle was Stuart Wurtzel, the film's production designer, who dressed Piermont's Main Street with false fronts, vintage signs, and antique cars to make it look just like a middle-American small town in the 1930s.

While movie lovers who visit Piermont may recognize some of the buildings on Main Street from *The Purple Rose of Cairo,* they will find one landmark missing: the Jewel movie theater, which played a major role in this story about a woman (Mia Farrow) who escapes the dreary realities of her small-town life by literally entering into the fantasy world of a film playing at the local movie house. The Jewel, it turns out, is now a parking lot. The Jewel, it also turns out, had been a parking lot before *The Purple Rose of Cairo* crew came to town and built a 1930s movie-house façade on the site. At the time it was all happening, Piermont locals watched with amazement as their town was transformed and then immortalized by Allen's cameras. It was an exciting ten days and nights. And then, practically as quickly as it began, the company wrapped its Piermont location, tore down the Jewel movie house and the other façades on Main Street, hauled away the vintage props and the antique cars, and Woody Allen and company picked up and disappeared, leaving Piermont pretty much as it had been before they came. In many ways, it wasn't unlike the ending of *The Purple Rose of Cairo,* where the film at the Jewel winds up its run, moves on to another theater in another town, and leaves Mia Farrow back in the real world again.

Piermont locals see their town transformed for Woody Allen's The Purple Rose of Cairo, *1984*

INDEX

PHOTO CREDITS

The Academy of Motion Picture Arts and Sciences: pages 24, 82, 119, 129, 133, 204 top, 207, 210, 250
The Algonquin Hotel: page 34
Richard Alleman Collection: pages 10, 26, 27, 38, 41, 67, 192, 229
The American Academy of Dramatic Arts: pages 166, 167
The American Museum of the Moving Image: pages 278, 280, 283, 290
The Bayside Historical Society: pages 287, 288 top and bottom, 289
Bogie's: page 161
The Brooklyn Bridge Centennial Committee: page 251
Alfred J. Butler/Theater Historical Society: page 291
Carnegie Hall: page 61
Cinema Collector's Collection: page 170
Erasmus Hall High School: page 265 left
Geffen Films: page 197
Tom Hanlon: pages 13, 14, 17 top
Terry Helgesen Collection: pages 25, 75
Kenneth Kneitel Collection: pages 36, 124
Library of Congress: page 7
Lincoln Center Library: page 107
The Marwall Collection: page 198
Michael R. Miller Collection: pages 8, 9, 70, 97, 98, 236, 237, 247 top, 254, 298 top and bottom
Michael R. Miller Collection/Theater Historical Society: page 267
Mitchell-Manning-Vatter Associates: pages 110, 116
The Museum of the City of New York Theater Collection: page 88
The Museum of Modern Art/Film Stills Archive: pages 2, 30, 47, 49, 95, 115, 120, 136, 138, 143, 146, 151, 160, 203, 215 bottom, 216, 218, 230, 234, 239, 242, 243, 255, 256 top, 258, 263 bottom, 267, 270 top, 272, 274, 281, 282, 286, 296, 300, 302, 310
NBC Photo: pages 39, 40, 284
Jerry Ohlinger Collection: pages 45, 54, 59, 206
Howard Ottway Zodiac Photographers: 188
The Collection of the Paterson Museum: pages 20, 21
Ken Peters, courtesy Cooper Hewitt Museum: page 142
Playbill: pages 79, 81, 83, 86, 93
Radio City Music Hall/Michael Miller Collection: page 35
Sally Savage: page 311
Joan Micklin Silver: page 174
Martin Walsh: page 305
Marc Wanamaker/Bison Archives: pages 5, 76, 87, 104, 148 top right, 148 bottom, 159, 162, 163 bottom, 177, 182, 201, 241 bottom, 268, 301
Warner Research Collection/B'Hend and Kaufmann: page 91
The Westin Plaza: page 57
UPI/Bettmann Archive: pages 62, 122, 139
U.S. Department of the Interior National Park Service, Edison Historical Site: page 4

Photographs by Richard Alleman on pages 7, 11, 15, 17 bottom, 29, 32, 42, 50, 52, 53, 63, 64, 74, 85, 92, 96, 106, 112, 113, 117, 118, 121, 123, 125, 127, 129, 131, 132, 134, 137, 148 top left, 150, 153, 154, 155, 156, 157, 163 top, 172, 173, 175, 176, 178, 180, 181, 184, 186, 194, 195, 200, 204, 205 bottom, 213, 215 top, 217, 219, 221, 222, 224, 225, 226, 227, 228, 231, 241 top, 244, 245, 246, 247 bottom, 253, 256 bottom, 257, 259, 261, 262, 263 top, 264, 265 right, 270 bottom, 271, 285, 292, 293, 299, 304, 307, 309